FORGOTTEN KINGDOM

by Peter Goullart

Yunnan Publishing Group Corporation
Yunnan People's Publishing House

This book is dedicated to

DR JOSEPH F. ROCK

This RU edition was produced in 1957 for sale to its members only by Readers Union Ltd at 38 William IV Street, Charing Cross, London W.C.2, and at Letchworth Garden City, Hertfordshire. Full details of membership may be obtained from our London address. This edition has been reset in 11 point Fournier type, leaded, printed and bound at the Aldine Press, Letchworth Garden City, Hertford-shire. The book was first published by John Murray (Publishers) Ltd.

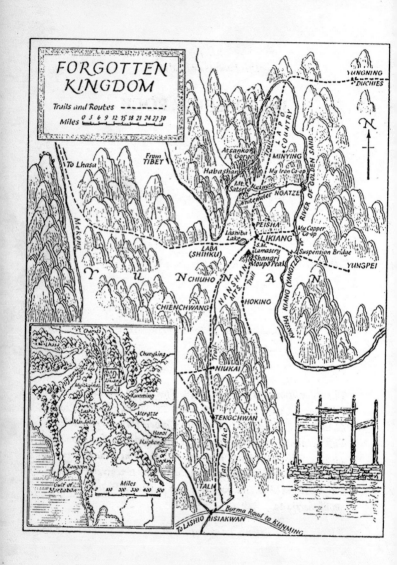

CONTENTS

Introduction   1

I   The Caravan Journey To Likiang   13

II   Likiang   31

III   The Market And Wine-Shops Of Likiang   65

IV   Further Afield   97

V   The Start Of The Co-operatives   107

VI   Medical Work   121

VII   The Nakhis   135

VII   The Tibetans   149

IX   The Boa, The Lolos And The Minkia   188

X   The Lamaseries   215

XI   Poltergeists   233

XII   Suicides And Dtomba Ceremonies   245

XIII   Marriages   262

XIV   Some Likiang Festivals   281

XV   Music, Art And Leisure Among The Nakhi   290

XVI   Progress   299

XVII   Hoking Brigand   319

XVIII   The Last Of Likiang   333

My grateful acknowledgment is due to Dr. Heinz Breitkreuz for his kind permission in allowing me to reproduce the photographs contained in this book.

INTRODUCTION

I WAS born in Russia more than fifty years ago. The upheavals, which have swept the world since the beginning of this century, caught me at an early age, and so sudden and violent were the changes that I can never think of my life as one connected and orderly process but only as a series of lives with little to connect them. Yet the years have not dimmed the recollections of my boyhood. My father died when I was two years old, and as the only child I became the centre of my mothers devotion. She was a wonderfully intelligent and sensitive woman, deeply interested in literature, music and the beauty of nature. I always felt that she was somewhat isolated from her many relatives, because none of them could equal her in intelligence, understanding or the breadth of her views. She wrote poetry and painted: she was psychic, and all this drew her and, eventually, myself away from the other members of the family. Among her circle of friends were many of the outstanding scientists and philosophers of

1

her time, and this may have had something to do with the method of my education which others considered peculiar and which was undertaken by a series of private tutors, including a philosopher and a theosophist. I remember clearly the vibrant life of Moscow and the sophisticated quieter refinements of Paris, although I was still quite young at the time.

I developed early an interest in the Orient, particularly in China, Mongolia, Turkistan and Tibet. It must have been in my blood and it undoubtedly came from my mother's side. Her father and grandfather were great and famous merchants during the past century, and their caravans went to Kobdo and Kiahta, and even as far as Hankow, to pick up China teas and silks. They ranged through Mongolia, trading in cattle, and dealt with Tibet in herbs, musk and saffron. All that was over when I appeared in the world and the only relic of the glorious past was my grandmother Pelagie, my mother's mother, who lived to the ripe age of ninety-seven. During the long winter evenings she used to tell me long stories of how her husband and his father made their journeys into Cathay and Mongolia and other fabulous lands where once Prester John and Ghenghiz Khan ruled. I listened starry-eyed; and all round her were old tea-chests painted with beautiful Chinese ladies proffering delicate teacups to bearded mandarins with fans and elaborate headdresses. There was lettering on the chests, like 'Hung Men Aromatic Tea', and there was still a faint fragrance of these brands floating in the heated air of her room. There were strange robes from Mongolia and Tibet in the long coffers against the walls, and Mongolian samovars, used by caravans, stood in the corner. I can still see the Shamanist drums and flutes hanging on the walls. This was all that remained of unrecorded travels: the men themselves were dead long ago.

I am glad that grandmother Pelagie died just before the Revolution — she was already half blind and was unable to walk, but her mind was still brilliant when she talked of her beloved past. Then the Revolution came. The subject is still painful to me, and there is no need to relate it here as it has been described so often. My mother and I were determined to get out of Russia. We rushed by train to Turkistan, only to find terror and bloodshed in Samarkand and Bokhara. The roads from there to Central Asia were blocked. We returned to Moscow to find the situation still worse. We fled to Vladivostok where we stayed for a year. On the way we were caught in the famous Czech uprising and it took us months to get through. The dangers and horrors we passed through best remain unrelated. At last we reached Shanghai.

In 1924 my mother died and I thought I could not survive her passing. In my grief I went to the famed West Lake near Hangchow and there, quite by chance, I met a Taoist monk. Our friendship was spontaneous, for I was already familiar with the Chinese language, and he took me to his monastery situated on a peak a few miles from town. There my friend ministered to me as if I were his dearest brother, and the Grand Abbot received me with wonderful understanding. With their guidance I found peace, as though by magic, and my heart seemed to heal.

I continued to visit the monastery for several years, escaping whenever possible from Shanghai, where at first I maintained myself by working for commercial firms as an expert in Chinese antiques, jade and rare teas. Then in 1931 I joined the American Express and acted as a tour conductor, escorting a wide variety of clients throughout

China, Japan and Indochina.

It may seem strange for a young man, working for a famous travel firm, to relax in Taoistic monasteries away from the brilliant lights of the 'Paris of the Orient'; but it was just because of the extreme gaiety of Shanghai night-life, which was an important feature of any tour, that I had to retire to such a refuge to restore my equilibrium and to regain my composure and strength.

I had only been at the American Express office a few days when an American millionaire, his wife and sister-in-law, booked me to take them to Peking. As a first step the millionaire instructed me to buy enough wines and food to last during the trip and to my embarrassment handed me ten thousand dollars in Chinese currency. This I had great difficulty in stuffing into my pockets. I stocked one of the cabins with two dozen cases of champagne and all kinds of fruit and canned delicacies. Unfortunately, as we put out to sea, a gale developed and the steamer rolled heavily. Several of the cases were smashed, and when the cabin door burst open bottles spun in all directions over the saloon and down the passages, crashing into the walls and exploding with deafening blasts. The good-humoured millionaire was highly amused, and this first excursion helped, oddly enough, to establish my reputation as a congenial courier and companion.

Then there was an eccentric American aviator of seventy-five, with a long white beard hanging almost to his knees. Whisking an aeroplane propeller out of his pocket he would shout, 'I am an aviator.' He was a true eccentric bent on his quest for an earthly paradise somewhere in the Far East. We flew to Lanchow, carried as cargo in a small Junker cargo plane, for in those days the Chinese airways system was still in its infancy.

Then we went to Peking and the old man rushed round amongst the other sightseers, twirling his little propeller in their faces and shouting, 'I fly, I fly, you see, like that!' He chartered an aeroplane for a flight to the Great Wall, took several reporters and gave secret instructions to the German pilot. The plane twisted and dived and sometimes the Great Wall appeared below us, sometimes on top of us and sometimes we seemed to scrape its very battlements. It was an unusual way of seeing the Great Wall and the reporters sat with faces as green as water-melons.

I travelled extensively at this time, for there were the routine tours and summer cruises as well as the more unusual journeys. China was a wonderful place to live in before the second Japanese war. I travelled also on my own and always stayed in Taoist monasteries through the introduction of my West Lake friend. I spent some time at Sian, the capital of the glorious Tang dynasty, and at Tungkwan, an old fortress of those days. I often spoke to my guru, the abbot, of my longings to go to West China, to live in that remote Tibetan country so little known to the Chinese and foreigners; but he always said the time had not yet come. Later, when the Japanese occupied Peking again and part of Shanghai, the guru told me that the moment had arrived. But how? I could not go there during war-time on my own. Then I suddenly came the offer to join the Chinese Industrial Co-operatives. I consulted the old abbot again and he made a detailed prediction of what would happen to me during the next seven years. Everything happened as he foretold.

Thus, as a member of the Co-operatives, I set out in September 1939 from Shanghai to Chungking, on what was to be the first stage of a long journey.

To get to Chungking, when the war between China

and Japan was in full swing, was a very complicated and dangerous business. I took a Dutch boat to Hongkong and thence a small French steamer to Haiphong. I was burdened with much baggage, and at Haiphong I met some missionaries who, with the University of Nanking, had been evacuated to Chengtu. They had scores of heavy cases, containing scientific instruments and other technical supplies, which they were taking to the university. Haiphong was a madhouse. American and British missionaries and business men were rushing along the streets and quays trying to identify their baggage piled like mountains everywhere. Public squares and parks were clogged with the trucks and cars of every description awaiting transportation. There was no highway to China. Everything had to go by the narrow-gauge train which took two days to get up to Kunming. Few of these people knew French and few French officials knew English. The poor missionaries were still sitting at Haiphong, although they had left Shanghai a fortnight before me. They could not explain to the Customs what they had, where it had to go and, what was worse, they could not fill in the forms in French. The French customs officials, crazed by the crowds, mountains of cases and bales, and the sea of documents, simply pushed out those people whom they could not understand. I filled their forms for them and led them to the Customs Commissioner. With a torrent of French, I pulled the commissioner outside and to a bar. I ordered all the aperitifs I could think of, whilst my friends glared at me, and in about half an hour the whole business was resolved and my baggage and their goods were on board the train in the afternoon. My poor friends were on the verge of collapse and I persuaded them to come with me to Hanoi to await the train there. In Hanoi I took them to the wonderful Hotel Metropole and made them relax with bottles of champagne which, I assured them, was a non-alcoholic beverage. In the morning we duly caught the train, and in the afternoon of the next day we arrived at Kunming, the beautiful capital of Yunnan.

All our baggage was piled into an ancient bus and I took the whole shipment to Chengtu. The troubles and breakdowns we had on the road were such that it was more than two weeks before I glimpsed Chengtu. I stopped off for a couple of days in Chungking to pick up my instrument of appointment as the Depot Master of Kangting, capital of Sikang. At Chengtu I caught a missionary truck for Yaan — the terminus of the motor highway to Sikang. We traveled by night, and at full speed the truck crashed through a rotten bridge. I was somersaulted and landed on my head and was fortunate not to break my neck; although I suffered from headaches for months afterwards. From Yaan we walked for eight days through the terrifying gorges of Sikang.

My two-year stay in Kangting or, as it was called in olden days, Tachienlu, was on the whole unhappy, though not without its moments of adventure and humour while on travel to the furthest parts of the province. The newly created Sikang Province had undoubtedly the rottenist provincial government and it was practically independent of Chungking. What they did to block my work and to embarrass me would fill a book. I was accused, in turn, of being a Japanese spy, Stalin's spy, Hitler's agent and, at last, a secret inspector of the Central Government. They tried to do away with me on several occasions, but each time I was miraculously saved. Finally I was put under house arrest. Luckily Dr. H. H. Kung, Finance Minister and President of the Chinese Industrial Cooperatives, intervened directly by telegraph and instructed me to return to Chungking. I was bitter, but I had to admit that this disagreeable experience had given me an unprecedented insight into the workings of Chinese officialdom at its worst. When I arrived in Chungking again I was no longer a simple and innocent foreign greenhorn, burning with the pure flame of idealism, but a real Chinese official with all the know-how to combat the machinations of the crooks with which the government teemed. I had not been without friends among the officials of Sikang, and they had certainly imparted to me confidentially a very useful knowledge of how the wheels within wheels worked in government circles.

I was received by Dr. H. H. Kung in Chungking and told him the truth. I knew he would be annoyed and he was. It was not the custom for a government official in China to embarrass his superiors by seeking redress from them. He had to work out his own salvation by becoming as wise as the proverbial serpent. In other words, he must become clever enough to outcrook the crooks. In Dr. Kung's eyes I was another stupid European who added to the friction, between the powerful Sikang Provincial Government and the weak Central Government, which the latter was trying to avoid at the critical period through which tile whole country was passing.

'I would like to go to Likiang to work,' I added timidly at the end of the interview, for although I had never been there, I had heard enough about the place to make me feel I would like it. The great man glared at me through his glasses.

'Is it I or you who makes the appointments? You shall go where I tell you to go!'

Somehow I could not suppress the feeling that there was

a hidden kindliness in his seemingly gruff manner. I was temporarily attached to the Co-operative Headquarters in the beautiful summer resort of Koloshan, about twenty miles from Chungking, where we were safe from the terrible bombing which was going on. At last an order came for me to join the Yunnan Headquarters at Kunming. This was a good sign, as the atmosphere in Kunming was much better than in intrigue-ridden Koloshan.

The days in Yunnan were comparatively peaceful as our headquarters were situated at a beautiful temple fifteen miles out of Kunming, not far from the Kunming lake. Then came a survey trip which I had to make to Paoshan and Tengyueh. Not saying a word to anybody in advance, I made a detour to Likiang and saw at once that this was the place for promoting co-operatives and not Paoshan or Tengyueh, both of which had no materials or workers, being merely military and trans-shipment points. I made my report accordingly, suggesting to Central Headquarters that they should send me to Likiang. There was a curt refusal to my request. I persisted gently but without result.

Then, quite suddenly, it happened. An order came from Dr.Kung appointing me the Depot Master of Likiang. I was packed off in a hurry and without the least ceremony. I was given only a little money, no stationery and not even the traditional seal of office. And no one was designated to accompany me. In the light of my Sikang experiences this appeared ominous. It looked more like an exile than an appointment. Usually there was a great fuss when depot masters were appointed to provincial towns. A seal and stocks of stationery were prepared for them, funds remitted and competent secretaries chosen to accompany them. I was willing to bet that somebody higher up was trying to get rid of me. The only man who was permitted to accompany me was my old cook Lao Wong, but he was no substitute for a secretary.

Later I found out that no Chinese candidate had been willing to take up a post in Likiang. They gave many reasons for their reluctance to work there. The place was too remote. It was, so to speak, outside China, the 'Outer Darkness', a no man's land lost in the sea of barbarous tribes who did not even speak Chinese. By all reports, the food problem there was impossible for a refined Chinese. The natives consumed things which to the Chinese were almost uneatable — mutton and beef, *sauerkraut*, yak butter and cheese. What was worse, everything was cooked in yak butter. Many Chinese there had been stabbed or otherwise disposed of, and it was dangerous to walk through the streets filled with fierce and animalistic savages who carried swords and daggers at the belt ready to be used at any moment. Why not send that crazy foreigner there? If he survives, it is all right; if not, it is his business as he asked for it. There were other, deeper considerations also. My immediate superior was not over-fond of me. He could not very well push me out of my job without a reason — that would have been a subtle insult to Dr. Kung. He knew better than to do anything so crude. But, if I could be sent up to Likiang all alone, without assistance or guidance, with only a small sum of money, what could I do in that strange, inhospitable and dangerous country? I should be terrified out of my wits and only too glad to return in a month or two humbly confessing my failure and praying for an asylum at the peaceful and safe headquarters. But then my fate would be sealed. A failure in Sikang and a failure in Likiang!

Yet I was filled with a sense of triumph, for it was in Likiang that I wanted to live, and I knew I could make

my work a success in spite of what they said or thought.
I was now armed with some experience, and to this I
resolved to add the practice of all the precepts and advice
I had imbibed during my long stay at the great Taoistic
monastery near West Lake. I was now one of the last
of a small group of foreigners who tried to work in an
executive capacity in the field with the Chinese Industrial
Co-operatives. All of them but myself had left of their
own free will or had been outmanoeuvred into giving
up. They were honest, idealistic, energetic and genuinely
devoted to their work. They all spoke good Chinese: but
they had not learned enough of the nature and mentality
of the Chinese to adapt their methods. The novelty of
their energy had kindled great enthusiasm among the
Chinese interested in co-operation, but they were unable
to sustain it for long because of the very qualities they
possessed. They did not recognize the moments when
it was more advantageous to slow down rather than to
push; to keep quiet rather than to talk. Instead of adjusting
certain irregularities adroitly, they ploughed straight
through them, causing both their friends and enemies a
severe loss of 'face' which, in China, has to be avoided
at all costs, as it arouses an unreasoning, uncontrollable,
destructive hatred. But the most important thing of all was
their lack of that intuitive ability to separate wheat from
chaff in their relations with the Chinese of all classes. A
foreigner who did not possess this sixth sense had a hard
time in China. Life and relationships between the people
in China are not what they appear to be. It is only the
man who knows the hidden meaning of such a life and
its relationships who can make his stay in the country a
success.

Thus I was now one of the 'Last of the Mohicans'

11

and, as Taoism had taught me, it would be important to practice inaction. Contrary to the ideas of some people in the West, who are unable to grasp the Taoist doctrine, this does not mean passivity and absence of all action and initiative. It actually means an active participation in life, but going along with its stream rather than battling against it foolishly, lest one be engulfed and destroyed. Many an obstruction which might cause a casualty can be circumvented. It is no good being too clever and pushing. The Chinese have a vast dislike of a smart busybody and always try to undermine him in a subtle way. Quarrelsome people are not tolerated. One could win a point and lose a friend. Taoism teaches that a man who does not quarrel has no one to quarrel with him. Another useful maxim, 'A man who does not climb does not fall,' does not really discourage advancement but implies that one should proceed carefully and circumspectly, step by step. My guru taught me that it is no good climbing a shaky ladder in a hurry; a man's position must be built thoughtfully and slowly to ensure permanency, success and respect.

Even with the right qualifications, the path of a foreigner in the employment of the Chinese Government was a hard one. Despite his credentials from Chungking and Kunming, he had to prove to the local authorities' and everyone else's satisfaction that he was the right person in the right place, especially as far as politics were concerned.

Thus I set out for Likiang realizing that the local people, not at first understanding the purpose of my arrival or of my work, would expect me to leave again shortly with empty hands, and that my Kunming headquarters were equally confident of the same outcome.

CHAPTER I

THE CARAVAN JOURNEY TO LIKIANG

*T*HE road to Likiang begins at Kunming, the busy capital of the Yunnan Province. From Kunming to Hsiakwan, a distance of some 250 miles, runs the famous Burma Road. From Hsiakwan to Likiang it is at least another 160 miles by caravan trail.

The prospect of travelling on the Burma Road used to fill me with dread. This great highway, although marvelously constructed, well kept and extremely picturesque, has been a notorious killer. It climbs several mountain ranges of about 10,000 feet by a series of hairpin bends and runs along the edge of giddy precipices. I traversed it for the first time shortly after it had been completed, and I can never forget the sight of countless heavy trucks lying at the bottom of deep ravines, smashed beyond salvage. This was during the war, when the road was the life-line for the supply of war materials and goods to China. Most of the drivers were Chinese and the majority of them from the coastal areas of China where the land is flat. The demand for drivers was urgent and insatiable. Licence or no licence, everybody was snapped up, either by the military or the commercial concerns, if he could demonstrate his ability to drive. Salaries were high and thousands of dollars could be made on the side. Unaccustomed to driving in these tremendous mountains, with their tricky weather conditions, steep gradients and breath-taking hairpin bends, hundreds of such drivers went to their death on their first attempt. Before my very eyes some of them went over the edge, a sickening crash echoing from below. Many, disregarding the warning of seasoned drivers, insisted on going on through certain dangerous defiles in heavy rain and were crushed by landslides. Almost all trucks were overloaded, many of them unchecked, with defective brakes which on steep climbs failed, letting the trucks roll backwards to their doom. Countless were the hazards that this road held for the traveller, quite apart from the ever-present menace of bandits.

I learnt the wisdom of making my round of old commercial firms in Kunming, before paying my fare, asking about the trucks to Hsiakwan with the most reliable drivers. To escape Japanese bombing raids, the start was usually made before dawn from some inconspicuous place in the countryside. On top of the merchandise, baggage was piled, and high on top of that we took our seats, usually twenty to thirty passengers — men, women and children. Whenever we came to a very steep climb and the truck could not take it, we jumped down and helped to push it up bit by bit, its radiator issuing a jet of steam like a locomotive. On the way down the hairpin bends we could only pray as the truck coasted, the driver saving petrol. This trip of 160 miles normally took from three to four days, and the nights were spent in roadside inns.

Hsiakwan was an unattractive, draughty place dominated by bare, forbidding mountains. Like Kunming, it was a beehive of activity, with the military — Chinese, American and British — dashing here and there in trucks and jeeps; merchants busily loading and unloading their cargoes from trucks and boats, and hordes of coolies, drivers and plain loafers idly sauntering about. Hsiakwan was notorious for its bedbugs — a specially hardy and big variety.

From Hsiakwan one could go to Likiang either by caravan or on foot. I have done both on several occasions, but I remember especially a return journey that I made by caravan after I had been in Likiang for some time. It was spring, the dry season, and before the excessive heat of summer.

Arriving in Hsaikwan, I had my baggage carried to a friend's house. Caravan men were called, who counted the pieces and decided how many loads they would make. Then the haggling started and continued for about two hours; the crafty men, apparently refusing my offer, would depart only to return at regular intervals, reducing each time their charge by fifty cents or a dollar a load. Finally we settled, gave them a deposit of one dollar and relaxed. Shortly afterwards, sturdy Minkia women appeared and carried the cases and trunks to the boats. In the evening, after a good meal, we went to check the baggage which was neatly stacked in a big boat, and when the moon appeared a huge sail was hoisted. Men and women produced native mandolins and guitars, a platter of cheese and a big pot of wine. While they played and sang, we had a drink. Then the ropes were cast off and we watched the boat glide off into the silvery vastness of the beautiful Tali Lake, accompanied by other cargo boats, leaving the passengers to proceed by bus.

I got up early in the morning and breakfasted on native ham and cream cheese with *baba* (flat round bread enriched with butter and ham shavings), washed down with Tibetan butter tea. My Nakhi servant Hozuchi appeared, and we took our hand baggage and *pukai* (bedding) and boarded a creaky, overloaded bus which brought us to Tali in an hour. Although considered by some to be one of the most beautiful places in the world, I have never liked Tali. Destroyed by an earthquake, it has never recovered and there was an air of desolation and death. Quickly we entered the south gate and passed through to the north gate. An array of 'chariots', with one or with two horses, was waiting. We agreed on the price, piled our baggage the best we could, and squeezed in among other passengers. I call them 'chariots' because I doubt that such vehicles could be found elsewhere in the world. Mounted on two wheels with old rubber tyres, they were oblong wooden boxes with the front open and two rows of planks to sit on, and shaded by a kind of blue tent. They were so primitive that I always thought of them as something that Pharaoh must have sent to fetch old Jacob to Egypt. The road was not a road at all but a trail of boulders, crossed by unbridged mountain streams, and along this the conveyance, creaking and swaying violently from side to side, was pulled by two sturdy horses at full speed. I prudently sat in front. Sometimes the bumps were so hard that passengers were thrown up against the ceiling and one man had his head nearly split open. Badly shaken and bruised, we reached our destination, Tamakai, at the other end of the Tali Lake, late in the afternoon. The only pleasure I had was to watch the marvelous lake, like a great emerald set in blue mountains.

As soon as we reached Tamakai we were met by the caravan man and conducted to his house. Other passengers were already there. We were made comfortable and informed that the cargo and our baggage were due presently as the boats had already been sighted in the distance. The house was new and beautiful. Doors, posts and furniture were of wood, exquisitely carved in filigree. Soon a splendid feast was served and many pots of excellent wine were produced. Our beds were covered with gem-like Tibetan rugs on which we spread our own bedding.

We were roused at four o'clock in the morning. There was a quick breakfast, followed by much shouting and sounding of the gong. The loads, securely tied to wooden frames, were spread in the courtyard. Struggling mules and horses were presently led in with many unprintable curses. Each load was lifted by two men, speedily clamped on the wooden saddle and the horse was permitted to trot out into the street. My hand baggage was quickly tied to a similar frame, the bedding spread in the form of a cushion, and the whole contraption hoisted on to a horse. I was then lifted bodily on to the top and the animal was shooed outside, the man shouting to me to mind my head when passing through the gate. Outside, other contingents of the caravan were also pouring out of neighbouring houses. To the sounding of the gong, the leading horse, gaily bedecked in red ribbons, pompons and small mirrors on its forehead, was led out. The caravan's leading horse moved forward and, having looked back to see that everything was ready, started walking down the road at a brisk pace. At once he was followed by the assistant leader, less gaudily decorated, but also full of authority. Immediately the whole caravan sprang after them, forming a file as they went along. The caravan men, in vivid blue jackets and broad pants, rushed after the horses. They wore picturesque broad-brimmed hats of translucent rain-proof silk with a bunch of multi-coloured ribbons.

It was a source of endless wonder to me to watch the speed with which the caravan proceeded. On the level ground or downhill it was very considerable, and the men saw to it that it was not slackened without reason. All the time the animals were exhorted onwards with the most obscene curses imaginable and encouraged by small stones and cakes of dry mud which were thrown at them. After three hours of such intensive march we came to a placid stream and a gentle meadow. The caravan was stopped, loads lifted and set in a row, great copper cauldrons were set up and the men started cooking luncheon. The animals were relieved of their saddles and given fodder and water. Neighing and screaming, they all started rolling on their backs. As the caravan fare included board and lodging, we all were given bowls and chopsticks and asked to join the men in the meal. We sat in a long row facing each other, taking food and rice out of large dishes placed between. Nobody was permitted to sit at either end of the row, for caravan men are extremely superstitious, and they say that anyone sitting at the end stops the way and a disaster may follow later.

In the late afternoon we arrived at Niukai and the caravan was split into three sections, each going into a separate caravanserai. We were lodged upstairs and a meal was served again. Afterwards we wanted to take a bath at the big hot spring for which the village was renowned, but the pool was filled with lepers. I tried to sleep, but could not. The grinding noise of feeding animals below was like the sound of a large flour mill, big rats ran over my face and the chattering of the caravan men round the fire continued unceasingly until it was time to get up.

Next day we crossed high forested mountains, the pass infested with robbers. This was the first robber ring before Likiang. In the evening we reached Tienwei and next morning we passed Chienchwang. All this land between Tali and Chienchwang was the site of ancient Minkia kingdoms, whose glory culminated in the establishment of the great Nanchiao Kingdom which was conquered and destroyed by Kublai Khan. Nobody really knows where the Minkia came from originally. The only work of note on the Minkia, Fitzgerald's *Tower of Five Glories*, gives some account of their customs and beliefs but does not reveal the secret of their origin. Perhaps, as some of them claim, they are indeed the refugees from Angkor Thom, but much research is needed to substantiate this claim.

Chienchwang was a small walled town, its streets drab and colourless. There was nothing to eat in its two restaurants except on market-day. The meanness of the Chienchwang Minkia was proverbial. Men and women dressed in black and they lacked the usual Minkia gaiety and insouciance.

The route followed the course of a river and, from one point on the road, it was already possible to see, through the gap in the mountains, the Likiang Snow Range, still fifty miles away, its peaks and glaciers glittering in the sun. The broad valley, planted with winter wheat, was narrowing. Soon we climbed a small hill, crowned with a white pagoda, and then descended to a picturesque gate. This was the frontier between the ancient Minkia kingdoms and the Nakhi Kingdom of Mu or Likiang.

Very soon we arrived at the village of Chiuho, where a market was in progress. The street was crowded with the Minkia from Chienchwang and from the Upper Valley, and with Nakhi and other tribal people. We met many friends who had come to the market, among them lamas, Nakhi students and several women from Likiang who had come to trade their wares. While lunching on fried eggs and some dried beef, washed down by Chienchwang mint wine, we saw Akounya's father with one of his sons. He was an old friend and his family treated me almost as one of themselves. They were the first of the Minkia I had befriended after my arrival in Likiang. I had gone one day to a furniture shop to order some benches and there I met a young Minkia carpenter, named Tzekuan, and his sister Akounya, who had brought some goods to Likiang for sale. Tzekuan and Akounya began to visit my house and I used to stay with them whenever I passed that way to or from Tali. Akounya was an energetic and bossy girl and I always thought of her as the head of the house in contrast to her mild, unassuming father and her quiet, self-effacing mother.

Akounya's father, who was awaiting our arrival, told us to go straight to his house at the top of the valley, where my horse was already waiting for me, saying that he would come back later in the evening. Again our caravan was swaying through the green fields towards the high forested mountains. The road became narrow and crowded. We were climbing imperceptibly but steadily, the air getting cooler and sweeter. The caravan leader began to beat his gong and deep sounds echoed throughout the valley.

The caravan gong was indispensable on the narrow, twisting mountain trail. It warned the approaching

Akounya. The Minkia girl at whose the author always stayed when travelling by caravan to Hsikwan.

peasants with their heavy baskets and prevented collisions with other caravans. Because of the speed with which caravans moved it could be disastrous for two caravans to meet without warning. The crash that followed was worse than a collision between two trains. The proud and jealous leading horses, unwilling to give way an inch, would head straight for each other and try to push each other into the deep irrigation canal by the roadside or against the rocks of a defile. Nor would the rest of the caravan stop. The animals would charge each other, screaming, pushing, throwing their loads off, and spilling the passengers in the *mêlée*. By the time they were disentangled by cursing caravan men, the scene looked like a battlefield. Bales were scattered about; fragile goods, like pottery, were shattered to pieces and dazed passengers hobbled into clearings to examine their wounds. For ordinary travellers on foot the only salvation, when they heard the ominous gong, was to dart to safety in some clearing by the roadside lest they be violently thrown into a ditch or have their legs crushed.

At last we arrived at the head of the valley, hemmed in by precipitous mountains. Again the caravan split into several sections and went into the appointed caravanserais. We bade the leader good-bye, giving him instructions for the delivery of our baggage in Likiang. Tile caravan fare was never paid in advance: that would have been a great insult. Only a small deposit, a dollar or so, was given and the balance was paid the day after arrival. The goods and baggage were not delivered to any central station or depot, but were distributed to patrons' houses or stores by the caravan men, who also guaranteed the integrity of the cargo, subject only to force majeure and the bandits' whim. This last lap before Likiang was the most dreaded, because the wild mountains ahead concealed the most powerful of the bandit rings.

Akounya's house was situated on the mountainside, overlooking the caravan road. She was there waiting for us, a husky girl, about twenty-two years of age, with a round face and rosy cheeks. Like all Minkia women in this part of the valley, she was dressed in a blue tunic down to her ankles, with a sash, and blue trousers. On her head she wore cunningly tied kerchiefs — blue, red and white. The ends were tied near tile temples to form perfect cat's ears. This feline appearance of Minkia girls never failed to delight me and I used to tell them that they looked like cats dressed in the Dutch national colours. Akounya disappeared into the kitchen, where her mother was already busy.

Her father and brother Ahtseng returned from the market late. The old man apologized, saying that he called on die home guard trying to arrange for an escort of ten for me on the following morning.

'There is a large band of robbers now and only last week a caravan was plundered,' he told me.

'Well, if it is a large band, ten boys are useless,' I said. 'It would be less conspicuous, surely, if I go just with Hozuchi and, perhaps, Ahtseng, who could come too.'

We talked and talked and finally agreed on taking five home guards just for the sake of 'face'.

Dinner was served by the light of mingtze — pine splinters — burning on special clay stands. A number of Minkia friends drifted in. A large jar of wine was produced for the crowd and a smaller one for me.

'This is your favourite yintsieu — the honey wine,' the father said. 'I bought it in Likiang last week specially for you.'

23

Typical Minkia dishes were put on the table, all in small saucers, according to local custom. There was home-cured ham, fried chicken, fried water plant, small fish, roasted eels, fried potatoes and salted pork. There was much joking and laughter and some mandolins were produced. How I enjoyed their sweet, slightly monotonous music and plaintive singing! It was very romantic — all about love, beautiful women and brave men. Every time a new dish was placed on the table by Akounya, one of the young men blushed.

'I think he must be Akounya's future husband.' I nudged Ahtseng. There was a roar of laughter, the young man turned crimson and others nodded knowingly.

The early morning was very cold and hoar frost covered the grass. We breakfasted heavily. I mounted my wild Tibetan horse; Hozuchi strapped on a basket with food and hand baggage, and we started. Almost at once we came to the sheer face of the mountain. There was a cobbled road, extremely steep, zigzagging upwards through the scrub. I dismounted and, parting from Hozuchi, I took a small path which was a short cut. It was a very long climb through rhododendrons and pines. Brightly plumed pheasants crossed the path now and then and hid in nearby bushes: distant trumpeting of deer and calls of mountain birds were the only sounds. The higher I went the colder it became and the more difficult to breathe. Whistles and catcalls came from above. Somebody was there. The view was magnificent: high mountains and dark green forests surrounded me, and on both sides of the path there were deep, rocky ravines. Far below there was an emerald lake and the yellow thread of the caravan trail to Taku. At last, panting, I reached the top of the pass where a dark, sinister gap led to the plateau

Path inside Atsanke gorge 11,000 ft, deep where the Yangtze River flows.

beyond. Five shivering youths with old-fashioned guns were waiting for me. 'Are you the escort?' I inquired, and they nodded. We sat for a while waiting for the horse and Hozuchi.

Then we started to walk along a narrow trail clinging precariously to the side of a breath-taking ravine. Soon we emerged on vast highlands pitted here and there with the devil's sinkholes. These were typical of the countryside around Likiang and were huge funnels with clusters of trees which camouflaged bottomless holes into the bowels of the earth. There was not a soul to be seen, nothing but a sea of pine forests and mountains around us. It was agreed that the escort would return home when we had passed the notorious 'Robbers' Temple', where the trail begins to slope gently towards Likiang. It marked the highest point on this plateau of 11,000 feet. Plodding hour after hour in the oppressive silence and utter loneliness, we stopped talking.

At last we came to a turn, after which the dreaded temple should have been visible. A band of ten men, poorly clad but each carrying an old gun, appeared as if from nowhere. We did not stop and they fell in with us. At last one of them spoke.

'*Zeh gkv bbeu?* (Where are you going?)' he asked me in Nakhi.

'*Ggubbv bbeu* (Going to Likiang),' I answered brightly. He pondered.

'*Nakhi koru chi kava* (You understand Nakhi),' he smiled.

A flood of conversation followed with my boy, the guards keeping discreetly silent. Hozuchi explained who I was, where I lived and where we were travelling from. I guessed at once who the strangers were, but kept my own counsel. I was not afraid of being killed, but I hated the idea of appearing in Likiang in only my underwear. We came to a pretty little clearing among the pines, where I dismounted and asked everybody to sit down. From Hozuchi's basket I extracted a jar and a bowl, filled it to the brim and said, '*Zhi teh* (Drink wine).' Round and round went the bowl and everyone became warm and mellow. The interest in my baggage and inquiries of how much money I had with me gradually abated. I prudently slipped in a word that I had no money with me at all as my funds had gone ahead with the caravan.

'We are poor people,' said one of the strangers, 'and have to live by our wits.' He took another draught of wine. 'However, you are a good man. We know much about your work. I have not met you before. But once you saved my life and that of my friend. Do you remember an old woman who came to you last year to ask for medicine for the men who had been burned by gunpowder explosion?' Saying this, he let his trousers fall down, exposing his scarred legs and abdomen. I remembered at once.

'So that was you!' I cried.

'Yes,' he said, slowly tying up his trousers.

The whole picture came back to me clearly. Once I came home late in the evening and found an old woman from a mountain village in my courtyard, crying bitterly. Between sobs she explained that her son and two friends had been making gunpowder, for hunting purposes, in a large cauldron that very afternoon. A man, absent-mindedly, had thrown a lighted cigarette into the cauldron...

'They are still breathing!' she infromed me, 'but all the skin on the thighs and addomen is burnt off.'

As Likiang had no hospital, she could only think of me and walked forty *li* (thirteen miles) to get medicine.

This was an extremely grave case, I thought, and the men must surely die with so much skin destroyed. What could I do? If I gave them medicine and the men died, I would be considered a murderer and my life would not be worth a penny at the hands of an enraged family and clansmen. Such was the custom here. And yet, I must do my best. I made the old woman swear, before my servants and neighbours, that the family should not bold me responsible for the death of these men and, I told her frankly, die they must if the injuries were so great. She understood and swore by the great god Saddok of the Snow Mountain, all other gods, and the spirits of the mighty Nagarajas who dwell in the mountains, lakes and trees, I gave her a generous supply of powdered sulphanilamide and cotton-wool, and told her to powder the men gently every day.

'But', I insisted, 'you must see that they drink water by the bucket all the time.'

She grabbed the drug and left. A week afterwards she appeared with a few eggs.

'They are still breathing and drinking the water,' she said.

I marvelled. Another week passed and she came again with a few eggs.

'Now they can eat a little,' she informed me.

A fortnight later she brought a small pot of hot honey and more eggs.

'Now they can walk a little. Thank you! Oh, thank you!'

Weeks later she came yet once more, carrying a chicken. She beamed.

'Now they can sleep with their wives,' she said exultantly.

So these were the men. They helped me gently to

Author's friend Hokuoto. A typical mountain Nakhi pcasant from Lashiba.

mount, wished us all a pleasant journey, and disappeared among the pines.

At the Robbers' Temple near by — a small half-burned shrine — we said good-bye to our escort, thanked them and gave them a small tip as is the custom. Meaning glances were exchanged, but nobody spoke about the encounter.

Again we travelled in utter solitude through a rolling country with nothing but forests and great mountains in the distance. Soon, however, the majestic Mount Satseto moved into view, with its glittering glaciers reflected in the beautiful blue lake of Lashiba. The village of Lashiba with its white, orange and red houses could be seen in the distance. When we reached it we stopped for a quick meal, and then followed up the shallow valley that holds the lake hemmed in by green mountains. Slowly we climbed up to the gap that led to Likiang.

CHAPTER II

LIKIANG

*D*ESCENDING from the pass, the loveliness of the valley hit me with staggering force, as it always did when I made this journey to Likiang in spring-time. I had to dismount and contemplate this scene of paradise. The air was like champagne; the weather, warm but with a tinge of freshness that came from the great Snow Range dominating the valley. Mount Satseto sparkled in the setting sun, a dazzling white plume waving from its top. Storms were raging high up there and the powdered snow was whirling up into the air like feathers on a cap. Below, everything was serene. Pink and white groves of blossoming peach- and pear-trees, interspersed with feathery bamboos, all but concealed white and orange houses of scattered hamlets. Roses were everywhere. The hedges were a mass of clusters of small double white ones: big white, pink and yellow climbing roses hung from trees and roofs: dwarf single roses spread themselves on meadows and clearings. The scent was overpowering and exciting. The fields were green with winter wheat, and between them ran deep, crystal-clear streams of icy water. Dark water plants waved in them like strands of hair. The water from glaciers divided and subdivided into innumerable streams and canals, and made the Likiang plain one of the best irrigated areas in the world. The gurgling of these swift brooks, the singing of larks and other birds was like the music of gods. The road twisted in and out of hamlets.

Likiang itself could not be seen: it was hidden behind a small hill, on the top of which a red and white temple was clearly visible. Crowds of peasants of the Nakhi tribe that predominated in Likiang were returning from the market: smiling men and women led horses, and we could hear their chattering and singing well ahead. Many of them knew me and their greetings were spontaneous and joyous, their faces red from the customary drink they had taken before returning home. Wine in clay jars was carried on horses and by women in their baskets, to be consumed during the cold evenings in the mountains. A group of young men, clad in short pants and jerkins of deerskin, appeared from behind a bend, playing on reed pipes and singing. They were the Attolays — a mysterious tribe living deep in the heart of the Nanshan range — who greeted me affectionately. There was a jumble of sounds ahead — tinkling of bells, clanging of iron, shouts, and tramping of animals. It was a Tibetan caravan coming from the city. Soon its owners came up on their broad, shaggy ponies. They were two Tibetan gentlemen, resplendently clad in red silk shirts and heavy coats tied at the waist by sashes, and wearing gold-embroidered hats.

'*Aro, konan ndro?* (Where art you going?)' I greeted them in Tibetan.

'*Lhasa la* (to Lhasa),' they grinned. Then, in perfect English one of them said, 'Have a cigarette, sir!' and offered me a packet of Philip Morris.

They went on slowly and soon the caravan came up. We pulled to the side of the road to let it pass. Unlike the Minkia caravans between Hsiakwan and Likiang, Tibetan caravans proceed unhurriedly and there is little danger of violent collisions. The horses and mules do not carry the heavy loads, of 140 to 180 Ib., into Tibet, but only 80 to 100 Ib.; unlike those in a Minkia caravan, the animals are unshod to prevent them from slipping on stone trails. The distance covered by a Tibetan caravan in a day is very short, twenty miles being the limit. The animals are looked after with loving care and always appear sleek and well fed. Light loads, short stages and plenty of fodder are imperative if the animals are to survive the trek of three months between Likiang and Kalimpong via Lhasa. There is no road, only a trail climbing and twisting up and down the steep mountains through dark rocky gorges, fording roaring glacier streams, sometimes wading in mud in tricky mountain bogs. Even with this care, mules and horses arrive at their destination exhausted and with hooves cut to pieces, and it takes a long time for them to recuperate.

The caravan we met was like any other typical Tibetan caravan. The leading horse wore a mask profusely studded with turquoise, corals, amethysts and small mirrors; red ribbons were arranged around its ears; and it carried a triangular orange flag, with green serrated border bearing a legend in Tibetan meaning 'Likiang-Kalimpong direct transit.' Each unit of twenty animals was accompanied by a walking Tibetan with a rifle, and a huge mastiff with a red woollen lei around his neck.

33

As we passed through the villages on the outskirts of the town, the women in the wine-shops waved and called us to have a drink. We had a cup of wine in each not to offend them. Greeted by neighbours, we slowly climbed half way up the hill and passed through the gate into a flower-filled courtyard. We were at home.

Our house was old but still in good condition, and spacious. All houses in Likiang had two storeys and were built with three or four wings, or more. Big or small, the architecture never varied. The lower part was of sunbaked bricks, whitewashed on the outside or coloured in orange, yellow or even light blue, according to the owner's fancy, with elegant borders traced in black or blue. In the centre there was a stone-flagged courtyard with three stone-lined raised flowerbeds. The lower rooms in the middle of each wing had four or six doors all beautifully carved in filigree. Other rooms had either carved or latticed windows. The back of the rooms was wainscoted in wood to conceal the ugly bricks. The upper storey was one vast room, sometimes quite low, and it could be partitioned into as many small rooms as one wished. Since few Nakhi liked to stay upstairs, it was usually used as storage for provisions, crops and goods. There was no ceiling and, as the wooden walls never quite reached the roof, breezes circulated freely. It had a few windows ill the outer wall and a continuous series of windows facing the courtyard which could be opened by tilting them upwards. As there was no glass but thin rice paper pasted on the lattice-work, like windows in Japanese houses, there was little protection in the evening, when the blasts of cold wind roared down from the Snow Mountain. The roof consisted of heavy clay tiles and the corners slightly curved upwards in the usual Chinese style. All tiles were of grey

Caravan from Hsiakwan to Liking. Author's baggage has just been delivered to the author's courtyard by the caravan lerder (standing).

colour, but sometimes the monotony was broken by white lines along the border.

It was extremely difficult for a newcomer to Likiang to get a house to himself. At best, the offer was to share the house with the owner by taking one or two wings. This was very inconvenient on account of kitchen arrangements, children and prying eyes.

When I first came to Likiang I made it known that I must have a whole house for my office and myself. Weeks passed and then, by accident, I heard of one; but there was a fly in the ointment. The owner was adamant on one point — her distant relatives, an old couple, who acted as caretakers, and their only son must continue living at the house. I had to accept. I was gratified to find it so speedily but, knowing the housing situation in Likiang, I became suspicious both of the hasty offer and the very low rental. It was true the house was far from the centre, but it was a large house conspicuously located on the main road from Lhasa and would have been very convenient for an inn; yet it had remained empty for a very long time. Discreet inquiries amongst my newly made Nakhi friends and those of my Chinese cook from Shanghai, elicited the fact that the house was haunted. And more sinister particulars were whispered into my ear.

It appeared that the house had been a prosperous inn owned by an elderly widower. He married the present owner who, it was related to me, was pretty, vivacious and a notorious flirt. Evidently she had other ideas about married life as, in a couple of years' time, the elderly man died in convulsions at night in one of the rooms on the ground floor. Bitterly weeping, the young widow assured people that he died of overeating. But, as he could not speak at all before he died, neighbours had a different

Author's house. Front gate and main street of Wuto village.

notion. They were sure that his death was due to the classic Nakhi poison, the deadly black aconite boiled in oil. The onset of this merciless poison was characterized by a paralysis of the larynx. In convulsions the victim could only stare frantically at his helpless friends without being able to utter a word. There was no known antidote. The young widow, with a small son, was left alone to enjoy her gain. The inn continued to do its business, but its popularity declined. The Nakhi are superstitious people and few local travellers, hearing the tale, wanted to stay at so inauspicious a place.

One night a weary military officer from Kunming stumbled into the inn. The enchantress cooked him a delicious meal and poured out for him many a bowl of strong clear *zhi*. Flushed with wine, the man talked, and continued talking far into the night. He was retiring from his business, he said, and he had money; as a matter of fact, big money in his saddle-bags. On the morrow he would continue the journey to his village, which he had not seen for many years, and where he would settle down, buy land and build a nice big house perhaps as big as Madame's; yes, and perhaps marry. The lady was very interested. It was late and there were no other guests. He drank more and more. He became amorous and she suggested a supper before retiring. She went into the kitchen and returned with a large bowl of delicious stewed pork, heavily seasoned with chillies, warm *baba* and appetizing titbits. After the meal she escorted him to his room. Late next morning she appeared very agitated. She explained to neighbours that one of her guests was still in the room and, in spite of her repeated calls for breakfast, there was no answer. They entered the room. The man was dead. There was an investigation, but nothing came out of it. Who cares much about a lonely stranger dying on the way, perhaps of a heart disease?

As no Nakhi would take the house, my arrival was God-sent. My cook implored me not to take it, saying we should all be dead in a year's time. I only laughed and went to see the lady in her famous noodle-shop. She was presiding over a stove with two enormous cast-iron Chinese boilers out of which she ladled greyish noodles into bowls for the customers sitting inside the shop. She was middle-aged and her face was of an unhealthy greenish-grey colour. Her dress was filthy and the shop itself fully matched her sloppiness. But her eyes were remarkable — bold, roguish and full of cunning. Although willing to get rid of the house almost at any cost, her inborn greed overcame her. She named an exorbitant rental and for one year only. Next year it would be double, and so on; certain rooms were to be reserved for her use; the old couple had to stay; the house could be used for her receptions on certain festive and ceremonial occasions and any additions I might make would become her property at the expiration of the lease. I launched my counter-attack. I said I was a high government official and that, if I wanted to, I could apply for a requisition order; then she would get nothing. Besides, I continued, the house was haunted and, therefore, useless to anyone else. But I did not mind staying there because I was a Taoist initiate, had much experience in dealing with the spirits, and, through a series of séances, could rid the house of its ghosts and evil influences. However, it would be a slow business, and I intended to stay a long time. I was surprised to see how quickly she climbed down. She was beaming. She told me that the idea of cleaning the house of ghosts and influences through my intervention was the

A view of Liking plain and Shwowo village from a lamasery.

best news she had heard for years. She herself proposed a very low rental, only forty dollars a year, much less than I had expected, and a contract for six years, renewable for another like period. On my part I agreed to the old couple's staying and to her use of the house for ceremonial occasions. Thus the deal was concluded and celebrated with a long drink of *zhi* on both sides.

I had the house cleaned, scrubbed and washed. The central room, where the unfortunates had expired, I made my general office. I partitioned the upper storey, facing the street, and made it my bedroom and my private office. The upper storey in the adjoining wing was made a guest-room.

A short climb along the stone-paved road led to the red temple on the top of the hill and to a wonderful view of the town and plains. Likiang lay snuggling between this hill and the foothills of the northern range opposite. It continued around the hill, spreading into the eastern valley and the main plain which sloped gently southwards. It was a sea of slate-grey roofs, with glimpses of orange, white and red walls of houses and official buildings. The square market-place below was packed with people and a babel of voices could be beard clearly. Trees and gardens were visible among the roofs and here and there a stream glistened in the sun.

The name Likiang means in Chinese the Beautiful River. This refers to the great River of the Golden Sand, more popularly known as the Yangtze, which flows to the west and east of the town and forms the vast loop in which Likiang is situated. The river is only twenty-five miles from the city in either direction, but it takes days to reach the apex of the loop in the north. The Nakhi call the town Ggubby. The epithet Beautiful River was more than deserved by both the river and town. Unlike most Chinese cities, Likiang had no wall. It was a large place as towns go in the sparsely populated Yunnan province. There has never been any census, but I reckoned that some 50,000 people lived in the town area. It was really a federation of closely knit villages and each street was called by the name of the village; for example, Main Street was Wobo village and the road on which I lived was Wuto village. The officious Chinese affixed to some streets such appellations as Chung Shan (Sun Yat Sen) Road and Chung Cheng (Chiang Kai Shek) Road, but no one paid attention to such innovations. Every town in China had streets with such names now probably changed into Mao Tse Tung and Stalin Streets.

Likiang was the seat of the Northwest Pacification Commissioner and the Magistrate, and enjoyed, therefore, a considerable standing in the Chinese officialdom. There was an efficient police force, but policemen were seldom visible in the streets. If there was a brawl, it could always be settled by the intervention of the interested bystanders or neighbours. If it was a case of theft from a shop or house, it could always be reported direct to the police station at one's convenience. If it was a pilferage from a food or sweetmeat stall, the culprit could always be chastised by the injured party, usually a woman, with a screaming barrage of most obscene words. Likiang was not civilized enough to have professional pickpockets or bank-robbers. Thousands of dollar in bank-notes or hundreds in silver were casually piled into open baskets by traders at one end of the town, the basket was hoisted on to the backs of women, slowly paraded through Main Street and the market and safely delivered at the other end of the town. Naturally everyone looked enviously and admiringly at the progress of this untold wealth within arm's reach, but that was all. Only when a wife was stabbed by her husband, or vice versa, did the police run to the scene of the crime.

The descent from our hill down to the market below was gradual, along a cobbled street with a stone-flagged path in the centre. The street was lined by dilapidated shops in which beautiful brass padlocks, in native style, were made; or those of Tibetan boot-makers, and the sellers of food. The mean exteriors concealed handsome, carved living-quarters behind.

Further down, the road descended in steep curves, which I used to tell my friends was the 'danger point' on my walk to or from town. Here, on the steps of their houses, sat sturdy Nakhi matrons spinning wool, knitting, selling fruit or just gossiping. I have always addressed the ladies, of whatever race they might be, as Madame. It has always worked in China and, I thought, why should not I continue the practice in Likiang? A few days after we had settled in our new house and my walks to town became a daily occurrence, some of these women began greeting me every time I passed with *'Zegkv bbeu?* (Where are you going?)' I always smiled in return and said, 'Madame.' A few days later I addressed one of these women again as Madame. She rose and advanced towards me threateningly.

'Every time you pass here you call us *Manda*! (fool),' she exploded. 'If you call us *Manda* again, I am going to give you a good beating,' she raged. The others roared with laughter. I gathered my dignity and tried to explain.

'Madame,' I said, 'I address you thus out of politeness. In Italian it is *Madama*, which is the same as in Chinese *Ma Ta Ma* (Mother Big Mother). Even among the Nakhi, elderly ladies are addressed as Dama.'

43

Whether they understood or not, I continued to call them Madame and every time some of them pretended to be angry with me. 'Again he called me Manda,' one of them would scream. 'Wait, we'll get at you!' they chuckled. Indeed they kept their word. Sometimes they would snatch my walking-stick or pull me by the seat of my trousers. But whenever this happened, they were repentant at once and consoled me with an orange, a couple of walnuts or a drunken plum (plums soaked for months in strong wine). On dark nights they escorted me half the way up the hill with burning *mingtze*(pine torches).

At the foot of the hill the road divided. One branch continued along the canal, skirting the hill, and the other crossed a small stone bridge and entered the marketplace. The market was a large square paved with cobblestones in the centre and great stone slabs along the sides. It was probably the only marketplace in the whole of China which was thoroughly washed every day, but this was done with the help of nature. Early in the morning the sluices of the canal which flanked the hill and was, therefore, slightly higher than other streams flowing through the city, were opened and about a foot of water was allowed to rush through the place for an hour or so. All rubbish was swept away by the water into a lower stream of the Likiang River at the other end of the market.

Likiang was covered by a network of these swiftly running streams which flowed at the backs of houses and, with the bridges, created an illusion of a miniature Venice. They were too shallow and too swift for any navigation and, anyway, there were no boats in Likiang, but they served the town well, providing fresh water for all purposes. The streets of Likiang were paved with stone slabs or stone bricks and were scrupulously clean. Sweeping was frequent and thorough and the refuse was swept into the streams, which also received the rubbish from the houses. One might think that these streams and canals would get clogged and polluted in no time, but the water rushed unceasingly, crystal clear, and nothing but pebbles were seen on the bottom. The force of the current was so great that all and everything was immediately swept down the stream out of the town. It was only further down the valley, where the current became slow and opaque, that one noticed how unclean the river was. Whilst the people were indifferent to the dumping of rubbish into the water in the city, they were careful about upper reaches of the river and tried to prevent pollution by all available means. This was not difficult as the river originated in a beautiful park, a quarter of a mile away, at the foot of the Elephant Mountain — a name derived from its resemblance to a sleeping elephant. Here, out of the mouths of subterranean caverns, rushed sweet, ice-cold water from the glaciers of the Snow Range.

From the marketplace one street branched off to the left and led to the houses of prominent merchants and to the yamen with its vermilion walls and red pillars. It was a long street and it merged gradually into the road leading to the Yangtze River. The street to the right was Main Street. Like all the streets in Likiang it was narrow and was paved with stone bricks closely fitted together. It was lined by a continuous row of shops, some bending backwards, some forwards, others leaning sideways on one another, as though frozen in an undulating and swaying movement of a ballet des boutigues. There were no pavements. Tibetan and Minkia caravans, going and coming from the busy market town of Hoking, thirty

Likiang Park

miles to the south, had to pass through this street and were a terror both to pedestrians and shopkeepers. Swinging loads scraped the shelves in front of the shops, sweeping the wares into the road, and scattering the baskets and pottery on sale by the roadside. The polished surface of the street was like ice, and the animals, with legs spreading, would sometimes crash to the ground, causing injury to some unlucky passer-by.

The shops were rather dark and mean. They had no plate-glass windows but only wooden counters, facing the street, with shelves below for the display of goods. Yet, considering that it was war-time, they were well stocked with all kinds of merchandise. Tibetan caravans were pouring in the goods from Calcutta, both for local consumption and for re-export to Kunming, at a prodigious rate. Best makes of British and American cigarettes were available and all kinds of textiles. Even new Singer sewing-machines could be bought. Of course, the prices were very high as the caravan is the most expensive mode of transport in the world. One shop had a small stock of imported beer at twenty-five dollars a bottle; few could aspire to buy such nectar. Matches cost fifty cents a box and were used only in emergencies. Some households always had a few live embers left in the stove from the previous day and neighbours would call in the morning to borrow a burning piece of charcoal. All the shops burned incense-sticks all day long at which smokers could light their pipes or cigarettes. Mountain people disdained matches even if offered. They always carried flint-locks and a supply of fluffy moss of which a tiny bit was placed on the tip of a cigarette or on to a pipe to catch the spark. Once I was trying to build a fire in rain and wind and had spent nearly two boxes of precious matches when a sympathetic mountain dweller came along and had the fire burning in no time at all.

The shops opened towards noon and the market-place began to function only in the afternoon. In the morning both the market-place and streets were deserted. Very few people had watches and there were few clocks. Even wealthy houses kept clocks more for decoration than for ascertaining the correct time. Indeed, there was no correct time. At the magistrate's *yamen* the clock might show nine o'clock, at another place it might be eight or ten. Who cared? People judged the time by the sun. When the sun was well above the eastern mountains it was time to get up and cook breakfast. When it was high in the heavens it was the time to go to market. It was quite impossible to make exact appointments, and if you had told a man to come at eight be might turn up at ten or eleven, or even at noon.

The shops were run, with very few exceptions, by women. They knew exactly what you wanted, where to find it, and what last ditch discount could be granted after a vociferous bargaining. They were shrewd and aggressive and knew how to clinch a bargain. When the woman had to go away, she asked her husband to take over. He was usually to be found at the back of the shop nursing a child and his emergence was a calamity to the business and a trouble to himself. He did not know where matches were kept or where to find the pickles or in which jar was the required wine. In most cases he gave up and requested the customer to call again later when his wife had returned. Even professional male assistants in some big shops lacked ability and salesmanship, for they were inattentive and rude and, when an important deal seemed on the verge of being lost, they rushed and called their master's wife to arbitrate.

The payment for merchandise was made in *pangkais* — Chinese silver half-dollars which were minted in Kunming specially for this region. Their value in the terms of American money was about eight *pangkais* to a dollar, but everybody had to look twice at the *pangkais*, for some of the newer vintage had more copper in them than silver and they were either rejected or accepted at a ruinous discount. During the last few years, preceding the fall of the Nationalist régime, Chinese paper money found its way into Likiang. It was brought by Hoking traders and government banks. These bank-notes were accepted reluctantly and not by everybody. Comparatively few people could read Chinese characters and one bank-note looked to them as good as another, and to simple mountain tribesmen some cigarette wrappers appeared like bank-notes. Many country folk were victimized by unscrupulous pedlars from Hoking and Tali. Ten-dollar notes were passed as hundred-dollar ones and hundred-dollar ones as thousands. I was constantly stopped in the street by peasants asking me to tell them whether it was a ten-dollar or a hundred-dollar note they had. Anyhow, the silver dollar always remained the basic currency and prices were calculated accordingly, and anyone with paper money always tried to convert it immediately into silver dollars. Exchange brokers flourished and they were invariably women.

The Tibetans, Lolos and other remote mountain tribesmen preferred to settle for their purchases in gold-dust, nuggets or the silver ingots they always carried with them. This procedure was most convenient and nobody suffered. The merchant, a woman of course, and the buyer would go to a goldsmith's shop near by; the gold would be analysed and the required portion weighed or a quarter or a half of the crescent-shaped silver ingot sawn off. Gold, silver and coins were not kept in a bank, as there were no banks in Likiang worthy of the name. They were kept in strong wooden chests, padlocked with heavy native locks, in the inner rooms of the house or, particularly in the villages, buried in clay jars in a secret place under the floor.

One of the streets off Main Street led to the Copperware Square. It was lined entirely with copper-smithies and the din was terrific, with every smith in his shop beating on a vessel with all his might. Likiang copperware was beautiful, heavy and extremely durable. It was all hand-beaten and hand-burnished and it possessed a wonderful lustre. The square was literally ablaze with the vessels. The gold content was high, for the copper was mined in tile rich gold-producing area along the River of the Golden Sand, a day's journey from Likiang. There were classical Likiang water buckets of rounded form with stands; jugs and tea-kettles of all sizes; and fluted trays with brass inlays and borders, which were used for sending as ceremonial presents. The samovars, of which each household must have at least one to provide the eternal boiling water for interminable tea sessions, were different from Russian models, having only one big handle and a long spout instead of a tap. There were also innumerable *houkous*, large and small, of which, like the samovar, each house, rich or poor, must have at least one.

The *houkou* and, to a lesser degree, the samovar were the symbols of Nakhi happiness and enjoyment of life. Without them no social function, wedding or funeral, or picnic, could be complete. The meals, during the cold days of winter, would be cheerless indeed without the warm companionship of the *houkou* and samovar. The *houkou* is a Chinese-style stove, like a large bowl with a lid and on a stand, and with a chimney through the centre. Water is poured into the bowl, charcoal burns in the chimney, and raw vegetables, meat and etceteras are put into the water and soon a delicious stew is ready. As the people eat, more water and ingredients are added, as well as more charcoal, so it can supply hot food for as long as is needed. The *houkou*, under different names but basically the same, is most popular from Lhasa to Shanghai and from Harbin to Djakarta: the Japanese version of it is the *sukiyaki*.

An elegant street not far from the Copper Square led to the palace of the Mu kings. A triumphal gate across the street marked the beginning of this aristocratic quarter. The palace itself was a rambling structure in Chinese style and was used as the District Primary School. Adjoining it there was a series of walled houses where the ex-king, his family and other royal relatives lived. A great stone arch, elaborately carved, was in front of the royal compound and bore two Chinese characters, 'Loyal and Righteous', bestowed on a king by a Ming emperor in the seventeenth century. The title of king or chief, still used by the people in reference to the head of the Mu family, was really an honorary one. During the Manchu dynasty the feudal status of the king had been abolished and Likiang became a *fu* magistracy. For a period the Mu kings continued to rule as hereditary *fu* (senior) magistrates, but even that was taken away from them and a succession of Chinese magistrates began. The Mu dynasty traced its origin as far back as the glorious Tang dynasty and produced many heroic and just rulers, interspersed with a few bad ones. Towards the close of the Manchu dynasty the royal family of Mu was well on the road of degeneration. They had absorbed the then new-fangled fashion of smoking opium and other elegant vices of the Chinese court and their downfall was rapid. Deprived of the revenue from their vast estates, the members of the royal family resorted to selling, one by one, their accumulated art treasures and the precious mementoes of their ancestors, to satisfy their insatiable craving for opium, and it was alleged that some princes had sold even their furniture and wives' wedding dresses. All the prestige and standing of this illustrious family had gone with the wind.

The king whom I met occasionally was a sorry-looking individual, pale, emaciated and dull, and was considered a nincompoop. He was seldom invited to big social functions, and even then was allocated a secondary place at the festive table. Other members of the family hardly presented a better appearance, although some of them were brilliant Chinese scholars. I had engaged a Mu king's cousin as the chief clerk at our office and he remained with us until my departure from Likiang. Sometimes he was absent for days and he never appeared at the office before the afternoon: but he was continually asking me for advances on his salary and trying to collect secretly, for himself, interest from our co-operative societies. He even stole an office clock and other articles and did everything in his power to squeeze a dollar or two from any source by hook or by crook. Yet I could not dismiss him: I tried, but found it impossible, for he was indispensable. His presentation of the accounts and his reports in Chinese for my head office were perfect, for he was a brilliant writer of Chinese official documents and knew all official usages and approaches.

It was only after I had opened our office in Likiang

that I realized how few Nakhi or Minkia knew Chinese
really well. Several men had been recommended for
the post of the chief clerk at my office. They had the
highest credentials teachers in high schools, secretaries
in local government and so on. Each was given a fair
trial, but their letters and reports were returned by my
headquarters as incomprehensible gibberish, hardly
worthy of comparison with a Chinese schoolboy's essays;
and neither head nor tail could be made of the accounts.
I was sternly ordered to find the right man. If they only
knew how difficult it was! Finally I got hold of Prince
Mu and everything went well. But what a smoker he was!
Opium was the essence of his life and he was ready to
do anything, and he did, to get it. His wife used to come
secretly to get what salary remained and she always
complained that she and her children were starving.
Everything that could be sold at the house had already
been sold. When he came in the afternoon, after his long
morning smoke, Prince Mu would plunge into work with
gusto. There were no problems that he could not solve,
He was one of the most educated and intellectual Nakhi
I have ever met. He knew Likiang's history and affairs
as few people did. He was an expert on Chinese history
and official life, and a brilliant conversationalist. He was
polished, urbane and charming, yet he was lost to all
decencies when the craving came.

In the vicinity of the Mu royal grounds there were many
marasions of the local rich, with streams gurgling in front
or between the buildings and roses spilling over the walls.
The houses were two-storeyes, with six or eight wings.
All the woodwork was lacquered in *sang-de-Bœuf* or
maroon colours, and the beautiful carving was gilded or
silvered. The stone-flagged *patios* were full of flowers and

blossoming bushes. The Nakhi were passionate lovers of flowers and always carried a blossom or a bouquet in the street. They planted roses, dahlias and cannas by the side of their homes and along the edges of the road and were always on the look-out for new varieties of flowers. I used to receive from America flower and vegetable seeds and my courtyard was a blaze of colour. Many were the requests for a seedling or a blossom. Sometimes my little garden was simply pillaged by the crowds of visitors: I did not mind that but I was really annoyed one day when they dug up and carried away my *incarvilia* and black aconite which I had brought from the Snow Range. They were native flowers, and all that they had to do was to take a walk to the mountain and get them there by the thousand, I wondered afterwards whether the black aconite was stolen for a hurried murder or suicide. Potted plants such as cineraria and calceolaria were much admired and coveted. Once I presented a pot of calceolarias to my friend, Madame Lee, who owned the best wine-shop in Main Street. She exhibited it on her counter and crowds of admirers viewed the flowers every day; women promptly christened the blossoms 'Testicle Flowers'. Particularly venerated were the peonies. There were certain exclusive gardens where they could be seen at their best: the enormous blooms were shaded by paper wrappers and, when enough had opened, a drinking party was usually organized by the owner in their honour.

Beyond the big houses the town terminated abruptly in a series of green fields, divided and subdivided by flowing streams. Likiang had no slums. There were no special quarters of the town where the poor predominated. There were no ramshackle one-storey buildings, no hovels made of kerosene tins, straw or packing-cases, and no mean, dirty and unpaved lanes. There was no West End and no East End, one part of the city was as good and aristocratic as another. Pigs were kept by each self-respecting household, but their pens were a convenient distance from the house: true they were permitted to wander all over the town, but they were well-mannered and respectful animals. They took care not to hinder traffic too much and slept mostly along the kerbs of the street where the sun was warmest. Pig manure was eagerly collected and sold at a good price as fertilizer for the fields: the pigs seemed to know this and the streets were seldom soiled. These highly intelligent animals left the houses, including mine, early in the morning and went to neighbouring meadows to forage for additional food, or to sleep in the sun. They returned late in the afternoon, grunting, and tried to poke the door open with their snouts. Whenever they were needed earlier, they could always be recalled by the owner shouting *'Nounal'* at the top of her (or, on rare occasions, his) voice. As in China, the pig was the mainstay and pride of the Nakhi economy and an acceptable companion to the housewife in the country when all the others were out. It always grunted so appreciatively, its little eyes twinkling, and punctuated its sympathy for the hard-working woman by gentle prods with its snout.

Thus Likiang, well paved and well watered, had no dust and no bad smells. Cooking and heating was done by means of charcoal and pine firewood. These two products were the greatest items of commerce on the market and a considerable source of income to the villagers. *Mingtze* — the rosin-impregnated pine splinters — were another important item, always necessary for illumination, and for lighting the home fires. As there were endless pine forests all around it was easy enough for any villager to gather them and to bring them to town for sale, either on horses or on his, or his wife's, back. In the morning there was always a column of fragrant pinewood smoke rising above the city.

Likiang had no cars, carriages or rickshas. Everyone walked, rich and poor, generals and soldiers, without distinction of caste or class. No millionaire had a chance to show off his Cadillac or Rolls-Royce and no Chinese general could roar in his armoured limousine through the peaceful streets of Likiang. The uniformity of locomotion had a wonderfully levelling effect on all classes of the population and promoted true democracy in relationships. A walking governor or general did not look nearly so formidable and inaccessible and could be greeted informally and intimately even by the humblest farmer.

Outside the town there was the outline of a motor highway to Hsiakwan, built years ago, but it had never been finished: there were no bridges, and torrential rains had washed away many sections in the mountains. The road had been initiated by the Provincial Government at the instigation of the Central Government, but the plan was successfully blocked by the Nakhi themselves through their powerful representatives in Kunming. The Nakhi did not want too much of Western civilization just yet. They said that the highway would bring much more trouble than benefit into their peaceful land. The little town would be swamped by hordes of Chinese crooks and loafers, in the guise of small traders, drivers and mechanics, just as Hsiakwan was. Native business and industry would be ruined by keen competition and home life disrupted by evil influences. There would be greater interference by the Chinese military authorities and other government departments with their peaceful and free existence. A form of regimentation might be imposed on them and, of course, the worthless paper currency. Alas, they were right, as future events have shown. The people of Likiang were not ignorant of the West. Many of them had been to India and Burma as traders. They had powerful commercial connections with Kunming and many Nakhi units were serving in the Chinese army. They were definitely in favour of building a powerful hydro-electric station for the town and nearby villages as Likiang had no electricity, and they welcomed aeroplane connections with Kunming, but not the ruinous effects of a new road.

There were no big factories in Likiang, but there was gratifying industrial development in a small way in later years through the advent of the Chinese Industrial Co-operatives. There were scattered all over the town many small factories where wool spinning, weaving and knitting was done by hand. Elegant European-style footwear and sports goods, all made from local materials, were displayed in many stores. The Minkia furniture shops could turn out anything from mahjong tables to ultra-modern wardrobes. Tibetan boots and saddle-bags were made by the thousand; in fact, the really fine Tibetan boots were not produced in Tibet but exported there from Likiang. In addition to these there were the copperware and brassware and the lovely hand-chased brass padlocks. By its huge trade through Tibet during the war and its newly developed industries, Likiang became very prosperous, and new buildings began to spring up overnight everywhere.

During my preliminary survey trip to Likiang I had found the people to whom I was introduced charming and hospitable, and there had been feasts and a picnic meeting organized in my honour. Thus, upon my appointment, I proceeded to the City of the Beautiful River with my head in the clouds. I chafed at every delay on the road, and even the fast caravan appeared to move too slowly, so anxious was I to plunge again into the atmosphere of welcome and geniality I had experienced. I was absolutely sure that, upon arrival, I should be surrounded again with friendliness and helping hands and my work be child's play, but alas, I realized only too quickly that my first impressions were wrong. The Nakhi proved to be truculent, unfriendly, mildly hostile and extremely suspicious, at the first arrival of all outsiders who were to take up permanent residence, whether they were of high or low rank. I found that to be received as a passing guest was one matter, but to settle and work among them was a totally different proposition. They especially distrusted all government officials coming from the capital, Chungking, as I did. They always thought that such men came— and came only for one purpose — to investigate their resources and wealth and make secret recommendations for additional taxation or the introduction of reforms curtailing their privileges or liberty. Every official, they thought, comes to take something. That there should be one who was ready to give something and help them, without expecting a rich return, was unthinkable and absurd. This new official, they said, intends to stay. He is a high officer, outranking the magistrate, so we must be civil to him but no more. Let us stand together and unobtrusively block his work, whatever it may be, and when he finds himself in difficulties, he will go away of his own will. Such was their reasoning.

It was only some considerable time afterwards that I fully

understood how cunning the Nakhi were. By no means were they the simple, innocent and child-like tribesmen which, some writers aver, still exist in some remote corners of the world. There may indeed be such tribes in existence but, in the light of my own long residence in this area, which more than qualifies for remoteness, and my subsequent travels in south-east Asia, I have come to the conclusion that nowhere can there he found the sweet and innocent natives of the romantic travelogues. An explorer or traveller who has stayed among such people only for a few weeks or months cannot assess accurately the character of such 'children of nature'. It is only by living among them for a long time, and associating closely with their mode of thinking, understanding their joys and sorrows and following their customs, that one may finally arrive at a glimpse of the truth.

My disenchantment had started soon after our arrival. We were lucky to be permitted to stay, for a while, in a room at the house of Dr · Rock, a resident of long-standing and much respected, and it was only by a fluke that I found my haunted house, after all other accommodation had been determinedly, though politely, refused me. Afterwards we had immense trouble in obtaining office furniture. There was nothing in local carpenter shops, and when we asked the carpenters to make us desks and other office furniture of the simplest design, they turned their backs on us. But with the greatest difficulty and much expense we had the furniture made by the Minkia carpenters in Chienchwang.

The next step was to win over and establish friendly relations with our immediate neighbours. The credit for this auspicious development went largely to my Shanghai cook, Lao Wong, whom I had brought with me. He was a tall, burly fellow, heavily pock-marked. Like all illiterate people, he was sagacious and, what is more, he was a born diplomat. But he spoke only that peculiar dialect which is used in Shanghai by the Chinese who come from the northern bank of the Yangtze. He had been frightened and dazed by the caravan travel and by his arrival among the 'barbaric savages' of the Western Regions of whom he knew only through that classic and interminable Chinese opera 'Hsi Yu Chi'(Travel to the Western Regions). He was much upset when we established ourselves in the haunted house and trembled at the least noise, expecting to be seized and strangled by two horrible ghosts. He planted burning incense sticks in every room and corner of the house before retiring for the night. Fierce-looking, skin-clad mountain men, with long daggers at the belt, who passed to and from the market, threw him into a cold sweat. However, seeing that neither he nor I had been stabbed or clubbed, he soon gathered courage and started going out.

Most of the Nakhi spoke a little Chinese, but to the end of my days in Likiang they never ceased to assure me that they could never understand what my cook was talking about. Undismayed he talked and talked. He was so voluble and his voice was so shrill, I could hear him from the top of the hill as I returned from the town. His constant visits to one and every neighbour, his talks and little gifts to children soon melted the atmosphere. Neighbours began drop in for a light for their kitchens in the morning, to borrow this and that or simply out of curiosity. Afterwards they would bring some peaches from their gardens or a few potatoes, a bunch of wild flowers or a rose. Soon we knew all about them and they about us and our doings. At last we felt we belonged, at least, in Wuto village.

Down the street, just before the gate which marked the boundary of the city, there was a great, richly ornamented mansion; It belonged to a Mr. Yang, a very rich Minkia merchant who considered himself a Nakhi by virtue of his lifelong residence in Likiang. He had many sons and daughters. He himself had retired long ago, but two of his sons had separate shops in Main Street and were doing well in textiles. They had branches in Hsiakwan, Kunming and Lhasa. The two younger boys, by his second wife, were at school. My cook made fast friends with the two merchant sons, and soon I was informed that Mr. Yang desired to make my acquaintance. I presented myself one morning. He was a handsome old man, stately and dignified, with an aristocratic face and long white beard and was immaculately dressed as a Chinese gentleman, in long gown and black silk makwa jacket, and he wore a black cap with a red button. He rose to greet me from a *chaise-longue* in which he was resting. It was on the patio; the air was filled with the scent of flowers, and there were rows upon rows of rare orchids and primulas and petunias in pots on marble stands. Roses and other flowering shrubs were everywhere, and there were brilliant goldfish in the marble-lined pond and in glass bowls. I was offered tea and wine of rare vintage. The old man was smoking a long silver-tipped pipe and sipped tea; slowly and unobtrusively he as looking me over. We chatted lightly and then I related the purpose of my mission to Likiang. He listened but said nothing. In a short while I rose to take leave; Mr. Yang rose too and, gently taking my elbow, led me into one of the hails. A splendid repast was laid out on a round marble table, with ivory chopsticks, silver pots of wine and silver cups. His sons and grandsons came in. I protested that it was too great an honour to be invited to a meal on my first visit, but I was gently pushed on to a chair and we all began to eat. The room was tastefully decorated with old Chinese paintings and scrolls. All the furniture was of blackwood; there was rare porcelain on stands and Tibetan copper jugs inlaid with turquoise, and a burnished brass censer out of which fragrant smoke curled in a spiral to the painted ceiling.

Mr. Yang liked me and invited me again many times. Sometimes it was a formal dinner at which one or two passing dignitaries were present, at others it was a festival meal, and once it was the wedding of one of his sons. Often we would just talk together of Likiang and its people, of local customs and of tile war which still raged far away; and often he would send me a gift of some fruits or a rare delicacy, or a joint from a newly killed pig. It was a gentle and enduring friendship. We understood each other even without speaking, and could be content to sit back and enjoy the peace of the little garden. He had early perceived that I was a Taoist and he himself had attained that mellow state through the lessons of his long life.

During one of my visits a few years later he led me to the back of his house and showed me a small pig in a separate pen.

'This pig is being specially reared for my funeral,' he said, chuckling. Then he led me to a disused corner room, opened the door and showed me a stout coffin, newly painted. I felt very sad, but he was smiling.

More than a year passed. I had gone to Kunming and returned after a month away. My cook was very excited when I stepped into the house.

'Mr. Yang has been asking all the time on which day

you will return,' he informed me. 'He will invite you to lunch tomorrow,' he added.

I entered the old man's house next day with foreboding. He was very glad to see me, but I noticed how frail he looked. His face had a strange luminosity. His two elder sons were with him.

'I was ill after you had left,' he greeted me. He invited me to see the pig. 'But I am too weak to walk,' he said. 'My son will show it to you.' The pig had grown enormously. It was now an exceptionally fat animal.

'My sons are now with me day and night,' said Mr. Yang lightly, 'but I knew how ominous this was. The old man was propped on the pillows and we had luncheon en famille, though he hardly ate anything. The leave-taking was emotional.

'I am glad to have seen you again,' said the old man. 'Good-bye! We may not perhaps see each other again,' and he feebly squeezed my hand. Next day at noon my cook rushed upstairs into my room.

'Old Mr. Yang is dead,' he announced with a show of emotion. I was shocked. Unloosing his tongue, Lao Wong flooded me with the details of his passing. It appears that the old man felt suddenly that he was going. His family gathered around him and dressed him in ceremonial robes. Then he spoke to all of them calmly. After that he lay down his head on the pillow and motioned to his son. As he breathed his last tile son placed a small silver coin on his tongue. Immediately he was put into the coffin.

According to Nakhi custom, when a man is about to expire a small silver coin must be quickly laid on his tongue. If this is not done, the man will never gain admission into the paradise where his ancestors dwell. Therefore, when a person is ill, weak or very old, there is always one of the family watching by the bedside day and night. Turns are taken by the members of the family, and woe to the son or daughter who does not perceive in time the moment of passing. Because of this belief, it is considered a calamity to die suddenly in an accident or a fight. The lost souls of such unfortunates are doomed to perpetual wandering in purgatory, until their entrance into the paradise is secured by special — and expensive — Shamanist ceremonies.

CHAPTER III

THE MARKET AND WINE-SHOPS
OF LIKIANG

*S*TARTING in distant villages early in the morning, the streams of farmers began to converge on Likiang soon after ten o'clock, along the five main roads. The streets were jammed with horses loaded with firewood; people bringing charcoal in baskets on their backs and others carrying vegetables, eggs and poultry. Pigs were either carried, tied up, on poles by two men, or led by women, who held the leash in one hand and gently prodded the animal with a switch in the other. Many other kinds of merchandise were carried either on the backs of the people themselves or on their animals. There was the noise of hooves on hard stone, loud talk, shouting and much laughter. In the market itself there was great tumult with all these crowds trying to pass each other and jockeying for the best positions on the square. On the previous night sturdy stalls had already been pulled out of the common pile, or dragged from surrounding shops and set in rows in the centre. Women and girls brought heavy bales of textiles and spread bolts of cloth on the stalls. Haberdashery, spices and vegetables were displayed in separate rows. Shortly after noon the market was in full swing and was a boiling cauldron of humanity and animals.

Towering Tibetans elbowed their way through the struggling masses. Boa villagers in their mushroom-shaped cloaks waved bunches of turnips. Chungchia tribesmen in their coarse hempen shirts and trousers, with peculiar little queues falling from their shaven heads, listlessly promenaded with lengths of narrow and rough hemp fabrics. Nakhi women ran frantically after some wayward customers. Many strange tribesmen and their women simply stood and gaped at so many attractive goods and at the elegant people of Likiang. At about three o'clock the market session reached its climax and then began to decline. Towards four o'clock the 'cocktail' session was in full swing.

Main Street was lined with dozens of 'exclusive bars' and thither thirsty villagers, men and women, turned their steps. Normally in China such a thing is unknown. Not that the Chinese do not drink, but wine in China is associated more with eating and the best time for drinking is considered to be at dinner with friends. The women in China do not sit down with men to drink, and therefore such meals are entirely male affairs. Generally, for propriety's sake, Chinese women do not drink much in public, preferring to have a sip or two in the privacy of their rooms. The usual refreshment in China, when concluding protracted transactions, is tea without sugar or milk. After a tiring day in the market the numerous tea-shops in Chinese towns and villages are crowded with congenial parties of men and women relaxing over pots of tea. In this respect, the customs of Likiang were quite distinct. There were no tea-shops, and if anyone drank tea at all during the day it was brewed in miniature earthen jugs on the brazier concealed somewhere in the back room. Everyone, men, women and children, drank wine, white or sweet yintsieu. No self-respecting child above two years would go to sleep without a cup of *yintsieu.*

The 'exclusive bars' were neither bars nor were they exclusive. They were general stores where, in addition to salt, sugar, salted vegetables and haberdashery, wine was kept for sale, both to be taken away in customers' own jars or to be consumed on the premises. The shops were uniformly small in Likiang and, in addition to the counter facing the street, there was a longer counter at a right angle to it, leaving a narrow passage from the door to the inner rooms of the shop. A couple of narrow benches were put before this counter and there the people sat sipping their wine. That the inmates of the house, including dogs, had to use this passage, sometimes spilling the customers' wine, was of no account. No one really minded such minor inconveniences in Likiang.

Anyone could have a drink at any shop, but some villagers acquired preferences for particular shops. These regular and faithful customers grew intimate with the lady owner, and always gave her the first option on whatever they were bringing to the market for sale. Similarly the lady favoured them with special discounts on whatever they wanted to buy from her. Actually such relations between the established clients and the shop owner were not so simple. The lady also acted as their broker, banker, postmaster and confidante. Baskets with purchases were left in her keeping whilst the customers went out for more shopping. Small loans were negotiated with her on the security of the next deliveries of whatever they usually brought to the market or against growing chickens or pigs. When clients could not pay for their drinks or purchases, credit transactions were permitted by the lady, who got her husband or son to record them in simple Chinese. Wallets with cash were sometimes deposited at the shop for safe-keeping by the farmers whose villages were not safe from robbers. As there was no postal service to remote villages, the wine-shop was a favourite accommodation address. Letters were duly forwarded to the recipients by safe hands. Confidential advice was sought by clients from the lady on the problems of engagement and marriage, childbirth and funerals. And, of course, every lady wine-shop owner was a Bureau of Information *par excellence*. She knew the *curricula vitae* of everybody within a radius of a hundred miles, and I doubt whether there ever existed a secret in Likiang that was not known to her.

I had humbly attached myself to three wine-shops. One was Madame Lee's in the smartest section of Main Street, another was Madame Yang's in the marketplace, and the third belonged to Madame Ho in the Tibetan quarter of the city near Double Stone Bridge. I faithfully visited all of them almost every day, when I was in town. About five in the afternoon I descended to Madame Yang's and stayed for an hour. At six I was at Madame Lee's, and went to Madame Ho's usually after dinner. However, I was not received into the inner circle of these ladies' clients until a much later date, when they had become sure of my respectability and integrity.

My debt to these clever and charming ladies is very great and it pains me that perhaps I shall never be able to repay it. The success of my integration into the life of Likiang and of my work is largely due to the sensible advice and infallible information supplied to me by these women. Had it not been for their vigilance and timely warnings, I would have made many blunders which might have led to my downfall. Every day at their shops added a valuable page to my experience and knowledge of this difficult region and its people.

The wine supplied by the wine-shops in Likiang was not imported or bottled in glass bottles. It was made entirely by the home method at each particular shop and according to an age-old formula which was kept secret. There were three kinds. The clear white wine, called *zhi*, was made from wheat and it was equivalent in potency and taste to gin. The sweet *yintsieu* was made of sugar, honey, wheat and something else, and was amber yellow, clear, and tasted rather like Tokay or sweet sherry. The older it was, the better was the bouquet. Then there was the plum wine, reddish and rather thick, which reminded me of Balkan *sliwowitz*. It was quite potent and I could not stand much of it. I preferred the *yintsieu* of a special old vintage which was best at Madame Lee's and cost a little extra, though the highest price per cup was only five cents. Anyone who wanted to take wine home had to bring his own jar or bottle. Bottles were very precious in Likiang, and an empty one might cost as much as two dollars.

Madame Lee was an old woman, very erect, stately and handsome, with aquiline features and large lustrous eyes. She belonged to the cream of Likiang society and was much respected both in the town and in the villages. Everybody knew her and she knew everybody. Her husband was a big, handsome old man with a long grey beard. He was purely ornamental and never interfered

Mme. Lee at her shop in the morning, facing the bar at which her customers sit.

with the affairs of the shop; whenever she went out and he had to take over he felt utterly lost and was as helpless as a child. He could not even find the right jar of *yintsieu* and I and my boon companions had to help ourselves. The couple had a son who was a school-teacher: he was married and had a daughter and an infant son. The daughter-in-law was a husky, simple soul and dutifully stayed at the back of the house, working hard. It was the old man who looked after the little girl and nursed the baby, which was always in his arms and yelled when his mother took him away for feeding. Old Mr. Lee also lent a hand in cooking, as was the custom with all Likiang husbands. He was always to be found in the back room, lolling on the bed or brewing tiny pots of tea, which he liked very much. Perhaps he did a little opium smoking too, but it was mostly for the sake of sociability.

Madame Lee was one of the most efficient and hard-working women I have ever seen. Besides presiding from morning till night over the shop, she also supervised the preparation of the stock-in-trade which consisted of a great battery of large jars with sauerkraut, pickled cucumbers, plums, peach, orange and quince marmalade, not to speak of wine. Everything was made at home with the help of the daughter-in-law. It was no surprise at all to meet Madame Lee carrying, early in the morning, a heavy sack of wheat or a basket of plums from a nearby village. Besides all these chores, there was the seasonal slaughter of pigs and the salting of hams, pigs' heads and pieces of pork for home use and for sale. She sometimes complained that she was tired, but at the same time she said that she was glad still to be able to work at the age of sixty-three.

Everything Madame Lee made was first-class, clean and

tasty. We could not live without her pickles, marmalades and jams, her succulent hams, Rocquefort-like bean curd cheese and palate-titillating sweet and sour garlic.

Likiang was a wonderfully free place, especially in commerce and industry. There were no excise taxes to be paid on home-made liquor or anything else manufactured either at home or at the factory, and no licences or permits to be taken out for selling it. People were entirely free to make what they liked, sell whatever they liked and wherever they liked, in the market, in the street or on the premises.

Although Madame Lee's shop opened at nine or ten in the morning she was too busy to appear until later. The shop remained unattended and anyone could come in, help himself to whatever he needed and leave the purchase money on the inner counter. This was true of the other shops in Likiang, and I never heard of this privilege being abused by the people or of this money being stolen.

It was not easy to get a seat at Madame Lee's shop in the late afternoon. In an emergency she permitted me to sit behind the counter on a small stool, facing the other customers. Men and women came to have a drink or two before starting on their trek back to the village: but in accordance with Nakhi customs, no woman sat down in company with a man. Women usually took their drinks standing in front of the shop and chatting meanwhile with Madame Lee. It was quite common for a woman to treat men to drinks; nobody tried to prevent her from paying the bill. As soon as his drink was finished, a man would go and somebody else would drop into his place. It was wonderful to sit at the back of the shop in comparative gloom, and watch through the wide window the movement in the narrow street, as though seeing on a screen a colour film of surpassing beauty. Sooner·or later everybody who had attended the market session had to pass through Main Street at least once or twice. Old friends could be seen and invited for a drink or new acquaintances made. Any stranger could be waved to and asked to share a pot of wine, without any ceremony of introduction, and I was sometimes stopped in the street by total strangers and offered a cigarette or a drink. No such liberties were allowed for women, but now and then one of them, who knew me well, would slap me on the shoulder and say, 'Come and let us have a drink!' and she would have to take her drink standing up so as to avoid a local scandal.

With the deep blue sky and brilliant sunshine, the street was a blaze of colour, and as we sat and sipped our wine from Madame Lee's porcelain cups, mountain youths, in the sheer joy of life, would dance through the street playing flutes like the pipes of Pan. They looked wild woodland creatures in their sleeveless skin jerkins and short skin pants. A woman would slowly lead on a leash a couple of truculent pigs whose progress was slow and erratic. They would get tangled with passing horses or try to push between somebody's legs, and there would be screams, laughter and imprecations from the outraged passers-by. A caravan would appear suddenly from behind a bend and women shopkeepers would rush to collect and protect their wares. The horses, heavily loaded with fire-wood, jostled men and women with baskets and stopped now and then before the shops whilst their owners tried to strike a bargain.

The company I met at Madame Lee's wine-shop was extremely diverse and interesting. Sometimes I sat in the company of a rich lama, a poor Boa, an even poorer Chungchia, men from Lotien, well-to-do Nakhi landowners from a nearby village and a Minkia caravan driver. At other times it might have been rich Tibetans, White Lolos, and other tribesmen similarly mixed up. There was no snobbery on the part of the wealthy or influential men and no subservience or cringing on the part of the poor. They all drank their fill quietly, smoked and talked, if they could understand each other. More often than not they invited me to a round of drinks and then I had to do the same. At the beginning I made some faux pas with those who looked very poor, by trying to pay both for my own orders and for the drinks they had stood me. The reaction in each case was swift and devastating.

'Do you mean that I an1 not worthy to stand a drink to a friend?' one man exclaimed indignantly.

'Do you take me for a beggar?' another fumed.

'I am as good as you are, and if I stand the drink, I mean it!' was the retort from a third.

Thereafter I was very careful not to offend the amour-propre of these proud and independent people. Nothing enraged them so much as an implication of superiority.

I must, however, admit that Madame Lee was a little snobbish, and did not encourage drinking at her shop by primitive tribesmen or by men whom she considered to be notoriously bad or thievish. She had her own marvellous intelligence system and knew exactly who was who. Sometimes I brought some new village acquaintance for a drink, only to be reproved later on and admonished not to have any connection with 'that crook'. At first I was sceptical of her judgment, but later on I learned to value her opinion very highly. If she said a man was bad, I invariably had proof at a later date to that effect.

Gradually she pointed out to me all the more undesirable characters of Likiang and the countryside. Some of them were sons of rich parents who had become notorious rakes, opium smokers, gamblers and even thieves. Others were village bullies who also smoked opium, gambled and were not above burglary or theft when opportunity offered, and I sometimes lost articles at my house when these rogues called on the pretext of wanting treatment for some ailment. But she sometimes became quite enthusiastic about some exotic tribesman sitting at her shop. I owe many friendships to her introduction.

I never saw any brawling in Likiang wine-shops and certainly never at Madame Lee's bar. But this is not to say that there were no quarrels in the town, for the people of Likiang were very sensitive and easily offended. Now and then a passionate quarrel would arise between two women or men in which their neighbours would take part. The women would shout dreadful things at each other and then burst out crying bitterly. Then the neighbours would step in and the parties would be speedily pacified and parted. Some quarrels, however, lasted throughout the day and night, with constant screaming, swearing and fighting. So many obscenities and insults were heaped on each other that it was beyond my understanding how the parties could ever look each other in the face again.

Occasionally something would happen to shock or amuse the town. Once, I remember, a stark-naked man appeared in the market and proceeded leisurely up Main Street. I was sitting at Madame Lee's. He went from shop to shop, asking for a drink or a cigarette. Women spat and turned away their faces but nothing was done to stop him. The truth was that the brazen Likiang women could hardly be shocked by anything, but they had to put on some show of modesty and embarrassment in order to avoid acid and biting gibes from the men. A policeman was never to be seen in the streets, and it was only at the end of the day, when somebody bothered to rout one out from the police station, that the demented man was led away. He was not jailed, for there were no laws or statutes in Likiang about indecency in public. Such matters were largely decided by public opinion. One could always go a few hundred yards towards the park and see dozens of naked Tibetans and Nakhi swimming in the river or lying on the grass in the sun in full view of the passers-by and in front of the houses. There was a lot of giggling and whispering amongst the passing women and girls, but there were no complaints. A line, however, had to be drawn against nakedness in the public market.

Another embarrassing case happened at Madame Lee' s shop one afternoon when I had retired there after a busy day. I was sitting with friends, sipping wine, and Madame Lee was busy with her chores. A poor mountain man came and stood at the door. Madame Lee asked him what he wanted. He said that he wanted me to examine him and give him medicine, as I had already earned a reputation for medical knowledge and was known to keep a cabinet of essential medicines in my office. This I always refused to do when I was at the wine-shops, as I did not want to turn them into clinics, thereby interfering with legitimate business. Madame Lee told him to come and see me on the following day at my office.

'What is wrong with you?' she asked casually. Before we could realize what was happening, the man let his trousers down to exhibit an intimate part of his anatomy. Madame Legs face reddened. Quickly she snatched a feather duster and struck the man.

'Get out of here, you fool!' she ordered peremptorily. But the damage had already been done. Madame Ho, who had a confectionery shop opposite, hooted with laughter. Madame Lee pretended to be very angry and reviled the stupid man. The story spread all over the town, and I was asked for full details about the incident at Madame Yang's rival wine-shop and at Madame Ho's.

Madame Yang's bar was definitely of a lower order compared with Madame Lee's. It was not even a shop at all, but rather a small space in the arched gateway of a new house that was being built. It was by a small stone bridge which crossed the clear stream of the upper canal, and the market square opened just below the steps of the bridge. Right in front was the busy street which led up and across our hill in one direction and to Double Stone Bridge in another. It was a very busy and highly strategic corner. A small low table stood near the wall just by the bridge and there were a few low benches. The rest of the space was occupied by stocks of new baskets, wooden buckets and tubs in which Madame Yang dealt. Behind was a courtyard and the house itself, partly finished. I used to sit at the table while Madame Yang sat on the stone step, sewing a garment or sorting out something. At first she had been very embarrassed to let me drink at her place. She thought it was very undignified for me, and bad business for her, as my presence might scare away her shy clientele. After a couple of weeks, however, everybody got used to me and I became a feature of the place.

Madame Yang was a shy, middle-aged woman. She was a widow and worked very hard to support her large family. But, by the very nature of her business, her profits were not big and she always complained of the shortage

A Tibetan buying pottery at Mme. Yang's shop inside the gate.

of capital. Once she had to ask me for a loan of fifty dollars, which I lent her. She specialized in catering to the poorest and most primitive tribes who lived in far mountain villages and hamlets, in Lotien and along the little-known Yangtze tributaries. She knew all the Boa, Chungchia and Miao, White Lolos and Lissu, and was friendly with the ghome-like Szechuanese squatters who lived in the forests of the Snow Range and in the strange village of Ngyiperla, in the awesome Atsanko Gorge, 11,000 feet deep, through which the great river roars in perpetual semi-darkness. The Minkia girls from Chiuho and Chienchwang were also numbered among her clients. She was very kind and had not the heart to beat down too much the semi-naked, shivering little men and women, who came sometimes from some far-off place, hardly known even by name to the local people, and whose only stock-in-trade was a small bagful of strange roots or a couple of crudely made little benches. I liked Madame Yang's bar more than any other wine-shop in Likiang, because here I was in the very midst of the drama of the helpless and declining tribes, and could watch their hopes and disappointments, and, perhaps, help a little in an unobtrusive way.

It was a hard existence for these slow-witted and incompetent people. They had lost their grip on life long ago and now did not know how to recover it. They were hungry, unclad and cold, and nothing they did helped to fit them again into the world. Their efforts to survive were pitiful and futile, because nothing they made or produced was vital any more to the changing economy of the world. Likiang was their world and Likiang was no longer primitive. Who wanted their crude benches or herbs? And, if somebody did, it was for almost nothing. What could they buy for their home with a few pennies earned after days of marching through drizzling rain or in biting wind? Of course, these unfortunates were not the only people who came to Madame Yang's. There were others, much more alive and dynamic in spite of their primitive dress and appearance, such as the mysterious Attolays from the Nanshan, who although clad only in skins, were tall, handsome, energetic and with a sparkle in their eyes. They looked like forest gods who had descended from their green glades for a spree among the mortals, and who could hardly restrain themselves from playing flutes and pipes, and dancing all the time.

At first the Attolays ignored me completely. They were very sensitive and as proud as the Black Lolos. I always watched them arrive for the market session. The men came first on splendid mules. The women followed afterwards, loaded with new baskets and wooden buckets for sale. They wore turbans and thick sheepskin capes with red woolen tippets on the shoulders, which the men sometimes wore too. This, I learned later, meant that they intended to stay overnight either at Likiang or at some midway village, using the capes as sleeping-bags. The women deposited their wares at Madame Yang's and returned from time to time with likely customers. When they failed to sell all their goods in one day, they left the remainder in Madame Yang's hands. Late in the afternoon both the men and women returned and enjoyed a drink. Afterwards the men rode off and the women started their weary trek on foot, their baskets loaded with purchases, topped by a heavy jar of the white wine, filled up by Madame Yang. They seldom reached their villages the same day and stayed overnight at Lashiba near the big lake.

One evening I was shyly offered a cup of wine by an Attolay, and as we talked I discovered that his name was Wuking and that he came from the furthest village in the Nanshan. His family was very large and one of his uncles was a colonel in the Provincial Army who sometimes sent them money and gifts. I soon came to know many of the Attolays through him, and he and his friends, sometimes accompanied by their womenfolk, used to stay at my house. My clinical facilities were a great attraction to them and were widely used. Wuking and his friends loved music and often danced to Western records, adding their flutes and pipes to tile music of the gramophone. I always sympathized with the Attolay women carrying those heavy baskets full of provisions and wine whilst their men went swaggering on horseback. One day I asked one of their women, who had just lifted a heavy basket on to her back:

'Madame, why do you have to carry all these heavy loads while your men always go home on horseback almost empty handed?'

She turned to me. 'What woman,' she said, 'would like a tired husband at night?'

I was always surprised to see the vast amount of wine carried by the women each evening to their villages. I pointed this out to a woman one day.

'Ah,' she sighed, 'husbands must be pleased. Without a husband a woman is nothing, however rich and powerful she may be.'

The stone slabs of the marketplace and the blocks of Main Street had been worn down and polished by centuries of walking. Poor Tibetans, in their top-boots with soft soles of uncured leather, walked like cows on ice. If a man tried to walk fast, he landed on the ground with his feet high in the air. The whole market shook with laughter and applause at such a misadventure. If a man fell off his horse, or was pushed into a canal, or a woman spilled her basket of eggs on the stones, the first impulse of everyone was to break into laughter. I was always surprised by this mirth over the misfortunes of others, but the people were not really cruel at heart and Soon went to the assistance of the victim.

Nor, indeed, were all the incidents comical. Going to buy a box of matches once from Madame Yang's neighbour, I saw in the corner of that shop what I thought was a Tibetan from some remote country, perhaps Hsiangchen. The man cowered and shivered, looking at me with terrified eyes. Some girls shouted a warning. As I leaned over the counter to take the matches, he gave a piercing yell and sprang at me with a dagger. It was due to the lightning action of the girls, who grabbed him, that I was not seriously stabbed. He had never seen a European in his life and thought I was the incarnation of a malignant *yidam*.

The shops around Madame Yang's were filled with merry girls, who assisted their mothers or married sisters in running the shops and at the same time acted as exchange brokers in their own right. Between spells of business they sat on the doorsteps, knitting loud-coloured woollen sweaters or embroidering, in multi-coloured silks, the seven stars which every Nakhi woman, married or unmarried, wears on the back of her traditional sheepskin jacket – the small pelerine – which protects her back from the eternal basket she carries. The fur is inside and a woollen tippet of dark blue colour covers the shoulders on the outside. These pretty circlets are about two inches in diameter. Formerly there were two larger

Likiang marker-place. A Hsiangchen Tibetan womam shopping.

circles, representing the sun and moon, hut they were now no longer worn.

These girls were carefree, impudent and eternally gay; and sometimes they were naughty. But at heart they were kind and their business acumen was prodigious. There was one group of about eight who formed a sort of club, always sitting and gossiping together. The youngest was Atsousya, about sixteen years old. She was pretty, very fair and puckish. Her cousin Anisya was about twenty. Her face was rounded and very white, with golden hair and green eyes. She was extremely sophisticated, and there was nothing that she did not know about the town and people. Another was dark-haired and bosomy, called Aszeha, with great smouldering eyes; then there was the heavy-featured and husky Ahouha and the gentle Lydya.

I did not know the others well, but always admired the beautiful Fedosya who presided over a spice stall in the market. She was already married and, with her black round mitre, which is the distinctive headdress of the married women, she looked exactly like Queen Nefertiti. I showed her the photograph of the bust of the famous and long-dead Egyptian queen and she herself admitted that the resemblance was remarkable. Madame Yang's own marriageable daughter Afousya was in league with these girls. But Afousya was very busy, assisting her mother, and had little time to participate in the gossip or pranks of the other girls. She was a sallow-faced, unfriendly girl and always screamed at her mother's clients at the top of her voice. I do not think she liked my presence at the shop and we always maintained a polite feud. Whenever she became too obstreperous I used to remind her that no husband would like a girl of her temper, which usually subdued her for a while.

Likiang market square. Mme. Yang's cakes and cigarettes.
Mme. Yang's shop is opposite.

Atsousya and Anisya always watched for my arrival at Madame Yang's and begged me for a cup of the sweet yintsieu. Afterwards the other girls would come up and it was difficult to refuse them a drink too. Finally I found the drain on my finances too heavy.

'Look, Atsousya!' I said one day, 'I cannot really stand drinks to all of you every day.'

'But you are rich,' she pouted.

'I am not rich,' I said, 'and I do not think I can afford coming here.'

Anisya came up.

'Let us make a compact,' she said, 'that one day you treat us and the next day we treat you.' So we agreed. But it did not work out like that; so I promised to give them drinks on Saturdays only. Even this arrangement was not strictly observed and, when I was happy over some good news, I invited them to an extra cup or two. Ahouha's grandmother, who passed in the evening from the market, was much flattered when I offered her also a cup of wine. She was eighty-five but still hale and hearty, and would give me a peach or an apple in exchange.

Like all Nakhi women and girls, Atsousya and Anisya were absolutely uninhibited and frank to a point of brutality. They were steeped in local scandals and related them to me with such gusto and enthusiasm that I, hardened as I was, could not suppress a blush. Soon they seized upon my sessions at Madame Lee's shop.

'You are in love with her, that's what it is,' they announced triumphantly one day. 'Be careful! Her husband is very jealous,' they warned. Silly as the joke was, the whole town picked it up, and some people winked at me knowingly when I said that I was going to Madame Lee's for a drink.

Both Atsousya and Anisya could not believe that I was unmarried.

'I am still looking for a wife,' I jokingly assured them.

'Atsousya why not marry me?' I asked her one day.

'Phew!' she spat. 'It's better to be a young man's slave than an old man's darling,' she said.

'Am I really so old and ugly?' I insisted.

'Of course, with your bald head and eye-glasses you look like eighty,' she replied brutally.

'What about Anisya?' I continued.

'Anisya has a husband already and the marriage will take place soon,' she confided to me.

Indeed, in a few weeks' time Anisya disappeared, and only much later I caught a glimpse of her in her married woman's attire. She looked unhappy and was much thinner. In a month's time she resumed her old place by the bridge.

'What happened?' I asked Atsousya.

'I'll tell you,' she said, 'but don't tell her I let you know.' Then she whispered, 'Anisya is being divorced.' I was surprised.

In a week or two one of my friends, Wuhan, who also knew the girls, told me that there had been a court case about the divorce. 'Why do you want to separate from your husband?' the judge asked. Anisya boldly stepped out and said, 'Your Honour, my husband is only a small boy and I shall be an old woman by the time he grows up. I cannot wait.' As this was more or less the truth, the judge granted the petition at once. Then, stepping down from the dais, he approached Anisya, and according to Wuhan said, 'Anisya, all my life I have been waiting for a woman like you. I am a widower and I want to marry you.' The marriage took place in a fortnight and this time

Anisya abandoned our little circle for ever. But sometimes we saw her, as a richly dressed young woman, the wife of a judge, passing through the market and greeting her old friends.

After six o'clock the market gradually emptied, and at seven the shops put up their shutters. The market stalls were gathered into a pile again. The streets became deserted, and it was time for dinner.

It was only after eight o'clock in the evening that Main Street began to fill up with people again, and the shops reopened. Some had ordinary oil lamps flickering with reddish light; others were lighted with pressure lanterns or carbide lamps. Pine torches were put up at intervals, while crowds of people promenaded to and fro, cracking sunflower or pumpkin seeds. On bright moonlit nights the street was jammed. Unmarried girls, locally called *pangchinmei*, in their best dresses and adornments, walked arm in arm in rows of four or five girls, just wide enough to block the street. In this way they charged up and down the street, giggling, singing and cracking their sunflower seeds. The unwary young man was soon engulfed by these Amazons and led away to an unknown fate. The more sophisticated boys lined the walls and doors of the shops and made comments on the marching beauties. From time to time a group of girls paused before one of them, there was a scuffle, a brief and ineffectual struggle, and off he was led, imprisoned in the ring of giggling and screaming furies. The destination of these prisoners, probably only too willing, was the park where dancing continued till midnight on the meadows by the river around the brightly burning bonfires.

Madame Lee's shop was usually open at night, but with a different clientele, made up mostly of the local blue-bloods, who refreshed themselves with wine before venturing into the perils of promenading, unescorted, on the street. The ordinary villagers and Tibetans, awed by these elegant, love-making crowds, walked slowly, also in rows and with arms linked. They usually scattered when the girls' brigades crashed purposely into them. There was some screaming and laughter, but no one really minded. The silvery moon smiled down from above, and fragrant smoke floated up to it from the pine torches. Later the market square was slowly transformed into an encampment by the erection of several large tents. Stoves were set up and benches and tables spread out on the stone floor. Delicious odours began to rise from a mass of pots and pans.

I would sit in one of these tents sometimes till midnight, browsing over a bowl of clumplings or noodles and watching heavily armed Tibetan caravan drivers or tribesmen. Eating in these tents was considered by the more sedate townspeople as a little dangerous. Sometimes bandits were present in exotic disguises, and brawls between drunken men were not unusual. On a very dark night, one of the girls near Madame Yang's shop would give me a bunch of the brightly burning *mingtze* to help me to find my way across the hill.

Down in the Tibetan quarter was Madame Ho's bar, high-class and exclusive in the sense that she catered mostly for the Tibetan trade. Her house was one of the most palatial mansions in the Tibetan section. Two of her sons were in Lhasa where they had a prosperous import and export firm. The youngest son, who was at school, was a silly and cheeky youth and always teased me with tactless questions. Her husband was a podgy, middle-aged man,

who smoked opium most of the day and was seldom seen
in the shop. Her greatest help came from her grown-up,
apple-cheeked daughter, also called Anisya.

Madame Ho was a plump and motherly middle-aged
woman, full of gaiety and *risqué* jokes. Her shop was
a replica of Madame Lee's and she kept it really as a
retreat from ennui, in addition to her legitimate business.
Her house was one of the largest in the town and it had
three separate courtyards, neatly paved with stone slabs
and decorated with flowers and shrubs in huge porcelain
pots standing on carved pedestals. The whole house was
exquisitely carved inside, spotlessly clean and beautifully
appointed, and there were spacious stables attached to the
main building. She had taken me early under her wing and
afterwards assisted me to solve many of my problems.
Her information was in no way less reliable than Madame
Lee's but, unlike that prim old lady, she loved to discuss
scandals, and punctuated her lurid recitals with pithy
comments on the parties involved. The result was that I
always left her shop with my sides aching from laughter.
She showered me with gifts, sometimes a cut of ham or a
pot of specially brewed wine or some new cabbages she
had received from Atuntze. I repaid her with free medical
advice for her children or with seedlings of American
flowers or vegetables, especially beetroot, though the
Nakhi did not like them to eat, saying that they were too
sweet for a vegetable. One evening Anisya appeared with
flaming red cheeks, and I remarked that she used too
much rouge. It was not the rouge, Madame Ho explained,
but the juice of beetroots which Anisya had applied to
advantage. The crazy fashion spread, and afterwards the
beetroots were cultivated by Anisya and her friends not
for eating but for the sake of the cosmetic value of their

juice.

The best time to go to Madame Ho's bar was after dinner. It was then crowded with the Tibetan merchants who stayed at her house. She always made a point of introducing me to them. These were very pleasant encounters and we always talked late into the night. Obsequious Tibetan servants appeared from time to time bringing some delicacies to go with the wine. Once there appeared a lama from Tongwa, with a big caravan and many trapa servants. He was as gross as he was powerful, and was, in addition, a great flirt. He scandalized even free and easy-going Likiang and the *pangchinmei* scattered, screaming and laughing in mock fear, when he tried to charge into their groups in the park. He even made eyes at Madame Ho, while drinking wine with me, and this reduced her to loud laughter. I teased Anisya afterwards.

'Why don't you marry him, you would be an abbess?' I suggested.

'Why don't you marry Madame Lee?' she came back at me like lightning.

Many rich caravans arrived at Madame Ho's house with introductions from her son in Lhasa. The caravan owners were courteously and cordially welcomed by Madame Ho and allocated spacious and comfortable quarters. Their horses and personal servants were also comfortably disposed of in the same building. The rest of the caravan drivers and horses either stayed with neighbours, if there was room, or camped along the road leading to my village. Further arrivals were treated in the same manner until the house was filled. But no merchant was permitted to feel cramped. The Tibetans like ample space, and several rooms for the exclusive use of two or three merchants was the rule. A profusion of expensive ornaments in silver and brass, burnished braziers and plenty of costly rugs were necessary to keep up the dignity of a Tibetan merchant and ensure his comfort. Good food was essential too, and it was served to each company separately in their apartments. The servants were left to their own devices in the matter of board.

Once in a while Madame Ho would give a regular feast for her merchant guests, to which I was usually invited. The food was ordered from a caterer and was stereotyped. But soon after the meal had ended the caravan men came, accompanied by their women friends. A small bonfire was lit in the courtyard and little tables were placed in the corners with jars of white wine and cups. Singing and clapping their hands, the men and women, confronting each other, went into lively dances. From time to time they refreshed themselves with a cup or two of wine. Faster and faster went the dancers the more they drank, until the dance became confused and changed into open flirtation. Similar dances went on in all encampments, and all through the night snatches of rhythmic singing floated into my windows.

Besides this spontaneous dancing by caravan men, there appeared from time to time small troupes of the Khamba vaudeville actors. They consisted of two or three women and about the same number of men. They had, as a distinctive mark, strings of beads suspended from their belts and they carried one-string violins, pipas (mandolins), flutes, tambourines and small drums. They went from house to house, and for a small fee, fifty cents or a dollar, they gave a lively performance, lasting about half an hour, of singing and whirlwind dancing. For a larger fee, they could drum and dance for a whole day if required. They stayed at Likiang a month or two, depending on business, and then moved on elsewhere. There was real artistry in their performances.

The Tibetan merchants who stayed at Madame Ho's did not pay for accommodation or food, although they remained usually for a month or two in Likiang. But Madame Ho earned a commission on the sale of their goods, probably from both sides, and that took care of the expenses of her hospitality. Once or twice a year one of her sons came himself from Lhasa with a caravan. The goods, if not sold at Likiang, were dispatched by caravan to Hsiakwan. But Madame Ho did not accompany them there herself, for no Likiang business woman ever cared to extend her operations, or travel so far.

The arrival of the members of a certain matriarchic tribe, living about seven clays by caravan north of Likiang, always created a furore in Likiang. Whenever these men and women passed through the market or Main Street on their shopping expeditions, there was indignant whispering, giggling and squeals of outraged modesty on the part of Likiang women and girls, and salacious remarks from men. They were the inhabitants of the Yungning duchies across the Yangtze at the apex of the great bend. The Nakhi called them Liukhi and they called themselves Hlihin. The structure of their society was entirely matriarchal. The property passed from mother to daughter. Each woman had several husbands and the children always cried, 'We have mama but no papa.' The mother's husbands were addressed as uncles and a husband was allowed to stay on only as long as he pleased the woman, and if he didn't, could be thrown out without much ceremony.

The Yungning country was a land of free love, and

all efforts of the Liukhi women were concentrated on enticing more lovers in addition to their husbands. Whenever a Tibetan caravan or other strangers were passing Yungning, these ladies went into a huddle and secretly decided where each man should stay. The lady then commanded her husbands to disappear and not to reappear until called. She and her daughters prepared a feast and danced for the guest. Afterwards the older lady bade him to make a choice between ripe experience and foolish youth.

They were a handsome race, tall and stately, with finely formed bodies and attractive faces. They were not unlike the Noble Lolos but, whilst the Lolos resembled more the classical Romans with their stern and aquiline features, the Liukhi were more of a classical Grecian type, warmer and softer and much less harsh in appearance and deportment. Like the Lolo women, their women wore long, full skirts of blue colour, red sash and a black fur jacket or a peplos, and hats or turbans. Sometimes they went uncovered, their hair done in Roman style, held in place by hair-nets. With their lips heavily rouged and eyes painted, they walked slowly, or rather undulated, through the streets, swaying their hips, smiling and casting an amorous eye on this man or that. That alone was enough to incense the less sophisticated Nakhi women. But when they walked slowly along hanging on the neck of a husband or a lover, and being held by the waist, this was too much for even the brazen Nakhi women, who spat or giggled nervously.

The Liukhi men appeared to be vain creatures, always preening and examining themselves in the mirror. They put rouge on their lips and powdered their cheeks and sometimes called at my place not so often for medical treatment as to inquire if I could give them some perfume, powder or cheap ornament. Turning around in front of me they would inquire whether they looked attractive enough. This was not so much a sign of effeminacy as of vanity and a desire to keep themselves spruce and smart-looking in a luxurious way that appealed to their womenfolk.

The Nakhi men were on the whole impervious to the charms of the Liukhi women. They were not insensitive to their wiles or beauty, but they knew well enough that most of the Liukhi tribe was infected with venereal disease, and it was only this dread of almost certain infection that made the Nakhi and other sensible men give a wide berth to the Liukhi enchantresses.

Only twice was my path crossed by Liukhi women and in both cases it resulted in a mild scandal. Once, passing Madame Yang's shop during the day, I was called by a well-dressed Liukhi woman who was sitting there drinking. She invited me to have a cup. I sat down. She said that she was from Yungning and that her name was Kwaisha. She was in Likiang on business, selling some gold and musk. She paid for my drink, for which I thanked her and then went away, not thinking much more of the encounter. In a few days she came to my general office and, in the presence of all my staff, told me that she thought she had syphilis. I explained to her that, if that was the case, she must have an intramuscular injection in the small of her back. Before we realized what she was doing, she had lifted her skirts and lay prone, naked on our large office table.

'Madame,' I said to her, 'please get up and cover yourself,' and then I explained to her that the injections had to be made in a special room and only if she came escorted by some female companions.

She came back later and was duly treated. Some time afterwards Madame Lee told me that Kwaisha came to her shop and got so drunk that she collapsed, and with great difficulty was removed with the aid of two Tibetans. I never saw her again but heard from Madame Lee that she had got entangled with a group of Tibetans, and was killed by a stone thrown by one of them during a quarrel for the possession of her charms.

On the second occasion two Liukhi women came into my office leading an old man. The elder one said, 'Please cure him. He is our uncle.' I examined the old man, who was very repulsive. He had ichthyosis — a rare and very difficult disease about which I knew little and for which I had no adequate medicines. I explained the situation to the women through my chief clerk, Prince Mu. The elder one stepped forward and said, 'You must cure him! You must! As a reward, I will pass the night with you.'

'Madame, I assure you that I can do nothing in that case,' I said, ignoring her offer. She appeared exasperated.

'Look!' she said again. 'Both I and my sister will spend the night with you.'

I began to feel like St. Anthony of Padua. The neighbours, who had drifted in, and my office staff could hardly contain themselves.

'Madame,' I said firmly, 'I am sorry I can neither cure the old man nor accept your generous offer,' and walked out of the office, leaving it to my people to get the disappointed women out.

For weeks afterwards I was teased in the market and in the wine-shops, for it was a scandal after the Nakhi's own heart.

FURTHER KINGDOM

CHAPTER IV

FURTHER AFIELD

*H*AVING entrenched ourselves in our own village, I was now determined to overcome the suspicions of the other Nakhi, and also other tribes, to make them see the value of my mission and my work, and to win their friendship. It was not the Likiang society of rich merchants and shopkeepers that I needed, but the hearts of villagers and ordinary folk who eked out their living by small industries and trade. It was only through their friendship and goodwill, I thought, that I could build up my work and carry out my duty to the Government which had sent me. I was right; looking back now at the years I spent in Likiang I can say that I succeeded, and succeeded gloriously beyond my fondest dreams. From Hsiakwan to the Kingdom of Muli far in the north, and from Lhasa in the west, to Yuenpei in the east, I gained hundreds, and perhaps thousands, of friends and well-wishers.

One thing I learned well: a Nakhi's friendship was not given freely or haphazardly, it had to be earned.

Neither could it be bought with gifts, because gifts were reciprocated and the more expensive the present the more burden it brought to the Nakhi in his efforts to match the value by his return gift. And yet, giving and receiving gifts was an important ingredient in friendship and social intercourse in Likiang; but the gifts come later, when friendly relations have become firmly established. A Nakhi peasant especially rejoices when he has gathered a good crop, slaughtered a fat animal or when the wine he has made is of superior bouquet. In his joy and contentment he always remembers his friends. So he brings a small basket of potatoes or a joint of pork or venison or a small jar of wine. He does not expect an immediate and rich return; but in friendship, being a partnership, an opportunity always presents itself to give in return something that he appreciates.

In courting friendship with a Nakhi a good deal of sincerity, sympathy and genuine affection was necessary, and also patience. They were very sensitive people. The Nakhi possessed no inferiority complex but neither did they suffer a show of superiority in anybody. They were not obsequious and did not cringe even in the presence of high-ranking officials or wealthy merchants. Unlike the Chinese in certain parts of China, they were not discomforted or disturbed by strangers of other races. A European did not awe them or excite feelings of antagonism or hatred. He was not regarded as a white devil or a Western barbarian, he was just another person like themselves, and was treated accordingly without any particular consideration or curiosity. Whether he was good or bad, mean or generous, rich or poor, he was judged by his subsequent actions and attitudes and the people behaved towards him accordingly.

Perhaps this indifference to racial characteristics was due to the extremely diversified population of this huge territory. The Nakhi were accustomed to the strange tribes constantly mingling with them. That a European might not speak Nakhi or Chinese did not make him an object of ridicule but rather of sympathy, for many other tribesmen did not speak either language. If a European, and for that matter anyone else, adopted a superior or patronizing attitude, nothing towards him changed visibly in the attitude of the Nakhi. He was treated civilly but with a greater formality, and soon found himself alone and isolated with only his servants to keep him company, except for an official invitation to attend a party once in a blue moon. He surveyed the lovely valley and the crowded city like a panorama, but he did not belong. The colourful life passed him by.

The Nakhi did not tolerate harsh orders or abusive language from anyone, much less from strangers. A particularly venomous word might lead at once to retaliation in kind, or by a thrust of the dagger kept handily at the belt, or a well-aimed stone. I had warned my cook, who was prone to fly into a rage, to be very careful about using his choice Shanghai invectives, especially to our native servants. Later on, when he had grown more opulent and arrogant, he was to suffer a lot on account of his loose tongue.

The servant problem in Likiang was very acute. Free and independent Nakhi did not want any menial jobs. There was no unemployment in the sense in which it is known in China proper or in the West. All the Nakhi, whether in the town or countryside, were small-holders first and merchants, traders or workers afterwards: all were devoted to their ancestral lands and farms. Those in the town who could not or would not attend to their fields and orchards in person, had farmed out the land to distant relatives or friends. However, poor farmer boys from infertile mountain districts were sometimes willing to undertake off-season jobs in the town, or when their families needed additional money for a particular purpose such as building a new house, buying extra horses or cattle, a wedding or a Shamanist ceremony. It was from a cadre of such youths that we used to get assistants for my cook.

At first we made our need of a servant known to some friends, then we were notified that a boy from one of the villages was willing to come out, and then the terms were discussed with the main condition that the boy should be treated with consideration and courtesy. Then the boy himself appeared accompanied by his father or uncle. They were good, hard-working boys, sometimes not too honest in small things, but that was overlooked for the sake of domestic harmony. Sometimes they left when they felt homesick, and sometimes they walked out when my cook could not refrain from saying something derogatory about them. 'We are as good as you are,' they would cry out. 'We are not your slaves and we have a home,' and off they would go. They were not poor in a conventional sense, for they had their farmhouse, a place to eat, a bed to sleep on and their friends to dance with when the sun had gone down beyond the mountains.

One sunny morning, a couple of months after my arrival, I was passing along a street and came to a little square with an old, shady tree. Enormous pink roses cascaded from its branches, around which an old vine was entwined. The scent was overpowering. A group of Nikhi young men stood around admiring the blooms. They all stared at me smiling.

'What beautiful flowers!' I commented in Chinese. At once they started talking to me. I noticed that one of them had red and swollen eyes.

'Come and I will give you medicine for your eyes,' I said at last.

'But we have not brought any money,' they protested.

'Who says I want money?'

'Where is your house?' they asked hesitatingly.

'Oh, just over the hill in Wuto. Quite near.' I reassured them, and we walked over. I administered argyrol and gave them a small bottle to take home. They were overwhelmed.

'No money and such kindness!' they commented. One of them was a tall, athletic youth with great liquid eyes and wavy chestnut hair. He looked intelligent and was particularly friendly. I gave him my card inscribed in Chinese. He said his name was Wuhan and the boy with the sore eyes was his cousin Wuyaoli. They lived in a village down the valley at the foot of the eastern range. They were students at the Provincial School, he added. With profuse thanks they went away.

A week later Wuhan appeared bringing a small pot of honey and a few fresh eggs.

'I cannot accept payment for my medicine,' I protested.

'It is not a payment,' he smiled warmly. 'My mother sent these trifles as a present. She says you are very kind,' he added. He said he liked me and wanted to be friends with me. Although he protested violently, I prevailed on him to stay for lunch. The reason for his protest, I learned later, was his fear that he would have to eat a European meal with knives and forks which he did not know how to use. When we sat down to an informal Chinese meal with chopsticks, he relaxed and, as the meal progressed, he began to use, haltingly at first, English which was taught at his school. Actually he spoke it quite well. In the end it was agreed that I should visit his home one Sunday.

I was very excited over the projected trip. It was to be my first visit to a Nakhi village as a guest. Everybody told me how difficult it was to gain an entrée to a farmer's home.

On the Sunday Wuhan came early to fetch me. We started at once and stopped only once at Madame Lee's shop to pick up a jar of *yintsieu* for our lunch. Then we marched out of town and along the main road to Hoking, due south. Soon the road branched off to the left and we were walking between green fields and along fragrant hedges of roses and wild flowers. We met peasants with baskets of firewood on their backs, leading heavily laden horses to the market. They all knew Wuhan and greeted him. His village was fifteen *li* from the city and we reached it in a couple of hours, stopping on the way to chat with the monks of a Buddhist temple situated on a nearby hill. The village consisted of only a few houses, built like those in the town, but with tall racks in the court-yard for drying grain crops before threshing.

Wuhan's mother was a sweet old woman and she was all smiles when I entered. She apologized profusely for not being able to talk Chinese. Wuhan led me into the central hall and seated me on a bench. He was an only son, his father having died long ago. They ran the farm, just the two of them, assisted by relatives and neighbours when needed. They had a couple of buffaloes, three horses, and pigs and chickens. A fierce little dog was tied in the corner. I was led upstairs where golden wheat was piled on the floor and lentils and peas heaped in little mounds in the corner. There were huge clay jars with rice, flour and oil, and pots of home-made white wine or gal. Slabs of rock salt, like cartwheels, leaned against walls. From the rafters hung hams and chunks of salt pork. There were baskets with eggs by the window. They had everything in plenty for themselves and for sale. Soon Wuhan left me sitting alone and joined his mother in the kitchen. Other guests began drifting in-Wuyaoli and Wuhan's other cousin Wukia, Wukia's father and elder brother and a couple of schoolmates.

The meal, which took a long time to prepare, was served in the courtyard which was scrupulously clean. Nakhi villagers preferred to use low tables for family meals and the guests sat on narrow benches a few inches high. It was only on more formal occasions that the standard square tables of normal height were used. We started with small fried fish, like sprats, and beautifully browned potato slices. Everything was served in saucers. There followed pieces of roast chicken, then fried walnuts, salted duck eggs, stewed eggplant, *sauerkraut*, sliced ham and many other delicious things. Every time a new dish was brought by the mother I thought it was the end. But no, as soon as one dish was finished, something else was placed on the table. And all the time we were drinking, toasting each other and laughing. I drank the sweet yintsieu, accompanied by Wuhan. Others preferred *zhi* — the strong white liquor made of wheat. It looked and tasted like gin and was just as potent. I felt well filled and slightly tipsy. I asked the mother to stop bringing in more dishes, saying it was a right royal meal. She only smiled; in the kitchen something sizzled and more things followed. Finally the meal was concluded with stewed pork and chicken soup, accompanied by a big copper basin of red rice which the Nakhi eat as well as bread. The polished white rice is used only for feasts by the well-to-do town people, but the red rice has the better flavour; it is highly nourishing and not conducive to beri-beri.

After the luncheon some of the elderly people retired and Wuhan suggested to the others of the party a walk in the mountains. A few steps behind the house we entered into a dense pine forest interspersed with all sorts of flowering bushes, mainly rhododendrons of several varieties. There were also other curious and beautiful flowers. One plant we met was called *lamalazak* and it was like a miniature Christmas-tree studded with red and blue bells. Slowly we climbed higher and higher among the trees until Wukia proclaimed that this was a mushroom zone. Indeed, all kinds of mushrooms could be seen pushing out of the short grass and between the bushes. The boys taught me which mushrooms were edible and which poisonous. There were some short and fat and branching into clumps that looked exactly like pink coral. These were the *akamus* — the most-sought-after mushrooms. Some looked like hard-boiled eggs stuck into the ground, the cracked shell showing a glimpse of orange yolk inside: these were the *alawous* — highly edible. Burdened with the loads of mushrooms and bunches of flowers we sat down to rest or lay upon the Tibetan rugs we had brought. It was wonderfully peaceful in these lonely mountains. There were no sounds but the whispering of pines and singing of birds. I was assured that there were many Nagas and fairies living in this endless forest. Afterwards we descended to a little spring of water gurgling out of a huge rock. Pointing to a pleasant meadow above the rock, the boys told me how a neighbour of theirs went once to this spring at night. Drinking the water, he saw three dignified and resplendently dressed ancients with long flowing beards. They were sitting in the meadow evidently discussing something. The old men, however, noticed his presence. They beckoned him to come to them and said that it was not well for him, a mortal, to see them. Much distressed, the man returned to his village and told the neighbours what he had seen. Shortly afterwards he sickened and died.

We returned home as the sun was setting. Oil lamps were tit when darkness fell. Not the kerosene oil lamps but little brass shells filled with walnut oil, cotton wicks protruding from the lip. These were supported on the brass stands like candlesticks. In the kitchen smoky *mingtze* burned on stone stands. The dinner was served in Wukia's home and was good too, although not nearly so elaborate as Wuhan's luncheon. Afterwards a bed was prepared for me at Wuhan's house. Tibetan rugs were laid on the bedsteads, sheets spread and a *pukai* (cotton quilt) provided. When the Nakhi retire for the night, they always shut tightly all windows and doors and place a charcoal-filled brazier near the bed. I admit that the nights in Likiang were cold, but to have a blazing brazier in a small, tightly sealed room was intolerable, and there was considerable danger of monoxide poisoning. I always horrified my Nakhi friends by removing the brazier and opening the door or window, risking, as they said, catching a mortal cold or the intrusion of evil spirits. Next morning there was a breakfast of sliced ham, fried eggs, *babas* and Tibetan butter tea. Then I walked home.

Afterwards I visited Wuhan's home many times just for rest and relaxation or to attend some ceremonies which he had to perform as the head of the house. I was also present at his wedding a few years later. Soon his relatives, scattered in the villages further down the valley, began inviting me too. Thus my friendships grew, and I began to be received into homes across the length and breadth of the main valley down to the south, almost as far down as the border between the Kingdom of Mu and the Hoking country.

CHAPTER V

THE START OF THE CO-OPERATIVES

A HUGE signboard, beautifully written by a local gentleman-calligraphist, adorned our gate. We were open for business. Such quick action on our part impressed the town. But I imagine our Kunming Headquarters experienced a shock at the receipt of our telegram announcing that the shop was open.

Now I was free to devote myself entirely to the promotion of industrial co-operative societies. Of course, everybody thought that, henceforward, we should be sitting grandly behind our desks all day long expecting the prospective cooperators to call. Had we followed this line of action, or rather inaction, we might have been sitting with crossed arms for years. Instead, every morning, accompanied by one of the office clerks, I tramped to all the wool-weaving factories we could find. Slowly and with infinite pains I tried to explain to these simple people what co-operation meant and how they could enlarge their tiny factories, improve their products and become prosperous. At first they did not understand a word, although everything was explained in Nakhi. Their minds could not grasp or digest all these technicalities. Day after day I persisted. When I mentioned that the loans could be given to assist in the improvement of their looms and in getting more stocks of yarn and dyes, this information seemed at last to touch a chord in the eminently practical heart of the Nakhi women.

We saw at once where our advantage lay and next time we concentrated our attention not on the men but on their wives and sisters. It worked brilliantly. It was the women who were the first to understand the idea of co-operatives and appreciate the benefits they promised. They became our most active protagonists. We did not know what they said or did to their husbands after our visits but when we came again the men seemed less obdurate and talked much more sense. We knew that if we could break the ice and establish one cooperative successfully, the results would be swift in this city where gossip was more effective than any advertising in the papers or radio broadcasts in the West.

I knew a Nakhi student by the name of Hochiatso. His father and two uncles jointly ran a wool-weaving factory on the hill just a couple of hundred yards from our office. Working through him and independently we at last succeeded in converting the factory into a co-operative enterprise, with others joining in on a share basis. Afterwards I sent Hochiatso to our Bailie Training School at Shandan, Kansu, where he learned how to make serges and good, woolly blankets.

The greatest event in the industrial life of Likiang was my introduction of the wool-spinning wheel of which, prior to my arrival, the Nakhi had no idea. I had brought

Wool-spinning Co-operative.

with me a model of the type of wheel which was used for ages in Europe before the introduction of mechanization. Even this simple machine puzzled them and it was only after many trials and errors that a really serviceable wheel was evolved. It caused a furore, probably as great as when the first chariot-wheel was constructed. It was copied and recopied and constructed, with and without variations, by the hundred. In a very few months the whole town was in a frenzy of wool spinning. Every shop had two or three whirring wheels at which the lady of the house and her daughters or sisters sat spinning whilst waiting for customers. Spinning-wheels lined the streets and could be found by the dozen in the larger houses. Everybody, men, women and children, began to spin. Varieties of wool yarn, hitherto hardly seen on the market, and then only good for sackcloth, were carried from one end of the town to another in women's baskets. There was the yarn for weaving and the yarn for knitting. All the pangchinmei now sat knitting the most fantastic and elaborate sweaters and pullovers I have ever seen for their sweethearts and for sale. Shops groaned with piles of these sweaters, socks and stockings, some so fine and fluffy that they could be compared with the best from abroad. The importation of wool from Tibet now jumped from the hundred bales a year, before my arrival, to two thousand bales a year, and more. Orders for woolen knitted goods were pouring in from Kunming, Lhasa and even Chungking. Likiang had now become a great centre of the wool industry in Yunnan.

There was no question any longer of my running after the prospective co-operatives in wool spinning or weaving. I was besieged with applications. But it was important to create spinning and weaving societies of quality, which would be genuine and strong, and this was not so easy as it might seem. I had to watch very carefully and not allow the formation of a society of members of the same family. Such co-operatives were not true co-operatives, for the loan from the bank to which co-operatives were entitled was, in the case of a family co-operative, negotiated and used entirely by the eldest male of the family, more often than not, for opium and other business in no way connected with the purchase of wool yarn or looms.

As the Chinese co-operative law prescribed a minimum of seven persons to form an industrial co-operative society, I required at the least seven separate families to join together. Each family nominated, as a member of the co-operative, a representative who could be a man or woman but who had to work with his or her own hands. I was very strict about this and never permitted anybody to act as a sort of honorary member, simply lending the use of his name to fill the list of members. The formation of co-operatives by the members of well-known local rich families was not permitted. They already had plenty of money of their own. Why should they get from the bank at a low interest the loan which was intended for the really poor? They would use this loan to lend money to somebody else at ten times the usual interest. I may say that I was not a great favourite with these avaricious merchant families who were without any pride. No matter how many times I snubbed their attempts to muscle in on the co-operative movement, always of course with the quintessence of politeness and decorum as befits a Chinese official, they always came back again and again, trying some other subterfuge or trick.

I can never forget one glaring example of such manœuvrings. One day I was approached by a great local gentleman who styled himself a general in retirement. He had an elegant house by the Likiang River across the bridge from Madame Lee's shop. He said that he heard much about my 'sublime and incomparable' work. He desired very much to assist me to extend it. Some of his friends wanted to form an Oil-pressing Co-operative Society. What they needed was just a small loan to put it into effect. As a refusal was, according to all the rules of etiquette, impossible, I had to agree. He informed me that the prospective members would wait for me at his house on the morrow at noon. I cordially assured him that I would be enchanted to attend this auspicious meeting.

I went with my trusted assistant Wuhsien at the appointed time. On arrival I was adversely impressed by the sight of food and wine prepared for me, as I had requested beforehand that no entertainment should be offered me during business conversations. Eight old gentlemen, very well dressed, sat around the room smoking their long pipes. They were refined and fragile-looking, with long, stained finger-nails. 'I have never seen a better collection of old opium smokers,' I managed to whisper to Wuhsien. I bowed and they rose and bowed. I had to take a sip of wine and a cake. Then we got down to business. In refined accents and high-flown terms the elders officially proposed to me to form an Oil-pressing Co-operative Society at a village near Likiang. Everything was almost ready—the presses, stocks of rape seed, etc. The only thing lacking, to start the operations, was money. They thought thirty or forty thousand silver *pangkais* would be a very modest sum to ask for as a loan. I looked round and composed myself.

'Do you mean to say, gentlemen, that you yourselves

are prepared to press the oil?' I exclaimed dubiously.

They were terribly offended, and were shaking with indignation.

'The very idea of it, sir!' exclaimed their spokesman. 'Of course not! We have enough workmen to do that for us.'

I made a very long pause, slowly sipping my wine. Then I spoke slowly and with infinite politeness.

'Gentlemen, the idea of this worthy co-operative society is beyond praise.' Again I paused, and then continued, 'I am rather worried about the amount you require. We never recommend to the bank to grant such large loans without referring the matter to our headquarters in Chungking, possibly to Dr. Kung himself.' They listened respectfully. They were greatly impressed by the exalted name.

'I will report the matter to my headquarters at once. As soon as I have a reply I shall be glad to inform you,' I said, bowing. We slowly filed out of the room.

Of course, I never bothered Chungking with such matters. But that was one of the correct ways of saying 'No.' I do not think these elders really expected any reply. They knew that I saw through their game, but there was no harm in trying. I do not think they were even angry with me: it was a legitimate gamble, a trial of wits. They had lost the first round, but hoped they might win the next.

When I first came to Likiang there was but one bank there and a very modest one at that. It was the Provincial Co-operative Treasury. As there were no co-operatives of any kind prior to my arrival, it had nothing to finance and, therefore, it seldom had any funds in its coffers. The cost of a remittance from Kunming to Likiang was, at least, 10 per cent; and to lose ten dollars on a hundred was a lot of money. Moreover, as Likiang used nothing but silver dollars, the problem of transporting and storing funds was acute. People either brought the money in their baggage by caravan or, if they had the connections, made transfers through the local merchants who had plenty of silver dollars[①] both at Kunming and Likiang, and so a loan of thirty thousand dollars, for instance, as the clever elders had desired, would have required quite a sizable caravan, as thirty horses would have been needed to carry the money, quite apart from the small army that would have been necessary as an escort from Hsiakwan. The bandits were no fools, and they had their own sources of information. They would mobilize all their friends and connections to make a concerted bid for so rich a prize.

Keeping such a precious cargo in the living-rooms of a wooden house, with no safes available, was another problem. Likiang had been plundered several times before by large groups of bandits, and a few hundred local militiamen provided doubtful protection. It was for this reason that the Co-operative Treasury held little capital and the local merchants tried to keep their hoards of silver coin down to a minimum. So there was always a shortage of ready money in Likiang and the purchase value of the dollar was, therefore, abnormally high. The interest on loans was fantastic: 10 per cent per month was considered a reasonable interest, and the $4\frac{1}{2}$ or 5 per cent charged by the treasury was regarded as extremely low and were much sought after.

As I had brought with me only a small sum of silver dollars, and as there were no other government banks but

---

① Whenever I refer to transactions in dollars it means it means silver halfdollars or pangkais, not paper currency.

the Co-operative Treasury, our Kunming Headquarters probably thought that this shortage of dollars would be a major stumbling-block in the development of my industrial co-operatives, even if I did manage to get a foothold in Likiang. They did not reckon on my powerful connections with the head-quarters of the Provincial Co-operative Treasury and with certain Yunnan provincial banks. My first Wool Spinning and Weaving Society, for instance, received a loan from the Provincial Co-operative Treasury in about a fortnight after their first constitutional meeting. As soon as other societies had been formed, they also obtained loans, though they were very small compared with the standards not only of European countries but even of such places as Kunming and Chungking, where values were inflated. The first loan was only for 300 dollars and the subsequent loans ranged from 200 to 500 dollars and they were all granted for a period of one year only. The loans were not needed for salaries or wages or any such unproductive purposes, for the co-operators lived in their own houses, ate their own products and carried on their duties without salaries or wages. They received their remuneration, according to the work done, when the profits were divided at the end of the year. With a few hundred dollars they could buy a lot of raw wool and make a number of looms and spinning-wheels. Their products were sold like hot cakes and there was no difficulty in making enough profit during the year to pay off the loan. I never had any trouble about loan repayments from the Nakhi people. The poorer they were, the more conscientious and particular they were about their financial obligations. Nor did I ever lose any personal loan I made to friends.

Luck was clearly with me. Something else soon happened which greatly stabilized and strengthened my position, and gave my work additional prestige. I received a telegram from the Bank of China in Kunming requesting me to meet and render assistance to their people who were proceeding to Likiang by chartered plane to open a branch of the bank there. This was great news indeed. I must mention in this connection that the bank's general manager in Kunming was a friend of mine and I also knew very well the secretary-general of the bank's headquarters in Chungking. I found at once a small temple for accommodating the bank's staff on their arrival. Then I assisted them in securing a good house for the exclusive use of the bank, which was so difficult in Likiang. The Kunming and Chungking branches were very grateful and gave a free hand in negotiating loans for my co-operatives at the incredibly low rate of interest of only $3\frac{1}{2}$ per cent per month. Unfortunately for the bank, however, all the loans made by them were in paper currency, which the recipients were at liberty to convert into materials or silver dollars. As the paper dollar was depreciating month by month, the societies had not the slightest difficulty in repaying even large loans when they matured. They made huge profits, as what they were repaying at the end of the year was in many cases less than a half of what they had originally received. It did not affect the individual branch bank itself as it was doing only its duty within the law. It was an overall disaster of a national magnitude with which even the Government was unable to cope. Only the silver dollar remained steady and, with this in circulation, life in Likiang remained stable and cheap.

The Bank of China stayed in Likiang only until VJ-Day

and then the branch was withdrawn. But by that time all my co-operatives had become the favourite children of the Co-operative Treasury and of several other provincial commercial banks which had hastily opened branches in Likiang, attracted by the rich caravan trade with Lhasa. Also, by that time, we had begun to receive some capital direct from our headquarters in Chungking.

In about two years my position had become so consolidated, and there were then so many first-class co-operatives, that there was no question of any withdrawal from Likiang. Dr. Kung was so pleased with my work that he honoured me with the title of commissioner and sent me a certificate to that effect. During my subsequent visits to Kunming I was received at our Yunnan Headquarters almost obsequiously, and it seemed that I was considered a power in the Chinese industrial co-operative movement.

I must pay my unstinted tribute to the National Government of China for its interest in, and sympathy with, the co-operative movement. Its laws and rules were wise and un-complicated. Simplicity in the organization, the accounts and in the supervision of the industrial co-operative societies was the rule. The disposition of the earnings was very sensible and it left a considerable latitude in their distribution. A reserve fund was insisted upon, but it was not retained by the Government at its pleasure. Upon the dissolution of any society, if a loan had been repaid and all claims satisfied, the reserve fund was returned for payment to members in accordance with the number of their shares and the length of their association with the society. The underlying principle was not to coerce the industrial co-operative society to continue for ever but to help poor craftsmen who had nothing with which to start to become prosperous and to regain their footing in society through co-operative enterprise. When they had reached the highest point of prosperity and security, it was up to them to continue their profitable association or, if they so wished, to dissolve, and enjoy the fruits of their labour individually and perhaps in other capacities, thus making way for another group of less fortunate people to repeat the process. It was a constant movement which slowly but surely was transforming Likiang and its district into a uniform community of prosperous and contented people. The results and proofs were there for all to see.

It was not difficult to start an industrial co-operative society if there were a number of people who knew the same line of industry. There were no great expenses involved in the preparation of account books. They were made of soft Chinese paper and the whole set cost no more than two or three dollars. The law did not require a set of printed and bound ledgers, or minute books made of expensive paper. Anyway, they would not have been procurable in Likiang. Whilst, under the uniform strictness of Western laws, a co-operative society is treated on the same level as a bank or a great limited company, and has to watch and comply with innumerable legal requirements, necessitating the employment of a highly qualified secretary and manager, an industrial co-operative in China was regarded for what it really was— an association of very poor people, often ignorant and illiterate, of whom not much could be asked. What trial balances or balance sheets could be demanded from a society whose members calculated the cost of materials and products with pebbles or beans and had never written a word in their life, as was the case of many co-operative societies in Likiang and elsewhere? They ran their affairs as well, if not better, than the societies with more educated members, though, naturally, a measure of supervision was necessary.

Whilst carefully avoiding the creation of the rich men's and family co-operatives, I had to be equally vigilant in not giving my sanction to the master and apprentice co-operative societies. There were several small workshops, especially in the padlock-making line, where the proprietor ran the shop with a few young apprentices some of whom were his relatives. They were not loath to proclaim their little factories as order to secure a loan from the bank, and were remarkably persistent in their efforts, inviting me for frequent inspections of their proposed societies, shuffling and reshuffling their apprentices and neighbours as prospective members. I never said 'No' to them, but merely mentioned that the banks had no money for loans at present.

Actually I was very fortunate with the material I had in Likiang for my co-operatives. The Nakhi were very independent and themselves never favoured the idea of a master and apprentice relationship. They had brains, though perhaps not very good ones by Western standards, but nevertheless capable of independent thinking and judgment. It was for this reason that large factories were impossible in Likiang, for no Nakhi would stand the peremptory orders of a manager or overseer for long, and when my co-operative movement had spread, many apprentices left their bosses and formed their own co-operatives.

The number of members in each of my co-operatives was not large. It was difficult to reach the necessary harmony of opinion and co-operation among a large number of people. Moreover, the Nakhi were so clannish that they could never work together with other people whom they did not know well. A successful co-operative could only be formed out of the people living in the same village or street. The plan of forming a combined co-operative of the Nakhi and the Minkia or some other tribes succeeded only in one case.

CHAPTER VI

MEDICAL WORK

*L*INKIANG had no hospital. There was a French-trained Nakhi doctor who, evil tongues said, assumed the title after a couple of years' work as a male nurse at a Kunming hospital. However, he belonged to a prominent local family, and that distinction alone opened the door for him into local 'society'. He was a nice, polite man, and we became friends. His younger brother, an army officer, was a devil incarnate, and also a bandit. He shot several villagers in cold blood, robbed an official escort of their guns and all but caused my own death. Once his brother invited me to an official dinner at his house. There were many guests and I was assigned a seat at the table opposite him. As was the custom, we all toasted each other from time to time. Although I had drunk in moderation, the fellow taunted me by saying that I could not take much more than another cup. I told him that I was quite all right for at least three more. He toasted me and offered me a cup which I emptied. I remembered no more. It was only late next afternoon that I regained consciousness. I felt like dying and was in bed for three days. Since there were no secrets in town that were not known sooner or later, I learned that the wretch had put chloroform into my wine. I was fortunate to have recovered at all, and never went to that house again.

As the Nakhi doctor was always busy with his wealthy clients and did not care anyway for the villagers' patronage, the poor people had nowhere to go to for medical attention except to some quack medicine shops. Having previously qualified as a doctor's assistant myself, I obtained from the American Red Cross in Kunming a small supply of drugs and medicines and my private office upstairs became also my clinic.

I had made it known far and wide that I was ready to treat all simple and easily recognizable afflictions and diseases, but nothing complicated or requiring surgical intervention. The treatment would be entirely free of charge as the medicines had been donated by the American Red Cross, and the clinical work was encouraged by my headquarters as a useful adjunct to the promotion of the co-operative movement. If I had expected a rush of patients, I was sorely mistaken. Nobody would come even if asked. The very fact that the treatment and medicine were free was a serious deterrent. Who would give something for nothing? people reasoned. They assumed that any free drugs were useless or, what is more, probably poisonous. However, I had already made a start with my friend Wuhan's cousin. His eyes had recovered and he was trumpeting my fame all over his village.

After a few days several women came with children. Some had eye diseases and the children had worms. They were all duly treated and supplied with medicine. In a week's time the marketplace was shaken with stories of miraculous cures, and long ascarides, wrapped in leaves, were exhibited to those who wanted to see for themselves. My reputation was made: and soon, from early morning till nightfall, the patients came, on the average about fifty a day, with no regard for hours or holidays. Most of my patients were poor village women afflicted with eye troubles of all sorts, caused by dirt and acrid wood smoke. Very soon, however, they began to complain.

'It is true,' they said, 'our eyes are much better, but this black medicine you put in does not seem to be good, for we do not even feel it. A really good medicine must be strong and painful—then we really know that we are being cured.'

Of course I used mostly argyrol, which was very efficacious in these cases, but it was not painful. To appease my wavering clientele, I mixed some chinosol with argyrol. Chinosol may also be used as an eye medicine, but it hurts terribly for a few minutes. When they came next time I put this desirable medicine in their eyes. They collapsed on the floor, writhing in their agony. I awaited their reactions with some trepidation after they had recovered. Wiping their streaming eyes with their aprons, they sang in unison.

'*Lah-da han! Hao da han!* (How peppery! How good!)'

They were absolutely delighted: it was a wonderful experience, they all said. 'This is the drug! It is precious!' And then they came in droves, bringing their friends with them and asking for that same medicine or nothing. In long rows they sat in the courtyard and fell, as if struck by lightning, as soon as I had put in the drops. Afterwards they always laughed and chattered in their delight.

Whilst the sore eyes formed almost a women's

monopoly, men came in an endless procession with their thighs and buttocks covered with scabies. They were so thick that they looked like fish scales. I had a big stock of sulphur ointment for this affliction, and at first I used to give them small pots of it, telling them to rub it in at night. In a week or two they used to come back complaining that the ointment was no good at all. Indeed, the awful scabs were still there. I had to change my tactics. With their pants down, I threw them on a low broad bench, face down, and rubbed them with all my might with powdered sulphur and vaseline, adding a pinch here and there as required. I rubbed until all the scabs were on the floor in little heaps, and the raw and bleeding flesh was clear. Then I rubbed some more sulphur in. The victims screamed and groaned, and staggered home hardly able to walk. After two or three such treatments their skin was as clear as that of a new-born babe. Of course, they were overjoyed and did not know how to thank me. It was hard and dirty work and I could not handle more than five such patients a day, so exhausting was it.

These skin diseases were, of course, a result of dirt and lack of personal hygiene. The Nakhi, both men and women, never took a bath. They washed only three times in their lives-when they were born, when they were about to be married, and when they were dead. In any other climate but Tibet and Likiang such a state of affairs would be intolerable. The people would smell like putrid corpses and would die of infections. But it was not really so bad in the dry mountain air of these high altitudes. The dirt simply dried and fell off in tiny scales. There was never any offensive odour from the people in the town and the villagers smelled like pinewood smoke. As for myself, I had a wooden tub made and took a hot bath in it in our little garden behind the house. I was partially visible over the wall and the women, passing along the crest of the hill, always laughed and shouted rude remarks. My cook took the bath after me in the same water, being too lazy to boil another lot. After him about ten of his Nakhi friends took turns until the water looked like pea-soup. Perhaps it was better than no bath at all.

Nakhi men also liked pain as a proof that the medicine or treatment was good. The men whom I cured of scabies were ecstatic in the description to their friends of the exquisite tortures they had endured at my hands and strongly advised them to come to my clinic with their sores. Some had deep ulcers on their legs. They said how much they suffered from these sores and hoped that I would cure them. Of course, they added, it must be awfully painful if the right treatment was applied, but they did not mind. I knew exactly what they meant. With big tweezers I tore off their scabs and dug out the wounds almost to the bone with cotton dipped in alcohol. They yelled and twisted. I filled the cavities with sulphathiazole, bandaged and sealed with elastoplast. Shaken but smiling, they always said what a marvellous experience it was. In three weeks or a month they were healed and I was invaded by others with still more horrible sores.

Goitre was a prevalent disease. However, it did not affect the Nakhi so much as the various tribes living along the Yangtze River and the Chinese emigrants from Szechuan who had settled in the forests and, of all places, in the great 11,000 feet deep Atsanko Gorge which the mighty Yangtze had cut for its passage through the Snow Range. Some goitres were of great size, pendant on both sides of the throat, creating an obscene resemblance to a backside. Of course, the best treatment for the goitre is its removal by

The Yangtze River is entering the 11,000 ft, deep gorge Atsanko.
The road throngh the gorge is on the left bank.

surgical means. To do this these poor people would have to travel to Kunming and pay high fees at a hospital there. It would be useless to suggest such a trip to a man whose whole fortune perhaps amounted to only a couple of dollars. Even a trip to Likiang, without a reason, was an expensive undertaking for them. They could not remain in town for the length of the treatment. So something quick had to be devised. I gave them as large doses of potassium iodide as I thought possible, short of killing them. I confess I had some very close shaves. A Lissu witch-doctor lay for two days in semi-coma after the treatment; others had attacks of iodism. However, all survived and I saw them again a month later. The goitres were half the size and, after a few more treatments, became very small and hardly noticeable, but, I must admit, they were still there, and I never succeeded in removing them altogether.

Leprosy, now genteelly called Hansen's disease not to offend the sensibilities of those who believe that a change in the name makes the disease less virulent and frightening, was not common among the Nakhi. If there was any, it had been brought from outside, and about this the people were very watchful. I remember a case when a Nakhi, who had been residing for years somewhere beyond Hsiakwan, came back to his village to rejoin his family. He was seen to be in an advanced stage of leprosy, and the villagers came to him *en bloc* and asked him either to go back or to commit the ceremonial suicide. He chose the latter. He was given a bowl of the dread black aconite boiled in oil. Afterwards they had his body cremated.

The Minkia, White Lissu and Szechuanese settlers had a few cases of leprosy: the Tibetans too. But it was not so common as the missionaries' reports would lead us to believe. There was a small leprosarium near Erhyuen,

150 miles south, in the Minkia country, but it was only half filled. I am not a scientist and have not conducted any systematic research or read much about the causes that produce leprosy. However, during my many years of residence and travel in China and along the Tibetan border I had time to observe and compare the conditions under which the people who had the greatest incidence of leprosy, and those who had the least, lived and worked. There were some verdant and rich valleys, which looked a veritable paradise to the eye, and yet the people there had leprosy. Why? There were other places, seemingly less fertile and fortunate, where the inhabitants were quite healthy. Why? I visited and stayed often in the Moshimien valley in the Sikang province, where a great Roman Catholic leprosarium, housing 500 inmates, was situated. This hidden valley was surely one of the most beautiful places in the world. At least 8,000 feet up it was hemmed in by great snow mountains and the climate was a perpetual spring. Two roaring torrents of pure glacier water cascaded down both sides of the valley. There were vast forests on the foothills: carpets of flowers covered alpine meadows and clearings in the forest: some of the rarest lilies in the world grew wild along the ridges: the air was heavy with the fragrance of so many flowers, myriads of bees buzzed around and the soil was black and rich. The Catholic mission had all kinds of fruit-bearing trees in its orchards and the vegetables of all descriptions in the well-laid-out and watered gardens. There were luscious tomatoes and big pimentos along the rows of cabbages and French beans.

And yet the valley was accursed. It had probably about 300 households or more of Szechuanese settlers and there was at least one leper in every house. So bad was Moshimien's reputation for leprosy that the people of Tachienlu, the provincial capital just across the Yajagkan Range, would not buy a chicken or egg, not at any price, if they knew it came from the Moshimien valley.

I decided to make a close observation of the people's habits and food in order to form, at least, a hypothesis of the cause of the dread disease in this happy corner. The inhabitants were dirty, in fact dirtier than usual, and the houses were dingy and filthy. Why? I asked. The water was too cold for bathing, they told me. As to their diet, they ate twice a day, late in the morning and soon after sunset, on bean curd, powdered chillies to make it palatable and soup made of sliced potatoes; and of course there was rice. Day after day and night after night they ate the same poor food. Sometimes it was a turnip soup, instead of a potato one, or boiled horse-beans were added to the menu. Once a week a slice or two of old salt pork might be added to the potatoes in the soup. I asked about eating chickens, eggs and fresh pork and vegetables, like those grown in the mission garden, which they could plant likewise. No, they said, it would be too luxurious to eat chickens, eggs and fresh pork—that was all for sale and they needed money. Yes, I thought, they certainly needed the money to buy opium which they smoked all day long. As for the new-fangled vegetables in the missionaries' gardens, their ancestors had lived well enough without them, and what was good for them is good enough for us, they said. Besides, they added, certain vegetables, especially the tomatoes, were reputed to be poisonous as they had originated as a fruit of the sin between dogs. What about the missionaries? I retorted. None of them has died from eating these vegetables. 'Ah,' men replied knowingly, 'you foreigners have different bodies, and what is good for you is death for us.'

They all looked weak, emaciated, with parchment-like skin, their eyes feverish with opium. What could one do to help them, to persuade them? The kindly Catholics certainly tried everything they could, but all was in vain against the dullness and obduracy of these people fanatically entrenched in their ignorance.

At the invitation of some Black Lolos I went from Moshimien to a village called Helluva further down the wonderful Tatu River. Then I had to climb to the mysterious Yehsaping plateau, 11,000 feet high, where these Lolos lived. Their houses were poor but very clean and they looked hale and hearty. I stayed with them several days. Even apart from the special feasts arranged for me, they ate well. They used pork, chickens and beef constantly — roasted, fried or boiler. They ate potatoes and buckwheat cakes and drank buckwheat and honey wine, called *zhiwoo*, with every meal. They did not smoke opium. They were dirty too, but very healthy. Not one of them had leprosy and the very mention of it made them shudder.

The Minkia around Likiang existed on a monotonous diet of rice with a little of bean curd or its equivalent, or rice and chillies only. And they had leprosy. The Szechuanese and White Lissu were also mean about their food and also had leprosy. It was only among the Nakhi, of the tribes in and around Likiang, who had such a varied and rich diet, both poor and wealthy, that there was no leprosy.

Whatever other factors cause leprosy, the disease seems to find fertile ground among the people who exist on a poor and monotonous diet. Dirt may or may not be a. contributing factor: malnutrition, due to unvaried food, certainly is. The Tibetans of lower classes also have an unvaried diet, consisting of the eternal *tsamba* — parched barley or wheat flour — and butter tea, and they too have leprosy.

The treatment of leprosy, even with the present-day revolutionary sulpha drugs, which had not yet appeared there in those days, was at best very slow and uncertain. I felt I was not qualified to handle such cases and passed them on to the missionaries in the south to their infinite delight.

I thought the real plague of Tibet and border regions was not leprosy but the venereal diseases. Judging from all reports and travellers' accounts, Tibet and Yungning region had at least 90 per cent of their population afflicted with one form or another of these souvenirs d'amour. Such a widespread prevalence was due, of course, to the practice of free love still prevailing in those parts. Likiang was comparatively free from this blight, thanks to the strictness of its marriage institution and the injunction that all Nakhi men should confine their amorous attentions strictly to the female members of their own tribe. If there were any Nakhi afflicted with these un-mentionable diseases, they certainly had picked them up outside Likiang. Returning soldiers were the most likely suspects in such cases.

The Tibetans, and to some extent the Liukhi, the matriarchic tribe living in Yungning territory, had during decades or perhaps even centuries developed very considerable immunity to syphilis. With most of them it now has a very mild form and even the third stage is not so destructive as it could be among other races. However, this benignity of the syphilis of the Tibetan variety does not extend to other races, particularly in the case of Europeans. In a European the virulence of the disease, contracted from a Tibetan, is so great that, without prompt treatment, a fatal ending ensues in about three months.

The prevalence of syphilis and gonorrhoea in Tibet and Yungning has a marked effect on the birth-rate. The population in Tibet is definitely shrinking, and the children in Yungning suffer from keratitis which is a result of congenital syphilis. The Tibetan Government has been greatly concerned and had plans for a wholesale treatment of venereal diseases, but nothing much has been accomplished because of the magnitude of the undertaking. This immense and heart-rending problem is further aggravated by the light-hearted carelessness and utter unconcern of the afflicted parties. They never think, for instance, that syphilis is anything more serious than a common cold and, since its first stage does indeed resemble the onset of a cold or flu, the ignorant man thinks that his own diagnosis is correct. Therefore, when they came for treatment they always said that it was just a cold and there was really nothing to worry about. They always got a shock when I told them that it was something else, and I remember a well-to-do Tibetan who came to see me with well-defined symptoms of this confidential disease. He was horrified when I told him the truth.

'No, no !' he cried. 'It is only a cold.'

'How did you get it ?' I asked.

'I caught it when riding a horse,' he replied.

'Well,' I said, 'it was the wrong kind of horse.'

In a long procession they came—the Tibetans, Liukhi and occasionally other tribesmen. But I do not remember really that I had any Nakhi with syphilis or gonorrhoea. As I have said, the Tibetan syphilis was benign, and after two or three shots they usually recovered, but in most cases it was an ungrateful and hopeless task. In two or three weeks they returned with a fresh infection. It was a SisytShean work for the most part, and I must admit I got tired of it.

Such was my clinic. Sick people came all the time, day in and day out, year after year. There were other diseases too. I tried my best to diagnose them and help. There were even attempts to make me attend difficult childbirths, but I drew a line at that as I had not had any experience at all in such matters. All the time I was extremely careful, and I would have been murdered if one of my patients had died.

The clinic made me acquaintances far and wide, and a number of pleasant and enduring friendships developed. I never took a cent for my attendance and medicines, but sometimes the people did bring a few eggs or a pot of honey, and it was not easy to decline these simple gifts. I remember I tried to refuse some eggs an old lady brought me, and she was quite indignant.

'Why do you refuse ?' she asked in a shrill voice. 'These eggs are fresh and good. I am not offering you anything dirty.' What could I say?

However, to run this clinic was not all plain sailing, for the cunning merchants and shopkeepers of Likiang were always after my medicines. Some were disarmingly frank. Said they: 'You get your supplies from the American Red Cross'—later it was the International Red Cross—'free of charge and you give tile medicine away also free of charge. These are good valuable medicines and cost a lot on tile black market. Why not sell us at least a half? Nobody would know. We are prepared to pay well and a goodly amount of hard cash will not harm you'; and they rubbed their hands in anticipation. I was neither angry nor did I show them to the door. My Chinese etiquette was as near perfect as is possible for a foreigner. I do not remember exactly what I said, but it was something infinitely polite and completely satisfying as to why I was unable to part with the medicines.

Then unsuspected attacks came from other quarters. Women started dropping in daily asking for ten tablets of santonin for a child at home, twenty aspirins for an ailing husband, ten or twenty sulphadiazines for somebody else also confined to bed, and so on in infinite variety. At first I did not hesitate, admiring them for walking so far over the hill to help their relatives or friends. It was when my cook had reported that he saw our santonins, sulphadiazines and aspirins being sold on the market at fifty cents a tablet, that I sat up and took notice. Immediately a notification was posted on the door, requiring all patients to present themselves to my clinic in person if they wanted any medicines. This helped, and afterwards I was careful not to give much medicine for follow-up treatment except when I knew for certain that the patient could be trusted: but there were wild scenes and much reviling whenever I refused point-blank some grand lady's request for packets of medicine.

Another favourite trick to the same end were the notes from very highly placed officials demanding that so much of a particular drug should be sent to him by bearer, usually an orderly. I always did send a few grains, profusely apologizing that momentarily that particular drug was almost out of stock. Even my charming Nakhi doctor friend quickly learned the way to my door to borrow this or that drug, promising to return its equivalent in a few days, though, of course, nothing was ever returned. Very soon I had to invent all sorts of excuses to stop the drain on my stocks of medicaments which were intended solely for use among poor villagers.

CHAPTER VII

THE NAKHIS

*T*HE Nakhi had strange convictions that some localities were bad and others good. At first I did not believe in such sweeping opinions. Nevertheless, with the passage of time, I learned that their assertions were essentially true. For example, Shwowo was a 'good' village and Boashi was 'bad'. Both these villages were in the northern valley and Lashiba, the village with the lake which I passed on my way to Likiang, was definitely 'bad'. But all the villages clown the main valley were 'good'. I asked my Nakhi friends how it was possible that the people in the whole village could all be uniformly bad. Wolves run to wolves and dogs to dogs, they told me, and bad men do not feel comfortable to stay with good ones: a paraphrase, in fact, of 'Birds of a feather flock together.' Collectively, Likiang was known as a 'good' town and Hoking and Chienchwang as 'bad' towns.

Somehow the bad reputation of Boashi village always distressed me. After all, the northern valley saw much

135

of the Nakhi history and the great temple to the patron god of Likiang, Saddok, was in Boashi. The name itself, Boashi-Dead Boa-was heroic. It was here that the invaders from Yungning were defeated and annihilated. They were led by a renegade sister of a Nakhi king, who had been given in marriage to a prince of Yungning. The woman had been captured and interned in an iron cage on a tiny island in the neighbouring lake. She was permitted to eat all kinds of solid food to her heart's content, but was not given a drop of water to drink, although there was water all around her. She died of thirst, suffering horribly. Such was her brother's revenge.

It was probably through the passes near Shwowo and Boashi that the Nakhi invaded the Likiang plain from the north many centuries ago. There is a reference to them and to Likiang in the Han dynasty and even earlier chronicles, but they were not known then as the Nakhi and the name and site of the present Likiang was changed several times. Dr Joseph Rock dealt with these ancient records in his monumental work on Likiang and surrounding territories called *The Ancient Nakhi Kingdom of South-west China*, but they are too long and complicated to be quoted here even in part. One fact emerges clearly, the Nakhi did come down from Tibet. Their sacred literature, written in pictographs, refers to Lake Manasarowar, Mount Kailas, to the yaks and living in tents on alpine meadows. They call the Tibetans their elder brothers and the Minkia their younger brothers. Their ancestors are curiously linked with all the gods of the Indian pantheon and their claim that the majority of their ancestors and heroes came out of the eggs magically produced as a result of a series of copulations between the mountains and lakes, pines and stones, Nagarajas and human females.

Old Nakhi villagers, formally attired.

The Nakhi, Burmese and Black Lolos, along with the Tibetans, belong to a racial subdivision called the Burmo-Tibetan stock. They do resemble each other to a degree, their languages and dialects have a common root and it is only in the manner of their dress and food that the difference becomes pronounced. The Nakhi, since the Tang dynasty, had begun the adoption of the Chinese civilization and culture of their own free will and the process is not yet over. In the matter of masculine dress it is practically impossible to distinguish between a Nakhi and a Chinese, but fortunately women have stuck to their picturesque Nakhi clothes and head-dress. The absorption of the Chinese etiquette and ceremonial was completed long ago and to advantage. With a correct approach, it is difficult to find a more polite and restrained people than the Nakhi. Secure in their knowledge of correct conduct, they judge strangers by their behaviour and judge very severely. Even during the visits to poorest homes in the village it is not meet for a person, however high his rank may be, to forget his good manners.

Of course, the Confucian ethics superseded and modified the original Nakhi customs, but a few of the latter still persist. Women may not sit in the presence of men or eat together with them. Also women never sleep in the upper rooms or remain there long. They are considered traditionally unclean creatures and it is not right for them to walk above men's heads. Local laws did little to protect women. Wives could be bought and sold by hundreds, and widows could be disposed of by the eldest son, although the latter practice occurred very rarely and was condemned as depravity. Continuous manual work was the women's lot. They did not revolt; they did not even protest. Instead, silently and

persistently like the roots of growing trees, they slowly
evolved themselves into a powerful race until they utterly
enslaved their men. They learned all the intricacies of
commerce and became merchants, land and exchange
brokers, shopkeepers and traders. They encouraged their
men to loaf, lounge and to look after the babies. It is they
who reaped the golden harvest of their enterprise, and
their husbands and sons had to beg them for money, even
if only a few pennies to buy cigarettes. It was the women
who started courting men and they held them fast by the
power of their money. It was the girls who gave their
lovers presents of clothes and cigarettes and paid for their
drinks and meals. Nothing could be obtained or bought
in Likiang without women's intervention and assistance.
Men knew nothing about the stocks in their own shops or
of the price at which their goods should be sold. To rent a
house or buy land one had to go to those women brokers
who knew about it. The owners would not negotiate direct
for fear of losing money without the women brokers'
expert advice. To change money you had to go to tile
rosy-cheeked girls – the *pangchinmei*. Tibetan caravans, on
arrival, surrendered their merchandise to the women for
disposal, otherwise they ran a risk of heavy losses.

Because of their manifold activities and of the heavy
loads of merchandise they transported on their backs
from house to shop or from one market to another, the
race of Likiang women had developed superior physical
characteristics. The women became tall and husky, with
great bosoms and strong arms. They were self-assured,
assertive and bold. They were the brains of the family and
the only foundation of prosperity in the household. To
marry a Nakhi woman was to acquire a life insurance, and
the ability to be idle for the rest of one's days. Therefore,

Ahouha--one of the pangchinmei (girls)of Likiang in formal everyday wear.

the market value of a Nakhi bride was very high, and as the Nakhi men outnumbered women by five to four, a man was lucky to find a wife at all. A single woman of almost any age would do; there were youngsters of eighteen married to women of thirty-five. What did it matter, the boy was secure for life? She was his wife and mother and, moreover, she kept him in clover. What more could a man want?

There was not a single woman or girl in Likiang who was idle. They were all in business from early morning till night. No family could possibly have a female servant. It was utterly unthinkable. Why should a woman slave for somebody at a few dollars a month when every day of her time was worth so much more? The wives and daughters of the Nakhi magistrates and other high officials, of the wealthy merchants and landowners, worked as hard as any humble village woman. Either they specialized in selling the Tibetans' merchandise at the local market or went down to weekly markets in Hoking, carrying the goods in baskets on their backs. Or, perhaps, they heard that some villages had cheaper potatoes or pigs, and off they would go, bringing the loads back and making a tidy little profit. Many a time I met Madame Hsi, the magistrate's wife, carrying on her back a heavy basket of potatoes or a sack of grain. Among the 'society' leaders of the West this concept of work would provoke a sensation perhaps greater than an invasion of the Martians. Imagine a Mrs. Astor or a Mrs. Vanderbilt lugging a sack of potatoes on her back through Fifth Avenue! Yet it is a fair comparison; for, in Likiang, the following day you might meet Madame Hsi at a wedding reception at some general's house, gorgeously bedecked in brocades and silks and festooned with costly jewels.

Thus the women in the little Nakhi world were despised creatures in theory but powerful and respected in practice. Men were the privileged beings, but weak and of little account in the economic life. Even in physique they seldom appeared the equals of their husky mates. When young, they sponged on their mothers and sisters and spent the time in picnicking, gambling and dalliance. When old, they stayed at home, looking after the children, talking to cronies and smoking opium. Like drones, they would have quickly died of starvation had their wives stopped the money-making.

In extolling the physical strength and business acumen of Nakhi women I do not wish to imply that Nakhi men were effeminate or cowardly. Since the earliest days of their history they have been renowned for their bravery, courage and loyalty. It certainly needed pluck and resource to come clown all the way from Tibet and defeat the aboriginal tribes which dwelt at the time in the Likiang plain. The contingents of Nakhi soldiers have always been the mainstay of the Yunnan Provincial Army, and when called upon they fought to the death. It was through the participation of the Nakhi troops that the famous Taierhchwang victory over the Japanese was won. They never turned their back on the enemy and very few survivors were left. They are intrepid horsemen, tireless walkers, and can exist for months on a meagre and monotonous diet.

In appearance the Nakhi men are as a rule handsome and well built. Many are of average height and a few are quite tall, although they seldom approached the gigantic stature of the Kham Tibetans. The complexion of both men and women on the whole is somewhat darker than that of the Chinese, but there are many exceptions. In some cases they may be as white as South Europeans. Other characteristics destroy any illusion that they have connections with the Chinese racial stock. Although the cheek-bones may be high, the face is essentially European in its contour. The nose is long, well shaped and has a prominent ridge. Unlike the Chinese, a Nakhi gentleman could wear a pince-nez if he wanted to. The eyes are light brown and only in rare cases greenish; they are not almond-shaped, but wide and liquid. The hair may be dark but it always has a reddish sheen; in most cases it is *châtain foncé* and it is soft and curly. All in all, a Nakhi reminds one strongly of a farmer from South Italy or Spain.

The Nakhi are passionate, frank almost to a fault and choleric. The latter characteristic was undoubtedly due to high altitudes. All the people staying above 8,000 feet, I observed, were irritable. This irritability was ever present and it was utterly unreasonable. The rarefied atmosphere was not conducive to good sleep and probably this factor was, to some extent, responsible for hot tempers. Otherwise the Nakhi, like the Tibetans, were one of the most cheerful people on earth. They smiled, laughed and joked all clay long, talked and shouted, and, at every opportunity, danced in the evening.

They were born gossips, both men and women. They simply could not keep their mouths shut. There was not a secret, whether a family one or political, that would not be known to the whole town within a matter of days or even hours. Especially enjoyable were the family scandals, and they were frequent. The more piquant a scandal the more it was discussed, with gusto and delight, in all wine-shops and on the market. Likiang was not, after all, such a small town and it always astonished me to observe how intimately its inhabitants knew each other. In time, I and my household came to be included in this happy community. Everybody called me by my first name, stopped to chat or greeted me with a smile; and, strangely enough, I seemed to know everybody too. Even the people from nearby villages seemed to be known to everyone in the town and were affectionately greeted when coming to the market.

The Nakhi, like the Tibetans, were the despair of missionaries. Like the proverbial bad pennies, they were inconvertible. For years the Roman Catholics and other denominations have vainly tried to establish themselves in the district, although one of the British sectarian missions managed to retain a precarious foothold in the city for a short while. It was in the charge of an English couple. They had a comfortable house and a small church with a corner-stone bearing the legend 'Lot No. 1 until He cometh.' They wrote communications on special letterheads overprinted with the title: 'President-Lord God Sabaoth; Vice President-Lord Jesus Christ; Treasurer - Mr. X (the missionary).' Business was poor and they had only a few converts among the Chinese emigrants from Szechuan. However, they used to make trips into the mountains up the Yangtze River, where they were compensated with some success among the primitive White Lissu tribes.

The failure to convert the Nakhi, one of whose religions was Lamaism, to Christianity, is inextricably bound up with the failure to evangelize the Tibetans. The reason for this lack of success in the spreading of the Gospel, undertaken by the missionaries from the western and eastern borders of Tibet, becomes clear if properly assessed. The Tibetan Church is just as well organized and powerful as tile Roman Catholic Church. Its tenets are rooted in Buddhism—a great and highly philosophical religion. It is controlled by the lamas and is headed by the Dalai Lama who, like the Pope, is both spiritual and temporal ruler. In the West the word lama is applied indiscriminately to all Tibetan monks. In Tibet and among the Nakhi it is an honorary title when addressing an ecclesiastic, but actually it takes an ordinary monk (commonly called trapa) diligence, learning and much of his lifetime to reach the status of a lama, if he ever does. All the real lamas are thus highly educated men, profoundly versed in Buddhistic philosophy and theology. They may or may not be saintly, but certainly they are always shrewd and, as a rule, they are good administrators and organizers. For comparison, it would not be inappropriate to liken the lower ranks of the lamas to the deacons and archdeacons, and higher ranks to the bishops, archbishops, patriarchs and cardinals. The lamas may or may not be the Incarnations or Living Buddhas (*trulkus*, also called *hutuktus*), but every Incarnation is a lama and the Church sees to it that he is properly educated to live up to the title. Each lamasery of note must have at least a few real lamas to give it direction and prestige and to train the novices who, later on, may go to the great monastic colleges near Lhasa where they have a chance to pass the examinations and become lamas.

It was with this type of opposition that missionaries had to deal. It was easy to declare to the people that the statues of the Buddhas and saints in the lamaseries were idols and that the lamas led men into superstition and to perdition with the bright fires of hell as the ultimate destination, but it was very difficult to prove that it was so. The type of missionary who went to the Tibetan borders to show the true light of salvation to the ignorant 'savages' was, with a few exceptions, a poor sort. They all claimed the 'call of the spirit', but had little education or knowledge with which to give it practical effect, and as often as not they were members of the less educated strata of European society. Not even knowing their own language well enough, they had great difficulty in learning Tibetan or local dialects, and it was seldom that they acquired enough fluency in the language to preach clearly and coherently. Perhaps unconsciously they did everything to maintain that superiority which was so resented on the border. They lived comfortably in European style and went forth only once in a while to distribute tracts and talk to the people. They invited to their meals the local *élite*, leaving the other people to gape at the gate. There was a widespread joke among the natives on the border that the missionaries reserved the first-class heaven to themselves and promised only the third-class paradise to the heathens. Theological contests between the lamas and missionaries tended only to enhance the prestige of the lamas with their greater knowledge of the theological and metaphysical aspects of both religions. Also it must be admitted the Tibetan Church was no more willing to permit the conversion of its adherents to Christianity than the Roman Catholic Church was willing to permit the Protestant missionaries in Spain and Colombia to seduce people from Catholicism. Any Tibetan who embraced Christianity became automatically an outcast, was driven away from his home and his very life was in jeopardy. The only possible Tibetan converts were the bastard children of Tibetan mothers and itinerant Chinese fathers whom nobody wanted and who could be picked up and reared in the missions.

With the Nakhi the matter of adherence to the Christian religion was somewhat different. They were in many ways similar to the Chinese who are not a religious people *per se*, in the Western sense of the word. The Chinese believe simultaneously and sincerely in Buddhism, Taoism, Ancestral Worship (Confucianism), Animism and willingly accept Christianity if need be. The Nakhi, likewise, had accepted Lamaism (Tantric Buddhism), Mahayana Buddhism, Taoism and Confucianism in addition to their ancient religion of Animism and Shamanism. To coin a phrase, they had a departmentalized belief, with each religion serving some particular need. Buddhism was useful in connection with the funerals and prayers for the repose of the dead. Taoism satisfied mystic and aesthetic cravings. Ancestor worship was proper and necessary to keep up the contact with the departed. Animism was the recognition and definition of the unseen powers and intelligences in Nature and provided a method of dealing with them. Shamanism was indispensable for the protection of the living and dead from the evil spirits. On top of these religious beliefs they had inherited from their ancestors a deep-rooted and eminently practical Epicurean philosophy. It taught them that this was, indeed, a transient plane of existence but nevertheless very material and substantial. It was not perfect or free from sorrows but, on the whole, it was not a bad place and, while life lasted, it was the bounden duty of every Nakhi to make the best of it. Although the tradition and scriptures asserted that the next world was a blissful and restful place, there were certain doubts about it, and there was little enlightenment about the conditions there from the few people who returned for a brief while through mediums. It was best not to take chances on future joys but to enjoy oneself to the hilt whilst on this plane. The happiness, which every Nakhi should strive after, was described as the possession of plenty of good fields and fruit orchards, cattle and horses, a spacious house, an attractive wife, lots of male and female children, barns chock full of grain, yak butter and other edibles, multitudes of jars with wine, abundant sexual strength and good health and a succession of picnics and dances with congenial companions on flower-strewn alpine meadows.

We must remember that the Nakhi were simple people and to them these rustic pleasures have always been the acme of existence. Looking at it from this angle, it must be admitted that the tribe, as a whole, has indeed attained the objectives charted in their philosophy. There was no area for hundreds of miles around which attained such prosperity and well-being as the Likiang valley or where the people enjoyed life more. What could the missionaries, of the sect which had established itself in Likiang, give these people? They insisted on the abandonment of all that was near and dear to the heart of a Nakhi; wine and tobacco were prohibited: so were the dances and dalliance with pretty girls during interminable picnics. All the séances and intercourse with the dear and helpful spirits were taboo. Ancestor worship was under interdict and so were all relations with the beautiful lamaseries and temples. 'What is left to us then?' the Nakhi asked. This is nothing but a living death, argued these fun-loving and life-loving people. Thus no Nakhi has become a Christian.

CHAPTER VIII

THE TIBETANS

$\mathcal{T}$HE Tibetan population of Likiang was considerable. Although they were at liberty to reside in any quarter of the city, the Tibetans always preferred the houses near Double Stone Bridge which spanned the Likiang River not far from the park. The meadows along the lonely road, which connected my village with this part of the town, were used for the encampment of arriving caravans. The Tibetan community in Likiang enjoyed an importance and standing quite out of proportion to its numbers. Tibetan merchants and dignitaries occupied the best houses and there was no service too great or too small which the Nakhi would not perform to make them comfortable and contented. This preferential attention and affectionate relationship was due, of course, to the racial affinity between the Tibetans and Nakhi; the latter always referred to the Tibetans as 'our elder brothers'. The fact that at least one people of their own race still remained completely independent and possessed a civilization and culture of widely recognized standing had a strong appeal to the Nakhi's *amour-propre*. However, brotherly affection was not the only reason and, I strongly suspect, not the main reason for such a felicitous reception.

When all coastal China was in Japanese hands and Burma was going fast, there remained only two 'ports of entry' for China for commerce with the outside world: Likiang in Yunnan and Tachienlu in Sikang. At the other end was Kalimpong to which the goods were shipped from Calcutta and Bombay by rail. Lhasa was the clearing centre and, being born merchants, members of the Tibetan government, great and small lamas, abbots of lamaseries and lesser lights did not hesitate a moment when the golden opportunity so auspiciously presented itself. All available financial resources had been speedily mobilized and even, I was told, a sizeable portion of the Dalai Lama's private fortune had been invested in the great and lucrative venture. Letters of credit, remittances or plain cash-on-delivery poured into India. Armies of Tibetan merchants, small traders and mere hawkers descended from the icy altitudes of Phari Dzong and Jelap-La and invaded the steamy bazaars and inns of Calcutta. Everything was indented, contracted or bought outright that could be conveniently carried by yak or mule. Sewing-machines, textiles, cases of the best cigarettes, both British and American, whiskies and gins of famous brands, dyes and chemicals, kerosene oil in tins, toilet and canned goods and a thousand and one varieties of small articles started flowing in an unending stream by rail and truck to Kalimpong, to be hastily re-packed and dispatched by caravan to Lhasa. There the flood of merchandise was crammed into the halls and courtyards of the palaces and lamaseries and turned over

A Tibetan buying haberdashery at Likiang Market.

to an army of sorters and professional packers. The least fragile goods were set aside for the northern route to Tachienlu, to be transported by yaks: other articles were packed for delivery at Likiang, especially the liquors and cigarettes which were worth their weight in gold in Kunming, crowded with thirsty American and British troops. To survive the three months' haulage over the rocky paths, across the highest mountains on earth, in rain or under the scorching sun, the merchandise had to be packed expertly and with infinite care. And so it was. The uniform weight of each package was of particular concern. No horse or mule could carry more than 60 catties[1] and no yak more than 50 on the long trek. At first the merchandise had been arranged in compact piles, then the piles were wrapped up in wool mats and some even in rugs and carefully sewn up in wet hides. The hides, drying up, shrank and squeezed the contents into one monolithic mass, which could be dropped, thrown about, shaken or sat upon without injury to the goods inside. It was impervious to the scraping of rocks or bushes and quite weatherproof. The cases with cigarettes or crates with sewing-machines were similarly strengthened with a network of wet strips of hides, sewn together.

Transportation by yaks was more hazardous than by mules and horses and, therefore, the merchants always tried to avoid sending fragile goods by these animals. Although some people refer to 'yak caravans', I would hesitate to use such a definition. A caravan, to my mind, has always meant an orderly progression of loaded animals or vehicles in a single file. And that is how the horses and mule caravans, descending on Likiang,

---

[1] 1 catty=$1\frac{1}{3}$lb.

appeared. But there was nothing orderly about the yaks, and they never proceeded in single file. They were nothing but silly, primitive cows, and they behaved like cows, progressing as a widespread herd in an erratic manner. Sometimes they slowed down, sometimes they rushed ahead, jostling and pushing each other. They did not seem to know or care where they were going, trying to squeeze between two rocks or between two trees, although there might be plenty of space around. I remember how a friend of mine lost a valuable cast-iron cooking range he was expecting from India. Just before reaching Tachienlu the yak which was carrying it had a mind to pass between two rocks. He did it with great speed, much energy and an obvious determination. Afterwards they could find only some chunks of iron, the plates and its legs. The yaks were not the gentle animals one might think. They were suspicious and truculent and always went after horses or strangers in a most threatening manner. I had many close shaves when encountering a herd of yaks un-expectedly. Yaks cannot stand warm weather at all, and therefore their operation is confined to altitudes over 10,000 feet, and they are at their best when they graze on the alpine meadows above 12,000 feet.

It was estimated that some 8,000 mules and horses, and probably 20,000 yaks, were used during Operation Caravan, when all other routes into China had been blocked during the war. Almost every week long caravans arrived in Likiang. So good and profitable was the business that even the rainy seasons failed to stop some adventurous merchants. This was a considerable risk and, in their avarice, they took it. The rainy season is much dreaded in Tibet and on the border, and all caravan and pilgrim traffic usually stops for the duration. The trails become muddy and swampy, rivers and streams swell to incredible proportions, mountains are wrapped in mists and avalanches and landslides become the rule rather than the exception. Many a traveller has been buried for ever under tons of rocks or swept to his death by a raging torrent.

Few people have realized how vast and unprecedented this sudden expansion of caravan traffic between India and China was, or how important. It was a unique and spectacular phenomenon. No complete story has yet been written about it, but it will always live in my memory as one of the great adventures of mankind. Moreover, it demonstrated to the world very convincingly that, should all modern means of communication and transportation be destroyed by some atomic cataclysm, the humble horse, man's oldest friend, is ever ready to forge again a link between scattered peoples and nations.

The dangers of the rainy season, sickness and other un-expected and unforeseen calamities were not the only hazards which threatened a caravan during its slow progress from Lhasa to Likiang. There were the powerful bands of robbers operating in eastern Tibet which constituted the vast third province, known as Kham, of the holy land. Kham is so remote from the Central Government in Lhasa, so little known and explored that, even to an average Tibetan in the Holy City, it is still a land of mystery and enchantment. To the dwellers of the remaining two provinces, U and Tsang, where Lhasa is located, with their dry gaunt mountains, arid plateaux, dust and howling winds, Kham is an embodiment of the beauty and charm of nature the like of which cannot be found elsewhere in the world. There the world's greatest rivers, crystal clear and unsullied, flow through marble gorges side by side, amidst the vast and stately forests which cover mountain slopes. Sparkling snow peaks, virgin and unattainable, soar into the blue sky. Even the gods love these paradisical vistas as almost every peak is the throne of a popular deity or *yidam*, of which the Yidam Demchuk is the best known. Much gold is reputed to be found in Kham, and its lamaseries are said to be particularly wealthy and beautiful. The Khamba (the people of Kham) never fail to excite the awe and admiration of other Tibetans. The men are, as a rule, of gigantic stature and very good-looking and the women are fair to look at and very white.

A goodly portion of this immense province had been detached by the Chinese at the beginning of the present century and placed under the Szechuan Provincial Government, later becoming a part of the newly created Sikang Province. However, in the olden days, when Tibet had not yet been converted to Buddhism, even Likiang was under the sway of the powerful Tibetan conquerors. It was the advent and dissemination of Buddhism that had emasculated the proud country and brought it to its knees.

Kham was infested with robbers and other lawless elements. The dual control, under which it had been placed, was certainly propitious to such an unhappy development. The bands, which had committed crimes in the Tibetan section of the province, could cross into the Chinese territory, and vice versa. The wild character of the country, with its high mountains, impenetrable primeval forests and turbulent rivers made it an ideal hiding-place. However, not all Khamba were robbers; there were many of them who were of sterling character. Banditry in Tibet was a time-honoured profession and was usually confined to the members of certain tribes or clans. The usual concept of Tibet, owing to the lack of precise information, is that the country has a homogeneous population, all speaking alike, dressed alike, with the same customs and religion, and all owing an undivided allegiance to the Dalai Lama and his government. Actually it is not so. Tibet is divided and subdivided into many tribes and clans, little kingdoms, duchies and baronies, all on a feudal system, whose heads owe allegiance to the Central Government and prove it by sending levies of soldiers, tribute and rich gifts to His Holiness the Dalai Lama. Kham is no exception and includes many such principalities both on the Tibetan and Chinese side of the frontier. The most notable of these little states, which have been visited by explorers, are the Kingdom of Mull, Principality of Liking, Grand Duchy of Kanze, Duchy of Tsoso, Duchy of Yungning, Principality of Bongdzera, not to speak of innumerable Black Lolo, Black Lissu and other tribal marquisates and baronies. In Mull, Bongdzera and Litang not all the people are of the Tibetan race but they are ardent lamaists just the same, and a steady stream of gold used to flow from their rulers into the Dalai Lama' treasury. Incidentally the King of Mull was a Mongol. His first ancestor was a general in Kublai Khan' army which invaded Liking and Tall via Mull, and in recognition of his services the Great Khan appointed him the King of Mull in perpetuity.

North-west of Likiang and to the west of the Mull Kingdom there is an isolated mountain range called Konkkaling. It consists of three peaks, about 23,000 feet high. It had been discovered and photographed by Dr. Joseph Rock, who used to make expeditions to Mull where the king was a great friend of his. These mountains are a veritable breeding place of the most ruthless brigands the world has ever known. To the west of these mountains there are two vast territories known as Hsiangchen and Tongwa. They are peopled with two Tibetan tribes whose members are professional robbers and cut-throats. So wild, untamable and treacherous are they that not even other Tibetans dare to venture into these areas. Although of an enormous size, rivalling some of the large European states, none of these areas has ever been visited by a European and probably will not be for a long time to come. There is no doubt that much of interest to explorers and scientists is concealed in these inaccessible and unmapped regions. There is, for instance, a great snow peak in the bend of the Yalung River in Hsiangchen, called Neito Cavalori. Those few privileged explorers who have been lucky enough to contemplate it from a distance, compute its height at something like 28,000 feet, and it may yet prove a rival to Mount Everest.

It was these Tongwa and Hsiangchen brigands who always lay in wait for the rich caravans coming from Lhasa. Of course all Tibetan caravan men were heavily armed, and when the caravan was big enough these rascals did not dare to attack them. It was when the caravan was small or poorly armed that their chance came. Madame Alexandra David Neel nevertheless describes the Tibetan bandits as 'Les Brigands-Gentilhommes' in her book. I have known this great lady since 1939, when I met her in Tachienlu, and have a profound respect for her. She is certainly one of the greatest travellers the world has known, and I am glad she received such fortunate mercy from these robbers, who even showed a certain gallantry towards her because she was a helpless woman and a *detsuma* (Reverend Abbess) to boot. Personally I would rather deal with a Chinese or a Nakhi robber than a

Tibetan one. A Chinese or a Nakhi robber seldom kills his victim. He robs you but he does it with a degree of finesse and delicacy, and at least leaves you your underwear to enable you to reach the nearest village with a modicum of decency. He usually forbears to search a lady, and may even listen to her protests about taking away certain items of her toilette. Not so with the Tibetan robbers. Their motto is 'Dead men tell no tales'. They shoot first and then look for anything of value on the dead man's person or in his baggage. I once heard an interesting story of how one of these Tongwa shot a man walking in the distance, only to discover afterwards that it was his own father.

I am prepared to admit that the Tibetan brigands of some other tribes may be 'gentlemen' to some degree but, from what I heard from reliable Tibetan and Nakhi friends, the Tongwa and Hslangchen cannot be idealized by any stretch of imagination. They are so avaricious and unprincipled that even the bonds of friendship mean nothing to them, and there have been cases when a man has killed a bosom friend for the sake of a couple of rupees in his belt. Everybody in Tongwa and Hsiangchen robs, steals and kills-lamas and trapas, merchants and serfs, men and women: even children learn the trade at a tender age. It is not a question of whether this Tongwa or that Hsiangchen is a robber, but whether the man is a Tongwa or Hsiangchen.

When the caravan has been plundered and witnesses eliminated or scattered, the goods, arms and animals are taken to the robbers' lair. There the merchandise is carefully repacked and reloaded and, lo and behold, the robber chief, resplendently dressed, enters Likiang as a peaceful and affluent merchant, at the head of a sizable caravan. No questions are asked and no explanations are vouchsafed. Of course rumours do travel, and travel fast; but rumours are rumours and proofs are proofs. The bogus merchant knows that the people know and the people know that he knows what they know, but everything proceeds according to form. The merchant sells his goods, gives generous parties right and left and acquires merit by rich donations to the local lamaseries.

I was very curious to find out what these Tongwa and Hsiangchen men looked like, and was surprised to find that quite a number of them came to Likiang, some accompanied by their wives, for the peaceful purposes of commerce. The men looked, and were dressed, like any other Tibetan. They appeared a little dirtier and more savage looking. The women were dressed after the fashion of the nomads' wives, but with a difference. The nomadic women carry a large number of metal disks attached to their hair, braided in small queues and spread evenly clown the back: the disks of the wealthy are all of solid gold or silver and those of the poor are of brass or copper. This is their way of carrying about with them their fortunes, which may weigh anything from thirty to sixty pounds or even more. Thus even these simple women were willing to endure suffering for the sake of fashion like their sophisticated sisters in civilized China and the West who had endured smilingly the tortures of bound feet and corsets. But the Hsiangchen and Tongwa women, probably to ensure mobility, were content to wear earrings made of large bunches of small cubes woven of multi-coloured bark. These earrings looked unusual, attractive and very *chic*.

I met a group of Tongwa youths at Madame Ho's wine-shop. One of them, named Dorje (Thunderbolt), became very attached to me and called on me daily. Soon his friends went back but he remained. One evening I found him waiting at my door with a bundle. He said that he had to stay behind to complete a business transaction. He found the inns of Likiang very expensive and wondered whether I would permit him to stay at my house for a few days. My cook and neighbours were horrified at the idea and dearly indicated with the palms of their hands across their throats what kind of fate I was courting. I decided to take a risk, so much did I want to know something about these mysterious people.

Dorje wag only seventeen, but looked too tall and big his age. He was slim and supple. His face was classically Grecian in profile with a high nose, bold outline, finely chiselled mouth and expressive eyes. His hair was brownish, long, and held in place with a red scarf wound around his head. In his left ear he wore a silver ring. He wore an ancient grey jacket with breast-pockets which clearly had belonged once to a Chinese officer. Perhaps this jacket could tell a story of its own; of how it got into the possession of a Tibetan boy in so distant a place. Tied around his waist was an ordinary tunic of unbleached wool, affected by some Tibetan tribes in Kham. Quite unlike the usual run of the Tibetans, who all wore long trousers tucked into their boots, this boy wore very short skin pants. So short were they that, over-lapped by his jacket, he appeared to have no pants at all. He certainly excited a great deal of merriment among the brazen Nakhi females when he appeared in the street. To complete his costume he wore a pair of tall soft boots tied at the knees, the tops being of red wool cloth and the bottoms of uncured soft leather. He carried several silver and brass charm boxes suspended from the neck by sword thrust through the belt leather thongs, a short Tibetan and

a curved dagger in a leather sheath. Such was Dorje —
an unexpected Ganymede from the Tongwa Olympus. So
light was his complexion that, dressed in Western clothes,
nobody would have guessed that he was a Tibetan, or an
Asiatic at all for that matter.

Contrary to all expectations, he was well mannered,
modest and unobtrusive. After supper, when I retired to
my apartment to read a book by the light of a carbide
lamp — a luxury reserved only to myself — he usually
came up. The wine we always drank in the evening
loosened his tongue and we talked intimately. One
evening he unrolled his tunic and showed me a number of
musk-pods.

'This is my merchandise,' he explained, 'but the dealers
here are trying to beat me down. This is the reason I am
staying longer than expected; I am biding my time.' Next
evening he leaned towards me and pulled out a small
leather pouch tied to his neck. He opened it and I saw
several gold nuggets and a quantity of gold dust.

'Please keep it secret,' he pleaded, 'but with these I
hope to buy some merchandise to take back.'

He was very pious and superstitious and constantly
touched his amulets to assure himself that they were still
there, murmuring the classical mantram, '*Aum, mani padme
hum*.' It was clear that he developed great confidence in
me and accepted me as a friend, perhaps a more intimate
friend than it would be possible or prudent to have in his
own country.

Gathering my courage I began asking him questions
about Tongwa, its people and robbers. I did not have to be
tactful, or approach the subject in a roundabout manner.
He was not a Chinese and my use of Chinese etiquette
would have been wasted on him. The Tibetans, if they

wish to conceal something, remain silent or, if they wish to talk, they talk frankly and directly and expect a similar attitude from others.

Although I had expected an interesting confession, I was shocked when he calmly confirmed, in all frankness, that all the Tongwa were robbers, thieves and, on occasion, murderers. He admitted, though rather shamefacedly, that he was a robber himself, paraphrasing the old adage, 'When in Rome do as the Romans do'. But he hotly denied that he had been a party to any killing. 'I believe in Buddha too much for that,' he tried to comfort me, seeing my distress. Had then these musk-pods, this gold, been obtained by robbery? I inquired. But he would neither confirm nor deny. I stared in wonderment at this handsome youth, so calm, so self-possessed and seemingly so pure. By now I was accustomed to robbers and brigands. I had stayed for months among the Black Lolos in the Taliangshan mountains in Sikang, whose profession it was to rob and plunder. I had been a guest of a Chinese robber baron in Helluva, also in Sikang. But all those men looked their part at the first glance; there was no mistake about it. But I could not reconcile myself to the fact that this gentle and dignified boy was a brigand too. I decided to lay my cards on the table.

'Look, my friend Dorje!' I said. 'Does it mean then that, before you leave, you will clean up my house and, perhaps, stab me for good measure?'

'Ma re, Ma re!'(No, no!)' Cried out, brightening up perceptibly.

Then he assured me that never, never would such a thing be possible. First of all, he regarded me as his best, most valued friend. I had shown him too much kindness, he added, and even the Tongwa are not insensible to true friendships. But the main reason, he explained, was his and his tribe's standing in the great and free market of Likiang. No Tongwa or Hsiangchen would dare to commit a crime in Likiang. It would be a flagrant admission and material evidence of the fact that both tribes are indeed brigands and thieves. The authorities and people of Likiang of course knew their unsavoury reputation and did not discount the rumours of their depredations. But bad reputation and rumours were one thing and deeds were another. No robber was a robber and no thief was a thief in these border regions until he was caught red-handed. Whatever robberies or bloodshed happened in remote Tongwa and Hsiangchen were no concern of the Likiang authorities. That was a matter for the Tibetan Government to attend to. But to have such acts committed in peaceful Likiang was a totally different thing. The whole weight of militia, police and outraged public opinion would fall not only on the individual culprit but also on the whole tribe. To lose one's life by being shot was nothing, but to have all the members of the tribe, living and doing business in Likiang, expelled perhaps after a little dose of third degree, and the whole tribe debarred from future visits and business in this great market, the only market in fact, would be no laughing matter. The whole economic life of Tongwa and Hsiangchen, as the case might be, would collapse on account of a paltry robbery or theft. Where could the people of Tongwa take their plunder, after successful raids, for disposal? Certainly not to Lhasa where they were well known and where the goods would surely be identified by the injured merchants. They would be arrested and tortured before they could even open their mouths'. Try to prove to the haughty and ruthless Tibetan police that you did not do it, without a ruinous outlay in bribes? No, Likiang was priceless, indispensable. That was the underlying motive for the exemplary behaviour and sterling honesty of these ferocious tribesmen in Likiang. They knew their economics only too well.

After these talks Dorje and I became closer friends and he pressed me all the time to go with him to Tongwa for a visit. I thought this was like an invitation to the biblical lions' den. I told him that he was clearly playing the role of a decoy to lure me to my destruction. He laughed it off, but became pensive. Finally he confessed that he might not be powerful enough to protect me from other people in Tongwa who were not so friendly to him. It was rather a wrench for me when he announced his departure, as I had become very fond of his company. He gave me a small silver shrine and his dagger as a memento and offered a little gold dust to pay for board and lodging, which I did not accept. He promised to come back again in a year or so with Lhasa rugs and other goods. Perhaps he did keep his promise but I was not there.

My experience with the Hsiangchen tribe was on different lines. A Nakhi friend had informed me that a very rich and powerful Hsiangchen lama had arrived in Likiang and was staying in great state at one of the palatial mansions near King Mu's compound. He thought that it would be very interesting for me to meet him and that I should call on him to pay my respects. Lowering his voice, he added that the lama was the head of a large lamasery in the heart of Hsiangchen country whose monks were notorious brigands. What is more to the point, he said, was the fact that this very lama and his monks had waylaid and plundered a caravan of one hundred and fifty horses just a few months ago, and that now he had brought

Likiang street scene. A lama shopping.

the repacked stolen goods for sale in Likiang. It was rumoured that some merchants in the town had received a message from Lhasa to be on the look-out for such goods as could be identified as belonging to certain Lhasa shippers. If this could be done, a great and extremely pungent scandal was inevitable.

It was in such an electrified atmosphere that, with my friend, I called on the lama merchant. Passing through a labyrinth of corridors and verandas we were ushered into a spacious room where the great man sat cross-legged on the rich rugs spread over a raised platform. A brazier was burning in front and a huge inlaid copper pot of butter tea was simmering on the fire. Contrary to my expectation, he did not rise to receive me, but motioned to me to sit down on the rug next to him, evidently not considering me of sufficient importance to be worthy of a display of good manners. If I had been sensitive I would have walked out there and then, but it would have caused an unnecessary 'storm in a teacup'. I always tried to avoid such *contretemps* even if it involved a slight dent in my dignity. The man was huge and extremely strong. He looked at me with searching and penetrating eyes. He wore a silk jacket of golden-yellow colour, signifying that he was indeed a lama, and the wine-red lama robe was wrapped around his waist. His head was shaven. With an air of boredom he offered me some butter tea in a new silver-inlaid wooden bowl and sipped some himself: We offered the traditional *khata* — white gauze scarf — as a mark of goodwill and respect, and greeted him. My friend told him who I was and what was my work in Likiang. Seeing that I was not a missionary or local government official, his manner changed; his eyes became friendly, and he talked in a jovial manner about this and that.

Finally he exploded in a sharp command to one of the attendant monks and the man rushed out of the room.

'I like you both,' he roared. *'Ara tung!* (Let us drink wine!)'

The monk returned with a jar full of white wine, cups were produced and we started toasting each other, munching *kanbarr*—dried yak meat. We must have stayed at least one hour, having a really jolly time with this unconventional lama.

After a week or so we heard that his sales were going very well indeed under the able direction of Madame Ho in her capacity as a shrewd and well-connected merchandise broker. She made thousands on the deal as she had skillfully beaten down the lama with discreet innuendoes as to the origin of his goods. I and my friend were quite surprised when one day we received invitations to dinner from the lama, and before he left I was invited again to his house for an intimate drink. It appeared that he liked me and wanted me to come with him on a visit to his lamasery. I thought the best policy would be frankness again. I said that I appreciated very much his invitation and, for my part, I always wanted to see his mysterious country, but I could not go to my doom with open eyes, for I still hoped to live a little longer. He said he thought he could protect me but his voice did not carry enough assurance.

One day I was intrigued by the appearance on a street near Double Stone Bridge of a gorgeously attired Tibetan woman, accompanied at a respectful distance by two more modestly dressed women who obviously were her suite. She wore a gold-embroidered semi-conical hat, jacket of gold brocade and a petunia-shaped skirt of some kind of cloth-of-gold. She was of average height and appeared to be in her thirties. Her face was neither beautiful nor ugly, her eyes were cold and commanding and she walked with great dignity. I bowed to her respectfully and she just nodded in return. I met her several times later and once she was accompanied by a giant of a Tibetan who was also magnificently dressed. He wore a similar gold-embroidered hat, rich silk jacket of purple colour, with gold and silver-studded belt, a silver-sheathed short sword and black corduroy trousers. His hair had not been braided in the usual Tibetan style and his black curls fell freely on his shoulders. His face was rounded, with apple-red cheeks and big eyes. His teeth were dazzling. Several times in my childhood I had seen a life-size painting of Peter the Great and it had left a deep impression on me. When I saw the towering, athletic figure of this magnificent man, tile same rounded face with red cheeks, the eyes and the black curls falling on the shoulders, the resemblance to the long-dead czar staggered me. Even the dress conformed to that period. The same evening, after dinner, I rushed to Madame Ho's wine-shop and described to her the woman and the man. She laughed.

'She is a ruling duchess from Hsiangchen and he is her latest acquisition.'

'Don't you think she is a rather hard-looking woman?' I asked. Madame Ho poured herself and me another cup of *yintsieu* before replying.

'Yes, she is. They say that they are fighting already like cat and dog.'

'That's funny. He is such a powerful man,' I ventured.

'Well, it's not all gold that glitters,' was Madame Ho's cryptic remark, and she started putting up the shutters.

Next day I met my Nakhi friend—the same who had introduced me to the robber lama. I described to him the Hsiangchen princess.

'Oh, I know her quite well,' he said. 'She is rich and powerful and she came to Likiang to enjoy herself,' he continued. 'Let us go and I will introduce you to her,' he proposed. 'By the way, people say she is divorcing her present husband. Perhaps you will be eligible as the next one,' he teased me with a sly wink.

The duchess received me graciously. She was seated on a pile of gem-like rugs, surrounded by her ladies. She ordered wine and we chatted for a while. I addressed her from time to time as Wang Mo (Powerful Woman), which is an official title meaning princess or duchess. She was very pleased.

'O Powerful Woman,' I said at last, 'you have acquired such a wonderful husband.' Even before I completed the sentence I realized that I had committed a dreadful faux pas. She became very angry and her cheeks suffused with red.

'Are you coming here to insult me?' she demanded severely. I did not know what to say, so embarrassed was I.

'You have probably picked up some scandal about me,' she raged. 'Wonderful husband indeed!' she mocked me. 'He looks good but he is nothing,' she continued in a loud voice. 'I have given him another fortnight to regain his virility,' she almost screamed. 'Otherwise out he goes!'

I could feel that she was near hysteria. I apologized profusely and we had another drink. I reminded her that Likiang had a foreign-style doctor and several drug stores, so that the happiness of her conjugal life might yet be restored by a clever doctor and the judicious use of certain restoratives. She shook her head sceptically.

In about three weeks I chanced in the street to bump into the poor 'Peter the Great'. He looked sheepish and dishevelled and his eyes were listless. He did not stop to talk to me and disappeared into an inn. I called on my Nakhi friend.

'Haven't you heard the news yet ?' he asked me. 'She did kick him out. Now she is gone and the poor fellow has been left high and dry to shift for himself.'

I liked the Khamba Tibetans who came on legitimate business. It was always easy to spot these giants walking through crowds in the streets or on the market. Their fluffy caps of fox fur made them appear even taller than they were. They were friendly, cheerful and generous to a fault. They looked very manly indeed with their hats on, but without hats their appearance was peculiar. The hair was braided in many pigtails which were coiled around the head with the aid of red ribbons, and in this way they strongly reminded me of some heroic Wagnerian women of the Brunhilde or Kriemhilde type, dressed in men's clothes. Several stayed at my house as guests. Their faces, burnt by the fierce sun of high altitudes and coarsened by biting winds, were usually quite dark; but I had occasion to observe that their bodies were always wonderfully white and the skin was like velvet. They never took a bath but rubbed themselves with butter every night. This, of course, made their skin soft, but after their sojourn in my house, the bed sheets were quite black and so impregnated with rancid butter that they could never be-washed or used again, and for weeks the whole house smelled like burnt butter.

The highly placed Tibetans of Lhasa liked to come to Likiang for both business and holidays in spite of

The main street of Likiang with some Khamba Tibetans passing through.

the great distance. All Tibetans are great travellers, and caravan travel in that vast country, if properly organized, is extremely enjoyable. But one high-class Tibetan family from Lhasa had settled in Likiang. It consisted of two men, a woman and a child, and a retinue of servants. They were mild and gentle people, extremely courteous and thoughtful. One of the gentlemen was a shortish plump man with a beard. He usually wore a purple tunic over his shoulders, tied with a sash at the waist, and a yellow silk shirt which hinted at a connection with a religious organization. His companion was a short man also. His hair was short-cropped, he had a beard too, and his face was somewhat ascetic and extremely intelligent. His attire was openly lamaistic, but he did not often wear the usual lama cloak. The woman was tall, very white and beautiful. She was dressed as a Lhasa lady of high rank, wearing the traditional apron of multi-coloured silk strips. The child was about five years old and was the best-looking Tibetan boy I have ever seen. He was dressed like a little Tibetan gentleman, with high boots, tiny sword and all. They lived by Double Stone Bridge. In due course I was introduced to them and we became great friends. I learned in a roundabout way from friends and Madame Ho, who had become a confidante of the woman, that the elderly man was indeed a lama. He was the Steward of the Royal Household of Reting, the Incarnation of the Sakya (White) Sect and one of the four titular kings of Tibet. His friend, the man in the lama dress, was the Chaplain of the Incarnation. I was beginning to piece the story together.

It must have been quite a few years before the arrival of these men, that there was some kind of plot in Lhasa, the figure-head of which was Reting. He was arrested by the Government and put in jail. Some people told me that he was tortured slowly and died of his injuries; others insisted with equal vehemence that it was not true and that he died in jail from a disease. Anyway, the Steward and the Chaplain had time to slip away from Lhasa with a considerable fortune in gold and valuable merchandise. Whether they did it after Reting had died or whether Reting, as a precaution, had sent them away with his fortune earlier I could not find out. It was such an unhappy and tragic episode, and it would have been in the worst possible taste for me to broach the subject to the two men direct. It appears that they had travelled to Likiang in a long detour via Kokonor, where they had adherents and friends. On the way the Steward met an attractive Khamba girl of good family and, throwing to the winds his vows of celibacy, married her and had a son. It seems they had wanted to stay in the Tibetan Kham, but the slow-moving tentacles of the Lhasa Government were reaching for them even in that remote province. Thus they settled in the safety of Likiang, selling their goods and gold as needed.

Naturally the old man's marriage caused a scandal in Lhasa. The ruling Church in Tibet is the Gelugkpa, that is, the Yellow or Reformed Sect, of which the lamas and trapas are strict celibates. But the Tibetans are a warm-blooded and passionate people, and many of them become monks not so much out of religious fervour but because it is practically the only way to security and a career in the theocratic society. Every family with two or more sons sends one to a lamasery with the same hopes and motives as a poor family in Europe or America would send its boy to a university. In this respect Tibet is a very democratic country. The Government is essentially theocratic, and there is no limit or obstacle placed in the way of a poor but clever and ambitious monk to reach one of the highest posts in the realm. He may even become a Regent if he is brilliant enough. As a matter of fact the late Reting came from a lowly origin. Hard learning, sagacity and drive are the only ingredients needed for success.

An exemplary life and restraint are also required. A monk may have peccadilloes but he must be very careful to keep them hidden. Open bravado is not tolerated and the punishment is swift and just: It was a courageous step, therefore, for my friend, the Lama Steward, to have married openly, but also it was a folly and an outrage. I always had a suspicion of how *declassé* he felt in his heart. Naturally he could feel more at ease in Likiang. Likiang's Lamaism was entirely the old Unreformed Red Sect (Karamapa), which with the Skaya and Bon (Black) Sects had been the original Tibetan Church before its reformation. The Red Sect lamas are much more indulgent in their life. They eat and drink what they like and they can have a wife and children so long as they do not bring their wives into a lamasery for cohabitation. But any lama could have his aged father or widowed mother to live with him in his well-appointed apartment, and they helped by cooking, sweeping and washing clothes whilst the lama son was immersed in his devotions or studies.

The two lamas liked my calls and I enjoyed immensely the company of this aristocratic family. I spoke to them in my halting Tibetan. They were always delighted and the lady clapped her hands in glee whenever I turned out a particularly long sentence, mostly with the use of a dictionary I always carried about with me. I was wondering whether this approbation was only a delicate mockery, but they assured me that it was not. They said it tickled them not because a foreigner spoke their language—that was no novelty as they had met explorers and missionaries who spoke Tibetan—but because I spoke the few words I knew in the real Lhasa dialect and used the correct forms and expressions of the honorific language which is the language that should be used when conversing with the lamas and members of Tibetan society. I explained that I had been taught the Tibetan language by a refined Lhasa gentleman during my stay in Tachienlu, and that I had a little practice conversing with the Prince Grand Lama of Litang and with the Grand Lama of Dranggo. They liked me all the more on hearing that I knew such great lamas.

The older man seldom went out. He suffered from an itch, which I thought was a form of eczema, and rheumatism. I tried to help him with the medicines at my disposal and he was always very grateful. I usually came in the morning and sayed for an hour or two enjoying the atmosphere of an elegant Tibetan household. They lived very well and the servants waited on them hand and foot. The drawing-room was expensively decorated in very good taste. There was a profusion of rare and beautiful rugs on couches and chairs, inlaid copper pots, with butter tea, and braziers had been burnished with such zeal that they glowed with red fire in the diffused rays of the sun which filtered through carved windows and doors. Only jade teacups were used by the family, with delicate filigree covers of silver and gold. On the wall above the altar there was a large photograph of their dead master, when he was young, festooned with silk khatas. Below on the altar stood a massive gold shrine with a photograph of the young Dalai Lama. Whatever differences and intrigues there may exist between the different churches of Tibet or between a church and, the Government, the

Dalai Lama, God King, is above politics, doctrines and favouritism. He always remains the Supreme Head of all the churches, sects and of the Government. He is loved and revered by all and everyone is loyal to him.

The little boy Aja Pentso (Prince Aja) played with his nurse or the other servants. He was an affectionate child. During some of my afternoon 'cocktail' sessions with Madame Ho, he used to come with his nurse to buy sweets. He liked to sit on my knee and always asked for a sip or two of the sweet *yintsieu* I was drinking. As all little children in Likiang drink like little fishes, I did not mind giving him half a cup. Later on, however, his mother asked me not to do it any more, for it appeared that he got drunk every time and created a lot of trouble in the house trying to beat up his mother, father and the nurse.

To the Nakhi and other Tibetans, the presence in their midst of a high-class Tibetan family was very flattering. The Steward and his lama were constantly invited and fêted. To repay this hospitality these two gentlemen had arranged one day a truly royal party to which I also received a formal invitation. The invitation was, as is the custom, for three o'clock in the afternoon. But who would be idiotic enough to go at three? Three times the servants called on the invited guests, and at last we presented ourselves at about six. The whole house had been transformed. The walls had been concealed behind red silk tapestries and red woollen mats had been laid on the floor. Benches and chairs had been covered with priceless rugs. On the seven or eight round tables, reserved for the most honoured guests, there had been placed jade teacups with gold stands and covers. The small wine-cups were of chiselled gold, spoons of silver and chopsticks of ivory. Water-melon seeds, almonds and pumpkin seeds, to munch before the meal, were arranged in the centre of each table on gold and silver dishes. The lady of the house came out in full court dress, weighted heavily with gold jewellery. Her husband and the lama wore jackets of gold brocade. Quite unexpectedly several other elegant Tibetan ladies and gentlemen appeared. It was like a scene from the Arabian Nights. The feast itself was of course Chinese, and had been ordered from a famous local caterer, also called Madame Ho. Several kinds of potent wine had been ordered in plenty and were served out of gold and silver pots.

There is no such thing as a Tibetan cuisine. Owing to the limitations imposed by their religion, the purely Tibetan food is extremely monotonous and, as a rule, it is badly cooked. Tibetan women, attractive as they may be and clever in trade and finance, are not good cooks, and anything they cook is uneatable. It may seem too sweeping an accusation, but nevertheless it is true. I had many occasions to sample the efforts of Tibetan ladies and, though extremely hungry, I could not assimilate a single dish. The yak steaks could not be tackled with knives—only with sharp axes; fried potatoes were raw, and the soup was plainly a dirty dish-water with something indescribable floating in it. In Gardar, in Sikang Province, I had to exist for two months on a diet prepared by the Tibetan women of the Morowa tribe and, at the end, nearly gave up the ghost. They used to make a daily soup with almost unwashed pig's intestines, dried peas and rutabaga. I had to eat it as there was nothing else, and it was only by frequent forays into the neighbouring lamasery that saved me from utter starvation.

Like the rich Englishmen, who solved their culinary problems by the employment of French chefs, Tibetan society solved theirs by the use of Chinese cooks. It was only natural therefore that the Reting's Steward had ordered a Chinese feast on this occasion. Evidently he had given carte blanche to Madame Ho because there seemed to be no end to the courses. We sat down at seven and I do not think we got up before eleven. Every expensive and elegant dish that could be prepared in Likiang was there, although actually there was not much variety in the ingredients. There was chicken in clear soup, chicken fried and chicken roasted, and the same was true about duck and pig and fish. There was so much food left that it must have lasted a couple of clays for the servants' meals. Wine flowed freely and, perhaps, not too wisely, as many people were ready to go under the table. They were solicitously assisted by their servants, who led them home. All in all, the feast was. quite the event of the season. If the guests had not been surprised by the food itself, at least they commented favourably on the quantity. What had impressed them most was the display of wealth by a member of the Tibetan aristocracy.

The Steward and the Lama always spoke nostalgically about Lhasa. They admitted they were terribly homesick. No Tibetan is really happy unless he has at least occasional glimpses of the Holy City and of the God King. And they had been separated from all this by space and time. They admitted, of course, that Likiang's life was pleasant and free and easy. The men of high standing in Lhasa do not have an easy time. There, they have to present themselves every day before dawn to the State Council chamber for an audience with the Regent and other ministers. Business or no business, they have to sit there ceremoniously sipping cups of butter tea. The whole idea of this strict institution, they said, was really to keep an eye on the activities and movements of the powerful and influential persons. Without such supervision some powerful lord might slip out into a province, where he had influence, and engineer an uprising, not so much against the Dalai Lama, who was loved and revered, but against the Regent who was not liked by certain factions. The situation in Tibet was analogous to the pre-war situation in Japan when that country was ruled not by the Emperor, but by the men who had access to the person of the Emperor, and did all sorts of things in his name.

However, the Steward and the Lama were not sitting idly waiting for things to happen. I could not fail to notice that they were busy with messages and telegrams; there were arrivals and departures of messengers from Chiamdo and Kokonor and, probably, even from Lhasa. Evidently they were scheming and intriguing to have themselves restored and rehabilitated in the eyes of the Dalai Lama and his Government. I did not stay long enough to see what happened to them, but before I left a cruel blow fell upon this gentle family. The little Prince Aja fell ill. I saw the boy and, in my opinion, it was a case of a simple cold, for which I gave him some aspirins. At the end of the week he appeared to be much better. However, listening to ignorant neighbours, the poor boy's parents decided to accelerate the recovery by a series of the injections recommended by a certain quack doctor from Hoking. This bogus doctor made it known to all Likiang people that all and every sickness could be cured almost at once by his injections. Without telling me anything, the father had invited this scoundrel who administered to the poor child sixteen injections, of what I never found out, between morning and evening. By nightfall the poor little prince had died.

I think it was at the end of 1946, when the war had already become a thing of the past, that a debonair young Tibetan arrived in Likiang. He travelled in style, taking a plane from Calcutta to Kunming and a private car from Kunming to Hsiakwan. He stopped at the house of a friend of mine, who was half-Nakhi and half-Tibetan. I was duly introduced to this cultured Tibetan, who wore European clothes and spoke good English. His name was Neema. It turned out that he was the private secretary to Kusho Kashopa, who was a member of the Tibetan Cabinet. Neema said that he came to Likiang on business, but it was only later that I had found out the nature of this business.

The landlord of the house where Neema stayed had a very pretty daughter. A romance developed between the handsome Tibetan and this Nakhi girl and, in due course, she was 'sold' to Neema for a considerable sum of money or, in other words, they got married. They stayed for a couple of months in Likiang and then went to Lhasa. In about a year they returned and then I knew what Neema's business was.

As I have already described, an unprecedented caravan trade had developed during the war between Lhasa and Likiang which enriched immensely many Likiang merchants and their counterparts in Lhasa. But peace came unexpectedly with the capitulation of Japan, and with the reopening of the ports of Shanghai, Hongkong and Canton no one in the interior of China wanted any more expensive goods brought by caravan. But the great caravans, that had started from Lhasa a month or two before the armistice, began to arrive in Likiang. Most of the goods had been sent on a consignment basis by the profit-hungry Tibetan merchant houses. Dutifully the Likiang merchants were sending the merchandise as soon as it arrived to Kunming, where it was selling at a huge loss or remaining in warehouses. The frantic Tibetans in Lhasa sent telegrams daily asking for the remittances, but no remittances were sent. With a capital of nearly 500,000 Indian rupees sunk in the merchandise already in Likiang, the merchants and the Government in Lhasa found themselves in a tight fix. In addition to the capital of the commercial houses, there was a good deal of money invested in the caravan traffic by the Blue Treasury, other Government people and the minister Kashopa himself.

There had probably been some premonitions in Lhasa about this fantastically expanded caravan traffic to China and some wise people had probably felt that this golden shower could not last for ever. It was due to these considerations, I believe, that Neema had been sent in the first place to assess the capacity of the Likiang and Kunming markets and to probe into the integrity of certain Nakhi and Hoking merchants. It seems probable that the young man had done his work conscientiously and reported to his superiors favourably. Otherwise the caravans would have stopped. But poor Neema could not have foreseen the sudden collapse of the mighty Japanese Empire and the quick peace. After all, he was only a capable secretary and a business man and not the Nechung Oracle, and it is clear that neither his reputation nor his position suffered when the crisis came.

The Tibetans are reasonable people and are true merchant princes when it comes to taking a legitimate risk. The magnitude of the business disaster that had overtaken them was treated as an Act of God, as it should have been. Who could have foreseen the atomic bomb and the sudden armistice when the war seemed to continue year after year without an end in sight? However, they were not a gullible people and the cabled protestations from Likiang and Hoking that not a cent could be remitted had not been accepted at its face value. The Government had decided to conduct an investigation into the failure to pay for the goods duly received at their destination. Armed with proper credentials and a power of attorney from Kusho Kashopa and the chief minister, Neema flew to Likiang again, bringing his wife. At the same time Nakhi and Hoking merchants in Lhasa had to submit to a mild investigation of their transactions and a restraint on further remittances to India and China was imposed. As a matter of fact, they were looked upon as the hostages.

It was a greatly changed atmosphere that Neema found on his second visit to Likiang. The traditional sweetness and welcome of the principal Nakhi and Hoking merchants for their Tibetan brothers had gone. The cunning foxes had been quick in scenting the true meaning of Neema's visit. Instead of the sumptuous feasts, a game of hide and seek began. A call on one firm elicited the fact that its owner was at death's door and could not be seen. At another place Neema was told that the master had gone to Kunming a few days ago. At a third he was informed that an interview could not be arranged as all the directors were still in Hsiakwan. There were similar excuses elsewhere by the dozen. In a truly Oriental tradition, the polished Neema neither flew into a rage nor threatened anybody with the full weight of the law. He merely announced that he was in Likiang on a visit to his father-in-law principally on account of his wife's health and his business was merely accidental.

He said that he would stay indefinitely and possibly make occasional trips to Hoking and Kunming to call on the old merchant friends who had so unfortunately dispersed from Likiang. In the meantime he called on the local Government and began to make his own investigations. Finally the 'sick' merchants had to recover and others to return. Then the fun started. Clad in their oldest gowns, these millionaires piteously cried how poor they were on account of their immense losses; they hardly had anything left to eat at home. Accounts were produced to substantiate the crushing losses, and many tricks were used to frustrate Neema's mission and avoid paying even a cent. Almost every week Neema wired long reports to Lhasa. He swore me to secrecy and asked me to assist him in rendering these messages into English to make them less understandable to his opponents, who had bribed the telegraph clerk to give them copies. He certainly used some pungent expressions to describe these crooks.

A few payments were extracted with extreme difficulty, some unsold goods were located, stored by the crooks with their friends or in secret places. One or two houses were offered in compensation as evidence of bankruptcy of the firm's owner. This immovable property was not of the least interest to the remote Lhasa Government, and with the end of the trade boom, houses in Likiang had declined sharply in value. With the war's end the city had rapidly lost its importance as a trade centre and was reverting to its original status of a peaceful little capital of a forgotten tribal kingdom, off the main trail of the world's events. Finally, with the arrival of the Red regime in Likiang, Neema was prudent enough to interrupt his futile collecting of outstanding debts and left Likiang, together with his wife, on the same plane as myself.

Sitting in my office upstairs one morning, I heard the tinkling of a silver bell and rushed to the window to see who was coming. It was perhaps a bad habit of mine, but I could never refrain from dashing to the window whenever I heard the sound of bells, hooves on the stone path or some unusually loud or unfamiliar noise in the street below. This was from my desire to see everything worth seeing and not to miss anything going on in this magical city. I was so grateful to the Fates who placed me in this house so strategically situated on the main road which led to many tribal villages, to Hsiakwan and to Lhasa itself. From the early morning till late at night it was crowded with a procession of unique people and sights—colourful and enchanting and not to be missed at any cost.

Seated in a silver saddle on a magnificent black mule, led by a soldier in black woollen cloak and carrying a gun, there was a pretty young woman in dark blue pleated skirt and red jacket, wearing an enormous cartwheel turban of scarlet silk. Two women in light blue dresses, barefooted but weighted with silver ornaments, ran behind her. To my surprise the mule stopped at our gate and the soldier entered. I descended just in time to meet the lady as she crossed the threshold. She smiled at me and introduced herself.

'I am the Queen Awouchin of Lotien,' she said with an easy grace. 'I always wanted to see your house,' she added in a lovely, silvery voice.

She was *petite*, extremely pretty and vivacious. I bowed and showed her upstairs. She ran up, accompanied by the two ladies-in-waiting and the soldier. She went straight to my desk and seated herself in the chair. The barefooted ladies with the dark-blue turbans sat on the floor together with the soldier. I asked the queen whether she would take tea. She wrinkled her nose and said 'No.' Would she drink some boiled water? I inquired again. She laughed outright.

'Don't you have anything better than that?' she said, looking at me challengingly.

I understood. Cups were brought and I produced a jar of best *yintsieu*. She drank her cup very quickly and I poured her another. She pressed me to keep her company and gave a cup to the soldier herself, explaining that he was really her knight-at-arms. The two ladies-in-waiting drank their cups greedily. We all became merry. Very soon we began asking each other very personal questions. I told her about myself, my work and how old I was. She said that she was only eighteen and had just divorced her sixth husband. She had come to Likiang for shopping and to look up some relatives who lived near the village of Shwowo.

At last she got up and went to my gramophone.

'Can you play some dance music?' she asked. I put on a slow foxtrot.

'Can you dance?' she asked. I said that I could.

I do not remember how long we danced, probably more than an hour. Like all the Tibetans and Nakhi, who come from remote mountain regions, she was a wonderful dancer. Not once did she miss a step or a movement. Since the music and dances of the Nakhi, Tibetans and Black Lissu along the Yangtze River are essentially Western in rhythm and execution, there was no need for any preliminary explanation or demonstration. She particularly enjoyed my boogie-woogie records and we jitterbugged until I was ready to collapse.

Finally she sat down and we had a few more cups of

wine.

'You ought to come down to Lotien,' she said. 'Perhaps we could even be married,' she added nonchalantly. I pretended to be shocked.

'At my age!' I exclaimed. 'And with you so young!'

She brushed that aside.

'A foreign husband would give me a lot of prestige,' she continued. 'You would have a comfortable life and much money.'

I glanced instinctively at her good-looking knight and he gave me a dirty look.

'What about your knight?' I whispered, winking at her.

She laughed. 'It's nothing. He is only a friend,' and she rose to go.

'Well, I will think it over,' I said, not wishing to disappoint royalty. I escorted her downstairs.

'I shall drop in again.' She waved to me as the two ladies were helping her into the saddle.

I entered my general office. Prince Mu and Wuhsien, my interpreter and organizer, were smiling broadly.

'That was Her Majesty the Queen Awouchin of Lotien,' I announced proudly.

'I know her well,' said Prince Mu. 'She is a distant relative of ours.'

'Is it true that she is only eighteen?' I inquired. Both men laughed outright.

'At least twenty-six if a day,' they cried in unison.

'What about her husband?' I continued.

'She has just divorced her fifth or sixth one,' they said.

'And the soldier?' I asked again.

'He is clearly a candidate,' said Wuhsien, 'otherwise why should she drag him along.'

The next day I was surprised by a visit from the

handsome soldier. He went straight up to my room, sat down and unwrapped a small leather pouch. Then he took two small moon-shaped silver sycees and laid them before me.

'What is that?' I asked uneasily.

'This is my present to you if you will lay off the queen,' he said simply. I felt I was becoming red.

'What do you mean?' I gasped, trying to control a burst of laughter.

'I love her,' he continued, looking me straight in the eye, 'and I hope she will choose me for a new husband.'

'But where do I come in?' I tried my best to get it clear.

'Well, she is serious about marrying you. She thinks foreign husband would be an experience and it would add to her power.' He said it with conviction.

Now I was laughing so much that the people downstairs thought I had gone mad. I took the sycees and replaced them in the pouch. Then I handed it back to the knight and filled two cups with wine. I told him solemnly:

'My dear friend, I am not Adonis, and please do not consider me to be your rival for royal favours.' We took a sip, then I continued: 'I shall never marry your queen, not because she is not beautiful but because I do not want to spend my life in Lotien.'

He brightened up considerably, but still persisted in trying to give me the silver.

I conducted him gently downstairs. He came back yet once more in the evening and presented me with a jar of my favourite wine; but the Queen of Lotien never came back.

CHAPTER IX

THE BOA, THE LOLOS AND THE MINKIA

THE aboriginal inhabitants of the Likiang plain were the P'ou or, as the Nakhi called them, the Boa. The conquering Nakhi, coming from the highlands of Tibet, scattered the P'ou and pushed them into the surrounding mountains, grabbing the rich plain for themselves. The Boa were very primitive, and it is said that they had even practised ceremonial cannibalism in the remote past, consuming their dead as a mark of respect. In comparison with the Nakhi they were little civilized, and possessed a mild inferiority complex. They did not like to be called Boa to their face, and when asked who they were, they almost invariably answered that they were Nakhi. Also, when mingling with the Nakhi, they were careful to see that they were not discriminated against in the matter of courtesies or etiquette lest an impression be created that they were an inferior race. Being mountain people, they always wore black semi-stiff cloaks, made of wool matting descending to just above the knee, and blue cotton trousers. The cloaks were of a perfect bell shape and I was always surprised on seeing the Boa approach, for they looked like huge moving mushrooms. For long walks they wore straw sandals which cost very little and were thrown away on arrival.

I had several friends among the Boa from Mbushi (Pig's Flesh) village in the Nanshan mountains near the place where I had met the robbers on the way to Likiang. One of them was a young man named Wuchang, short, stocky and fat with a face like the full moon. He was always extremely polite and very dignified and used to bring me every time he came to Likiang a couple of big turnips or rutabagas and a tiny pot of honey which he presented to me with the air of a grand duke presenting a diamond tiara to his duchess. Then he took ceremonious leave, went to the market to dispose of the rest of his turnips and came back in the evening to have dinner and, usually, to stay overnight. Once he came when I had a party of Nakhi friends to dinner. Somebody must have said something uncomplimentary about his being a Boa because he cried bitterly afterwards the whole night through and I had. much difficulty in reassuring him that no offence was meant. He said he was much insulted by these proud town people. His greatest ambition was to invite me to his wedding, but, alas, I had to leave Likiang before it took place. But once, on my way to Shihku on the Yangtze River, I had to pass his village where there were no springs or streams and the only water they had was in the pools left after the rainy season. Wuchang received me in his poor dwelling as though I were a count and he a refugee feudal king who had to take a temporary shelter in this mean hut. Sometimes Wuchang's neighbours came with him to visit me. Wuchang disapproved of some of them and always whispered to me warnings to have nothing to do with them. I did not pay much attention but soon had occasion to regret it. A few weeks afterwards one of these undesirable Boa came in the evening, after the market, together with two friends. They looked primitive indeed as they glanced at me sideways like trapped animals. They all said that they wanted to stay overnight and would leave early in the morning. So I dined and wined them and led them to the guest apartment in the other wing. I gave them no bedding as the Boa and some other tribes-people always preferred to sleep on the floor, using their cloaks as blankets. Early next morning my cook rushed up to me almost blind with rage.

'Come and see! Come and see!' He gasped.

I entered the guest apartment. Our guests had already gone. All the walls were urinated through and through and there were 'visiting-cards' all over the floor. I never again permitted any Boa from that village, except Wuchang, to stay at my house.

In addition to the Nakhi, Boa and Tibetans, the Likiang valley and mountainous regions around were a hodge-podge of many other tribes, including the Black and White Lolos, Black and White Lissu, Minlda, Attolays, Miao, Chungchia, Sifan, Chiang, the most interesting of which were the Black Lolos and Minkia, who played an important role in the life and economy of Likiang.

In my long travels and sojourn among the tribes of China and Tibetan borderland, Turkistan and Siberia, Indo-China and Thailand, and other areas of south-east Asia, I have come to the conclusion that all the existing tribal peoples belong to two strictly defined categories—the outgoing and the on-coming. By the first category, I mean those who seem to have outlived their life span on earth, and to have lost their vitality. They have exhausted their evolutionary urge and have no more will or desire to make progress in life. They are not interested in improving their lot or in learning, or in fact in anything that goes on outside their sheltered nooks in the mountains. Even the age of aeroplanes and motor-cars, of improved methods of cultivation and miracles of modern medicine leaves them cold. They have no urge to investigate these wonders nor do they relate them to themselves. They just want to be left alone, to eke out their own primitive existence. When hedged in by their aggressive neighbours they surrender their lands passively and just retreat quietly and shyly into deeper recesses of the protective mountains. They resist feebly and ineffectually the efforts of governments and missionaries to draw them into the vortex of civilized life. They will even don foreign clothes and meekly go to church services in the mission, but only in response to gifts, persuasion and pressure. Their heart is not in it. They are static and cannot be pushed or elevated in any manner; and when the civilizing process becomes too rapid or violent they just cannot stand it and they die. Their role on earth has ended and they are bound to disappear, and disappear they will, in a few decades probably, under the surging onslaught of more aggressive and civilized races bent on expansion into the remaining corners of the planet in their search for more space. Either they will quietly die out or gradually they will be obliterated by intermarriage with other, more virile races. It is to this category of the moribund tribes that I would assign the Miao, White Lissu, Chungchia, Boa and many others, scattered throughout Asia from Kamchatka to New Guinea. Their struggle with the world, if a struggle it has been at all, is over and their doom is near in spite of all the spoon-feeding by governments and kind-hearted missionaries.

Tribes of the second category may also appear, at first glance, static or dormant, but the illusion disappears after a careful observation and analysis. First of all it must be noted that even their physical characteristics are vastly different from those of weak tribes. As a rule they are tall, strong and handsome people. They are very energetic in their own sphere of activity: there is nothing cowardly or shy about them, for they are aggressive, ruthless and cunning, if not actually clever. They may be awed at first by the wonders of civilization, but quickly get accustomed and try to put them to their own use. They are not afraid to mix with or travel among the people of an advanced civilization and are always ready to learn two tricks to the one practised on them. They are not averse to modern education and schools. They are always prepared to accept the benefits of modern medicine, new methods of agriculture and new varieties of vegetables and domestic animals. They learn the ins and outs of present-day commerce and are interested in politics in so far as they concern their borders and immediate livelihood. They are brave and intelligent and make excellent soldiers. There is little doubt that such vigorous tribes are coming into their own in the world and that they will play an important role in future events in Asia. If some of them have appeared dormant in the past, it was due to the isolation imposed by the lack of communications, the tyrannic despotism of their unenlightened rulers and, perhaps, the results of venereal and other diseases. As education spreads and medical facilities improve, there will be an immediate and spectacular resurgence of these virile, fresh and handsome races on the world stage. The world may yet be enriched by their music and dancing, their luxuriant artistic talents and their invigorating and passionate approach to life. To these tribes of the future undoubtedly belong the Nakhi, Tibetans, Minkia, Black Lolos and Black Lissu. The latter are but a sub-tribe of the Black Lolos and should not be confused with the White Lissu or White Lolos.

The home of the Black Lolos is in the Taliangshan, which is a mountainous country five hundred miles long and roughly one hundred miles wide which separates the vast Chinese province of Szechuan from the newly created province of Sikang. The Black Lolo always means the Noble Lolo or, as they call themselves in Chinese, Hei Kuto (the Black Bone). Actually the word Lolo is derogatory and should never be used to their face. It is best to refer to them in conversation as Hei Yi (the Black Yi), for an unwary choice of the word may mean instant death. I prefer to call them the Noble Lolos because they were, as a whole tribe, the most noble-looking people I have seen in my life. They are very tall and are of regal bearing. Their complexion is in no wise black but, like certain-mulattoes, of a chocolate and cream tint. Their eyes are large and liquid, with a fire always burning in them, and their features are aquiline and almost Roman. Their hair is black, slightly wavy and very soft; and its arrangement is a distinctive feature of all Lolos. It is gathered through a hole at the top of their dark blue or black turbans and hangs as a limp tail or, more often, springs up like a miniature palm-tree, supported by a sheath of black strings. The hair of the Lolo is sacred and no one is supposed to touch it under the pain of death. They believe that the Divine Spirit communicates with man through the exposed lock of his hair which, like upstanding antenna or the aerial of a wireless set, conveys the spiritual impulses, like waves to a receiver, to the brain.

The formal dress of a Black Lolo is a black jacket secured by a leather belt adorned with mother-of-pearl. The trousers are immense and are so joined together that the seat hangs almost to the ankles. Usually of silk of gay colours — scarlet, blue, poison green, yellow or violet — they are tied at the ankles with woven ribbons. When formally dressed, the man must also wear as an earring a piece of amber the shape and size of an apple with a cherry of coral hanging beneath. An ankle-long cloak, called *tsarwa*, woven of soft grey or black sheep wool, thrown over the shoulders, completes the picture. The women also wear the *tsarwa* over their dress. When I first encountered the Noble Lolo women my immediate impression was that I was in the presence of a group of Italian princesses and countesses of the Renaissance period. In their long flowing skirts, their jackets of lovely faded brocade, their black picture hats, their high silver collars and great mother-of-pearl earrings failing to the shoulders, they stood before me so tall, handsome and haughty, with their smouldering eyes and that slight smile playing on their aristocratic, chiselled faces, that my first impulse was to bow deeply and kiss their hands. It was only my training in how to behave among the Lolos, painstakingly given me by my sponsors before I was allowed to proceed on my trip through their dangerous country, that saved me from such a foolish action which would probably have ended in my death. A deep bow was enough.

The Noble Lolos have no king and they do not live

in towns or villages. Each clan occupies a well-defined section. of this vast land and each member family lives in its own castle, located usually on top of a hill, some distance from neighbours. The head of the clan, in accordance with its prestige and importance, has a title of prince, marquis or baron. The castle is nothing like the medieval castles of Europe. It is simply a wooden stockade, heavily buttressed with stones and earth, and it has a stout gate. It is located on a hill for defence, and guards are on the look-out day and night for the approach of an enemy. The buildings inside are singularly unimpressive and consist of a group of mean low huts of interlaced bamboo or branches with plank roofs. Inside everything is scrupulously clean; and even a small pin could easily be found on the meticulously swept earthen floor. The furnishings are equally austere—a square table, a few benches, a chest or two and a round stone hearth sunk into the floor, over which a kettle is usually boiling. There may be a large armchair in the main hut, with a tiger or leopard skin spread on it, and some shields and spears hanging on the wall behind. This is the throne of the ruling head. There are no bedsteads, for the Lolos sleep on bare floor around the fire, wrapped in their *tsarwas*. It is a truly Spartan existence.

The Noble Lolos in the Taliangshan lead a settled, pastoral life. But, to paraphrase the Gospel about the lilies of the field, the Lolos do not plough or sow or gather anything into their granaries with their own hands. In conformity with their Spartan life, their social organization is a replica of that of ancient Sparta. Both men and women are warriors to their finger-tips, and all the qualities and virtues which made Sparta such a distinctive nation of the ancient world are praised and practised by the Noble Lolos with equal fervour and strictness. So ferocious and ruthless are the Lolos in battle, so contemptuous of death or torture, so cunning in their strategy and terrifying in their lightning and stealthy attacks, that they are feared more than any other people in the whole of western China and down to the borders of Siam.

Since they are the aristocracy, the caste rules are enforced with utmost severity and important deviations are occasionally punished with death. No agricultural or menial work is permitted to the Noble Lolos—men or women; they may not even serve at table. Men practise the art of warfare from childhood. Womenfolk spin wool, weave *tsarwas*, sew garments, embroider and look after the household. All work is done by the White Lolos, who are the slaves—the Helots of ancient Sparta. It is they who cultivate the fields and gather the grain, rear animals and do the household chores. It is also their duty to act as go-betweens between their masters and the Chinese merchants in matters of commerce which, although despised by them, is nevertheless necessary to the well-being of the master race. Horses, cattle, grain and skins of wild animals are sent to local markets by the Noble Lolos through their White Lolo intermediaries, with the perennial instructions to be always on the look-out for any guns or ammunition, for which they are insatiable customers.

The Black Lolos like nothing better than to have punitive expeditions sent against them by the Chinese. By treachery or ruse they lure detachments of soldiers into the forests or defiles where they kill them from ambush and take their arms. Since early times, the Chinese have frequently had to take up arms against the Lolos. No battle against them has ever been decisive, and they have never been really conquered or dispersed. The famous Chinese General Chukoliang, who, during the era of the Three Kingdoms, carried out many successful expeditions into the western regions of China, fought many battles with the Lolos. They impressed him with their unparalleled bravery and savagery and, as he confessed in his memoirs, his victories were abortive; at one time he even had serious doubts about the human status of the Lolos and thought them to be ferocious beasts in human form. It is related that to satisfy his doubts he had one of the captured Lolos cut open and found nothing but grass and roots in the stomach. Evidently this discovery persuaded him of the futility of further warfare against these strange people on whom no military punishment had any effect and who made treaties, only to break them when the troops had been withdrawn.

Although China has consistently claimed suzerainty over the whole region of the present Szechuan and Sikang provinces since the beginnings of the Chinese Empire, the Lolos have never recognized any authority but their own. Since only the fringes of their country have been visited either by Chinese officials or foreign explorers, nothing much is known about its topography or its population. On maps the Taliangshan country is a blank space marked 'Independent Lolos'. Even with the aid of modern weapons and aeroplanes the conquest of the Lolos would be extremely difficult and costly, if not altogether impossible. There are no towns or villages to shell or bomb. The isolated 'castles' represent not the slightest value either to the conqueror or to their inhabitants. They are purposely built that way—to be abandoned at a Moment's notice. The invaders would not know where to go or where to find the Lolos as there are no roads to indicate the way, whilst the Lolos themselves know every nook and cranny of their own mountain fastness. Their tactics, bravery and treachery would certainly force an invading army into providing them with a ready arsenal to replenish their needs in arms and ammunition. They are as elusive as the will-o'-the-wisp and are ready to inflict death in many ways other than by use of arms. They are past masters in the use of the much-feared Yellow Poison, and it is nothing to them to poison all streams and wells used by their enemies with this slow-acting concoction.

Even at the present time, it is reported, the Lolos still remain unconquered. The new Chinese regime has demanded the surrender of their arms and their submission to the new government. Instead, the Black Lolos have arranged the withdrawal of all their clansmen and their families who lived on the outer, exposed mountain slopes, to the main ranges of the Taliangshan. At a great conclave a king was elected to lead them, a drastic and almost unprecedented measure which is only resorted to in a very grave emergency, when the existence of the whole race is at stake.

The White Lolos are not related racially to the Black Lolos. Originally they were of Chinese and other tribal stock, captured and enslaved by the Lolos. The process of the enslavement of fresh victims has by no means stopped, and it is this gnawing dread of such a fate which keeps in constant suspense all the Chinese living on the fringe of the Lolo-inhabited mountains. When I arrived in Yuehsi, ancient Tang capital of what is now South Sikang and northern Yunnan, I at once noticed this tension. Even when walking in the streets of this small but heavily walled town, Chinese shopkeepers and others looked nervously over their shoulder at the few Lolos buying and selling on the market. No Chinese ever dare leave the protective walls after sunset or before sunrise.

Leaving the town at dawn with my little caravan of two horses and a Lolo soldier in attendance, I noticed a Chinese youth passing through the heavily guarded gate. He carried a long knife in each hand and was shouting hysterically, 'Come! Come! I am not afraid! Come!' I thought he was mad and asked the Chinese sentry what was the matter with him. The soldier explained to me that the boy was on his way to the next village and was demented with fear of the Lolos. The narrow valley, in which the ancient town lay, was hemmed in on both sides with mountains where the Lolos lived, and to protect itself the village had strongly fortified stone towers to which families retired for the night.

Although the White Lolos were the serfs and had to work for their masters as required, I did not notice any signs of cruelty in the way they were treated. There was not much difference in the standard of living between the masters and serfs, as the former did not live in any great luxury. There was no difference in their diet, and when the Black Lolos had a feast everybody in the household had his share of food and wine. The distinction was emphasized in the difference of caste, and their functions. The nobility fought and plundered, and protected the household. The serfs did the field and household work and were afforded protection. No Black Lolo might marry a White Lolo, and did so only under pain of death. Romances between the castes were strictly taboo, because the purity of the Black Bone had to be zealously guarded. Punishment for disloyalty, and even for a breach of discipline, was swift and just, irrespective of caste.

Many White Lolos, through their perseverance, application and successful trade with the Chinese, have become more or less emancipated and established themselves as a sort of an intermediate caste in the no-man's-land between the commerce-hating and exclusive nobility and the profit-minded anything that is really valuable like a diamond ring or a gold wrist-watch. Such gifts are politely but firmly declined with an excuse that it is too valuable or of no use in their simple life. Utility articles, such as matches, silk thread, packets of needles, a jar of wine or a packet of medicine are accepted gratefully and with enthusiasm.

A great feast is as a rule given for a guest, with rich and tasty food, much wine, beautiful dancing, minstrel singing and exhibitions of fencing. Wine is drunk out of a big jar placed on the floor in the middle of the room, from which it is drawn by each person through a long bamboo tube. As the level in the jar sinks, additional supplies are poured in. Lolo singing is unusual and very beautiful; some of the men have voices of great range and power. Dancing and music are almost Western, the music reminiscent of Hungarian tunes and the dancing, in which I have never seen any women take part, is quite like czardas or Caucasian sword dances.

The Lolos' achievements in the realm of vegetable gardening and animal breeding were always puzzling to me. One would think that these people, so primitive in many respects and isolated for centuries in their remote mountains, would exist almost entirely on the roots and plants found in their forests, and on the flesh of wild animals, shot or trapped by them. It was a surprise to me to find that they planted and ate white and blue potatoes which compared favourably in quality and size with those produced in Europe and America. These potatoes, when grown by Chinese in West China, were originally small and diseased, and it was only after they had borrowed Lolo potatoes that they were able to improve the size and quality of their own crops. Lolo cattle were magnificent. Their bulls and cows were big, well fed and glossy with a peculiar greenish-red sheen. Their ponies were much sought after by the Chinese. They were of medium size and extremely hardy, and especially well suited to riding in the mountains. Sleek, lively and phenomenally intelligent, they could do almost anything but speak, being extremely sensitive to their owner's wishes.

I was presented with two ponies by my Lolo friend, Szema (Prince) Molin, before I started on my trip through the Tatiangshan. One was a red and white stallion called Hwama (Flowery Horse), and the other was a small grey one which carried my two suitcases and bedding. I had been warned not to use a whip unless I had to, and not to rely too much on the reins, but preferably to talk to the horse all the time and to indicate direction by touching the sides of his neck. Indeed, the little Hwama himself knew quite well where to go, when to trot or even gallop, and was extremely careful when descending precipitous rocky slopes or fording roaring torrents. Whenever I spoke to him, he replied with a gentle neigh. So human was this little horse and such a good, faithful companion that I felt his loss as keenly as that of a great friend when I had to sell him to the Governor of Sikang before my departure for Chungking.

The Lolos sometimes arranged horse-fairs in the neighbouring Chinese towns or settlements, which were invariably attended by the highest Chinese officers and wealthiest merchants anxious to secure good Lolo ponies and mules. There was wild feasting during those fair days, when the Lolos showed off their skill by galloping standing on the horse, picking up objects on the ground and displaying other tricks so well known in Europe from performances by the equally dexterous Caucasian Cossacks. The prices which pure-bred Lolo ponies fetched were out of proportion to those normally paid for other horses or mules. And they were not easy to get, as the Lolos kept the best animals for their own use.

Another interesting animal which the Lolos bred was their hunting dog. It was a lean, middle-sized dog, usually black, of such cunning and intelligence as to be considered almost fabulous by the Chinese. At night these dogs became good watch-dogs and gave an instant alarm of a stranger's approach. The Lolo chickens were, in their enormous size and weight, also a cause of envy, and it was the wish of every Chinese to be presented with a rooster by his Lolo friends.

The question of where the Lolos originally obtained the stock of such excellent animals and the seeds of superior potatoes even before the arrival of Europeans or missionaries, has not yet been answered.

The secret of the Noble Lolos' superior physique lies in the good food they eat and the fine country they live in. Beef, pork, mutton, chicken and fish are no rarities in their daily menu and a variety of Irish stew is particularly good. All this is eaten with buckwheat pancakes and washed down with pink buckwheat sparkling wine called *zhiwoo*. The only sweets known to Lolo children are fresh honey and brown sugar.

Since they live above five or six thousand feet the climate is always moderate and the air is pure and invigorating. Most of their country can best be described as a vast park with century-old oaks and flower-covered meadows, purling brooks and small blue lakes; though sombre forests clothe the steep mountain slopes. There are no snow peaks in the Taliangshan range, but snow covers the ridge in winter. With the castles perched here and there on the mountains, the gallant knights trotting on their sleek chargers, stately ladies passing on horseback with a small band of retainers carrying bows and arrows, and young girls running behind; and with the oak-trees and the meadows and the trill of nightingales, one feels transported by magic into the France dearly Middle Ages.

Such is the country of the princes of Black Bone – beautiful like the legendary Arcadia, but mysterious and very dangerous. And with my two ponies and the little Lolo soldier, Alamaz, whom Prince Molin had detailed to accompany me, in a mother-of-pearl studded leather jacket and enormous trousers and armed with a bow and arrows, I felt small and insignificant when meeting the brilliant cavalcades of the Noble Lolos. Alamaz, trembling with fright, always begged me not to speak, not to look and not to smile. But I am of a naturally cheerful disposition, and I always bowed to the passing knights, and they smiled back to me. Only once was I cornered in a dry river bed by a mounted man, who knew a few words of Chinese.

'Money, money!' he demanded.

I showed him the few Chinese bank-notes I was carrying.

'That's nothing!' he snorted, and rode away.

On the last lap of my journey which, Alamaz warned me, was the most critical, we turned aside to let a magnificently clad elderly lady, on a sleek black mule, pass with her large retinue of warriors and maidens. I bowed and she stopped, and addressed me with a smile. Alamaz translated in his halting Chinese. 'The lady is going to Luku too.' (Luku was the market-town where the Taliangshan road terminated.) 'She suggests that we join her party, and she guarantees protection.' I bowed again, thanked her and we fell behind the cortège. Once or twice we rested and she offered me a drink of *zhiwoo* from the horn she was carrying in her saddlebag. Finally she saw me safely into an inn at Luku. One of her warriors later came to collect a fee for her protection, a demand which I had not expected; but as it was evidently the local custom, I paid a few dollars, which were gratefully accepted.

The Lolos were not entirely confined to the Taliangshan, which was their ancestral territory. But it was only there, as I found out later, that they led a settled existence and were, so to speak, at their best. They also inhabited the vast region between the Kienchang valley, which formed the western border of the Taliangshan Range, and the Kingdom of Mull. The Duchy of Tsoso and other districts around Yenyuan and down to Yuenpei were all Lolo country. They also lived in the Siaoliangshan (Lesser Liangshan)—a mountain range following the Yangtze River along the bank opposite the Likiang district. Many of them had spread along the mountain ranges which abutted on Siam, and the Lolos, who periodically make raids into Siam, are known there as Haw Haw.

Those of the Lolos who lived in the forests of the Likiang Snow Range Were White Lolos, and those who stayed in the Siaoliangshan across the river were a mingling of the White and Black Lolos, with many Black Lissu scattered amongst them. As I found out after my arrival in Likiang, the Black Lolos of the Siaoliangshan were quite unlike those I had met in the Taliangshan.

They were absolutely savage and ruthless and, as far as I am aware, no one going there, with or without an introduction, has ever been spared. They had no habitual settlements and were used to roaming from place to place, burning the forest just to plant a single crop of buckwheat or of poppies. I could not find out for certain whether the Black Lolos on the Taliangshan grew poppy, and I had not seen any; but it is an established fact that the Lolos elsewhere are the principal growers of this profitable crop.

Opium made from the poppies was sold through the agency of the White Lolos and certain trusted Chinese merchants who worked hand in glove with the Chinese military. This was a vast and fabulously profitable trade for all concerned, and the main revenue of the Yunnan and Sikang militarists came not from taxes or even gold diggings but from opium. The wars waged between the generals were for the control of sources of supply of opium or of opium traffic revenue. The political reasons concocted for such hostilities were excuses primarily intended for the Western diplomats at the capital. The strictly worded and marvellously expounded laws prohibiting opium smoking and trafficking were equally deceptive and the high officials who presided over the enforcement of these laws were often themselves the greatest smokers. A poor farmer, wishing to make a small fortune with four or five ounces of the illicit drug, might be caught and shot as an example, but a caravan or truck loaded with tons of opium and escorted by a heavy military guard always reached its destination in safety.

A Chinese trader, normally a rather timid and law-abiding creature, becomes an intrepid adventurer ready to sacrifice his life and risk the welfare of his family if he scents the possibility of getting a good parcel of opium at the original grower's price. He will go anywhere, suffer cold and hunger, risk encounter with robbers and wild beasts to obtain the black gold. He may even go into the dens of some of the Black Lolos; but whether he returns is a matter of fate.

There was an interesting case in Likiang while I was there. Hearing of an accumulation of the drug among the Lolos of the Siaoliangshan, two Chinese and a Nakhi procured official blessing and left on an expedition with some local soldiers in sufficient strength to intimidate, as they thought, the savages and secure the loot. What actually happened, once they had crossed the Yangtze, no one really knows, but a week or so afterwards the corpses of the three merchants were found on the Likiang side of the river, and the corpses proved to be only their skins stuffed with straw and grass. Of the soldiers there was no trace.

The reasons for the exceptional ferocity, lack of faith and uncontrolled lawlessness of the Siaoliangshan Lolos were to be found in the loss of caste and home, after their expulsion from the Taliangshan. As I have explained, the Noble Lolos' sole occupation is that of being warriors. Probably to keep themselves in practice and to avoid going soft, they engage in warfare among themselves on any slight pretext. When one clan defeats another, they may make peace if the matter has not been very serious, but if the offence has been grievous and contrary to the general custom of the Lolos, all other clans may join together to punish the wrongdoers. When defeated they are usually driven out of the Taliangshan paradise, to become *declassé*, mere outlaws, without caste, without friends and homeless. They usually flee either to the Siaoliangshan or to other wild ranges of mountains, where they undergo a psychological change, losing all their codes of chivalry, mutual trust, loyalty and fair dealing even towards members of their own clan, not to speak of outsiders. Like beasts of prey, boiling with rage and humiliation, they rove and rave through the mountains, plundering, killing and torturing their victims to their heart's content. An outsider's visit to such a clan of outlawed Lolos is not possible, for they do not care for any *laissez-passer* or letters of introduction, and the only transactions, if any, that can be done with them, must be done through their White Lolo slaves or associates. A visit therefore to the Siaoliangshan, though comparatively near Likiang, was out of the question for me.

A number of the White Lolos from the Snow Range, and possibly from the Siaoliangshan, used to come to my clinic. They had a standing agreement with the Mu King to patrol the forest lands around the Snow Range infested with Szechuanese squatters, who were always suspected of robberies and murders. I do not know how useful the White Lolos were on these patrols, but they were certainly very destructive to the forests, burning them right and left without rhyme or reason. They always complained that they were very poor, and in appearance they were more filthy and grimy than other primitive tribes. Some of them pretended to me that they were Black Lolos, but their height alone and the wizened Mongolian faces precluded any possibility of so noble an origin. However, my medications and the white wine which was provided on their infrequent visits evidently made a deep impression on them and filled them with gratitude and friendliness. They enjoyed seeing me sometimes in the forests of the Snow Range on my way to the co-operatives or on occasional picnics, and sometimes they brought an egg or two or a small pot of buckwheat honey.

It was clearly the knowledge of my cures among these people that led to a rather delicate incident. Without any previous notice or warning, a real Siaoliangshan Black Lolo walked into my apartment one afternoon, accompanied by a couple of retainers. Even before he spoke, I recognized the aquiline features, flashing eyes and the upstanding lock of hair. He was very tall and had a sword and a dagger at his belt, and was dressed all in black. He said he was from across the river (I knew only too well what place he meant), that he was ill and wanted medicine. He would pay me, he added. I examined him and diagnosed a touch of malaria. I asked him where he was staying. He said that he had come to Likiang under a guarantee by Captain Yang, commissioner of the local militia, and that he had his baggage with him.

I served wine and we drank and talked. It was soon dinner-time, and as he made no move to go, I invited him and his retainers to share my own meal. After dinner I gave him a good dose of quinine and told him to rest until the next dose. He looked over my apartment with interest, and then announced that he would stay at my apartment over-night as he wanted me to check personally on the action of the medicine. This caused me some anxiety as I feared the consequences if he became dissatisfied with the efficacy of my medicine. On the other hand, I was well aware of the sense of insult which would be caused by refusing hospitality to a Black Lolo. A bed was prepared for him, with clean pillows and linen, and placed in the same room as mine. He undressed completely, put on the belt with the dagger around his naked waist and placed his sword under the pillow, with which he could quickly express any sense of dissatisfaction of the medicine.

However, all went well, and he left early the next morning with profuse thanks, saying that he felt much better. I supplied him with some more quinine to take at home, and had to refuse tile offer of a silver *sycee*. He was the last Noble Lolo I saw.

The Minkia people called themselves Pertse or Pervountse and the Nakhi called them Laebbou. They intermingled with the Nakhi both in the town and in the southern and eastern parts of the plain. They had their own villages or lived together near one another in Nakhi villages. Like the Nakhi and Tibetans, they were also a gay people, but voluble in the extreme and rather irresponsible. In facial appearance it was difficult to distinguish them from the Chinese. Men wore the same clothes as the Chinese, but women wore their own picturesque dress. Their Maung Khmer language sounded like Chinese but was sweeter when sung, and sing they did from early morning till late at night, whether working or not. They were very romantic and indulged in flirtations at all times. It was nothing serious — just a joke, a wink or a burst of song. The girls usually took the initiative in teasing or wooing their coy and sheepish men. Born coquettes, they always managed to create a situation where a man had to speak to them whether he wanted to or not. Purposely pushing a man with her basket, a girl would reproach him for being awkward, another would scream that he had stepped on her toe or tried to upset the bottle of wine she was carrying. There would be some repartee and finally the whole group would sit down, have a drink and sing.

The main trouble with the Minkia was that they were all very mean and much more calculating than either the Nakhi or Tibetans. Both men and women worked, but the women worked the harder. Whilst the Nakhi women also worked hard, they did it in a truly capitalistic spirit, expecting a good profit from every transaction or unusual exertion. They never carried anything too heavy for them and what they carried was for their own commerce. Their Minkia sisters did not possess such brilliant business ability, they were real transport animals carrying goods or objects from one town to another for a small fee. They developed an even stronger physique than the Nakhi women (which is saying much) as they always tried to carry heavier and heavier loads, which were paid for according to weight. They became champion carriers, some of them carrying anything up to 140 Ib. It was nothing for a Minkia woman to carry a heavy cabin trunk from Hsiakwan to Likiang, and they would carry their disabled husbands or sick parents on their back thirty or forty miles to the nearest hospital.

But the greatest renown of the Minkia did not lie in the ability of their women to carry their husbands or of their men to run the caravan traffic to the Burma Road. It was their uncanny skill in masonry and carpentry that made the whole tribe famous throughout the Yunnan Province and far beyond the borders. They built speedily and well anything from a humble village house to a palace or a great temple. The precision and excellence of their work would be a credit to any Western architect. Steeped in the tradition of centuries, passed by example and word of mouth from father to son, every Minkia was a born artist. Every house, wayside shrine or bridge, though conforming to a set style, yet was an individual work of art. But it was in carving stone and wood that the artistic genius of the Minkia race found its finest expression. Even the meanest house must have its doors and windows beautifully carved and its patio adorned with exquisite stone figures and vases arranged with striking effect. The subjects of the carvings were always mythological, and perhaps their symbolism had already been forgotten, but their felicitous meaning was always plain. The process of stone and wood carving was laborious, but the execution was perfect, no detail being left unfinished. In Likiang only really poor Nakhi built their houses themselves.

It was the Minkia who were invited to build and decorate the houses of the rich in Kunming and other important cities. The beautifully carved and gilded tea-tables of the Dalai Lama's household and his famous carved and painted stables, I was told, were executed by specially imported Minkia artisans. The King of Muli and other lama potentates always placed orders with the Minkia for tea-tables and other carvedobjects according to their own specifications.

If it is true that the Minlda had migrated into Yunnan from Angkor Thorn, this seemingly inborn propensity to artistic work in stone and wood is strong supporting evidence of the migration. Their facial features too, when they are pure-blooded Minkia, bear strong resemblance to the carvings on Angkor War. Their language is Maung Khmer and, although strongly adulterated with Chinese words and expressions, is nevertheless a distinct one. The name of the city Tali is not Chinese, but a perversion of the Khmer word Tongle, which means Lake. Tali is situated by a large lake.

Of all the tribes of Yunnan the Minkia are the closest to the Chinese, having adopted the Celestial Civilization almost in its entirety. They have no writing of their own and Chinese is used in all written communications and records. The intermarriage with the Chinese is extensive and unhindered either by tradition or jealousy. As a matter of fact, it is rather difficult to trace or identify a Minkia of really pure blood. It is only against the background of the morose, supine and rather unfriendly Yunnan Chinese that the Minkia become easily distinguishable by their inborn gaiety and levity. Not that Minkia women are judged as dissolute by their Chinese sisters, but no Chinese woman would dare to be so easy-going and friendly With men. Certainly few, if any, Chinese women would exchange double-edged jokes with a group of men or take part in drinking bouts.

My friendships with the Minkia were extensive and agreeable, but, looking back, I now realize that at no time were they so genuine or selfless as with the Nakhi. There were always strings attached to their gifts, and invitations to visit their homes were very infrequent; they usually preferred to enjoy my hospitality. There is no doubt in my mind that they were a calculating and purse-tight people. The quality of their hospitality, with a few exceptions, left much to be desired; once or twice I was stupid enough to accept Minkia invitations, only to find the doors of their village padlocked on arrival. Afterwards I never went out to Minkia homes unless accompanied there by the host himself or his deputy.

However, I often went in the evening to visit groups of the Minkia carpenters whom I knew. They were always working till nightfall on some new houses due to the building boom in Likiang, and would be eating their supper when I arrived. As a rule they sat in a circle on a half-completed first floor and I was always very careful when climbing up their makeshift ladders. To them such hazards appeared non-existent. Their women always came to visit them, bringing some home-made delicacies such as pickled cabbage or turnip, and would stay in town for a day or two until replaced by other relations. Of course these visits to husbands, brothers or lovers were not the primary object in travelling to Likiang. They either had been hired to bring some loads up or had come with their own merchandise to sell. And it was so much nicer and less expensive to spend the night with their own folk, as a kettle bubbled on the hastily constructed hearth and sparks from the fire flew up into the uncompleted roof. There were straw mats or wooden stumps to sit on while a jar of white wine was passed around and a big pot of bean curd and cabbage soup, perhaps a tiny fish, plenty of chillies and red rice. Afterwards people relaxed on the mats; more wine went around, mandolins were produced and sweet nostalgic songs were sung late into the night. I loved these plaintive rhythmic songs.

The most frequent Minkia visitors to my house were Akounya's father, her two brothers and their friends. They felt quite at home and after dinner always came up to my room to have more drinks and to listen to my gramophone. They liked opera records best, and of these they preferred *La Traviata* above all others, and pretended that it contained a number of Minkia words. They asked me to tell them what *La Traviata* was about. To have explained it to them literally would have been easy, but they would have lost much of the meaning of the libretto. At last I had a bright idea and, as the opera progressed, told them the following story:

'A beautiful Minkia girl from your village went one day with her friends to the crowded Chiuho market. There she met a handsome Minkia boy from Chienchwang who also came to the market together with his companions. He persuaded her to accompany him to Chienchwang where a marriage would be arranged. She went. There was much rejoicing on her arrival. But her parents-in-law were cruel to her. She was disappointed and decided to flee back to her village. Her aria betrays her sadness at the inevitability of the parting. The man sings about the loss of his beautiful bride and of the purchase money he paid for her.'

My friends were delighted with this interpretation and said they could now themselves feel the emotions expressed by the singers. The music, they said, was clearly Minkia music. Crowds of Minkia came afterwards to hear the records. The only thing, they said, that they could not understand, was how foreigners could compose so true an opera about Minkia life. I said that many years ago an Italian explorer, who also was a composer, travelled through these parts and wrote the libretto and the music. I pray that the spirit of Verdi will forgive me for the liberties I took with his opera for the sake of the pleasure and joy that it gave to these simple people.

CHAPTER X

THE LAMASERIES

*L*IKIANG had five lamaseries which all belonged to the Karamapa (Red) Sect of the Tibetan Lamaism. They were beautifully situated on the hillsides surrounded by forest. Lamaism had been introduced into Likiang about four hundred years ago by the saintly Lama Chuchin Chone, who founded the first lamasery, Chinyunsze, at Lashiba behind the lake. The mystic doctrine of Tantric Buddhism, the colourful rites and the ecclesiastical connection with Lhasa strongly appealed to the Nakhi. Thus the faith, superimposed on their own Shamanism and in strong competition with Chinese Mahayanist Buddhism, spread in the valley. Some of the smaller lamaseries had been subsidized by the Mu King and, with the decline of the dynasty, they were left, so to speak, high and dry. Because they had not been built in strategic places, from the point of view of commerce and pilgrimage, they declined and had only a comparatively few lamas and trapas left to look after their vast but rapidly deteriorating buildings. The original lamasery at Lashiba was still prosperous because it lay on the Likiang-Lhasa caravan road and, in addition, was much revered as the mother of all other lamaseries. The Pouchisze lamasery, the one nearest to the city, was a small but beautifully grouped complex of temples and apartments. It had a saintly Incarnation, Shenlou Hutuktu, now dead, in whose honour a large white stupa still stands in the pine forest behind. I had the privilege of meeting him when I was in Chungking in 1941. This Grand Lama was a very kindly and enlightened man and at that time he had foretold that I should come to Likiang.

The Pouchisze lamasery was as cosy and intimate inside as it was beautiful outside. There were nooks and small courtyards filled with flowers and blossoming vines. A huge Tibetan mastiff guarded the place. He was so old that he tottered as he walked, yet he was still dangerous to intruders and his deep bark reverberated through the corridors like a lion's roar. The kitchen, adjoining the little flower-filled courtyard and guest hall, was spacious and clean, and was presided over by an old Chinese cook, also a convert to Lamaism. He always provided a delicious meal and a jar of wine for the frequent visitors who came to spend week-ends at this beautiful and restful spot. The lamas and trapas of the lamasery were gentle and courteous. Most of them were natives of a large Nakhi village below. Because of the gentle and learned Shenlou Hutuktu, the lamasery was remembered by the Likiang gentry and by visiting Tibetan merchants, with donations sufficient to keep it going in proper style. Moreover, the lamas had a hope that soon Shenlou Hutuktu might decide to reincarnate in some lucky child's body and bring the old glory back to his beloved lamasery and to Likiang. The only serious drawback to the lamasery was the lack of water, for the mountainside on which it had been built was dry and water flowed only during the rainy season.

I often went to Pouchisze for week-ends and the lamas were always glad to see me. It was wonderful to relax there with nothing but the rustling trees around, blue sky and the tinkle of a silver bell of a lama in prayer.

My favourite lamasery, however, was Yuenfoungsze or Shangri Moupo gompa. It was the largest and most active lamasery in the Likiang district, and was set half-way up from the plain to the sacred peak of Shangri Moupo, whose 14,000 feet high pyramid dominates the city on the south side. It was very strange that, whilst the great snow peak of Mount Satseto was only of local significance to the Nakhi, the smaller Shangri Moupo occupied a very prominent place in the Tibetan cosmology, being regarded as one of the sacred peaks of Tibet — the dwelling-places of the gods. The Tibetans believe that the gods reside alternately on particular peaks of western and eastern Tibet. High lamas keep a strict record of the cycles of these divine migrations and name the year and month during which the gods move from one to the other. When the gods have reached the Shangri Moupo and the Chicken Foot Mountain across the lake from Tall, which is also sacred, then it is time for the Tibetan pilgrims to turn their steps towards Likiang and Tali, to pay respect to these holy thrones of the gods, and to acquire merit by offering service or donations to the nearby lamaseries and shrines.

The Shangri Moupo lamasery was some eight miles from the city, along a narrow road which, passing fields and villages and crossing deep streams, led in a steep climb through the forest of pines and rhododendrons. The forest belonged to the lamasery, and was therefore a

Shangri Moupo Lamasety. senior lama with the lama Manager on the right.

sanctuary for animals; so that the climb, though arduous, was like a progress to paradise. Birds sang from tall, shady trees; crystal streams rushed down in orchestrated cascades; rare flowers pushed up from under bushes, and the air was heavy with the fragrance of blossoms. After the first mani pile, with the stones and slabs engraved with the eternal 'Aum, mani padme hum!' the road wove through a dense spruce forest. Then, suddenly the lamasery was there, lying in a hollow of the mountains like a huge bowl, with a green meadow in front and very old trees dotted around. There was a huge circular fish-pond, fed by mountain streams, and a flight of stone steps leading to an imposing gate, beyond which sat four giant grinning avatars, representing the four manifestations of power or energy; and across a vast courtyard was the great prayer hall itself, reached by two stone stairways. The courtyard was profusely decorated with flowers in pots and stone vases and there were rose bushes and old cassia-trees in the stone-lined tubs.

To the right of the courtyard there was a passage which led to a spacious dining-room decorated with huge mirrors. In front of it was another large courtyard, paved with cobble-stones, at the end of which were stables for the horses and mules, and a huge kitchen. Connected by a veranda to the dining-room was a two-storey wing, in which my good lama friend, the manager or bursar, lived below his trapa clerical staff. He was a convivial fellow, with bright intelligent eyes and a great forehead, and was quite bald. He came from a village not far from ours and, people said, he was happily married and had children. I asked him about it one day and he laughed heartily.

'Well,' he said, 'if nobody gets married, where are the

little lamas to come from?'

I had met him at Madame Lee's bar, where he always went when in town as he was very fond of a cheering cup. He was most hospitable, and often invited me for week-ends. I always brought with me my medical kit and some flowers and vegetable seeds for the lama himself, for, like the other lamas, he was very fond of gardening.

My arrival was usually on a Saturday afternoon. After a drink of the special white wine made by the lamas themselves, the bursar disappeared on business, and I made excursions into the surrounding woods, searching for flowers, particularly the kounpanyas, which are little purple orchids. On my return to the lamasery I called on a few other lamas I knew and offered any medical help that I could give. There was usually an inflamed eye, a touch of a skin disease, a bout of malaria or an attack of indigestion, and they were very grateful for these little tokens of attention. Then the evening came, with the cold of an altitude of about 1 1,000 feet, and we sat by the brazier awaiting the gong for dinner.

I was always placed at the large round table at which the senior lamas sat. They were very dignified elders, some with white beards, clad in their red togas. All victuals were produced at the lamasery and the meals were very good. There was beef, pork and mutton, sauerkraut, rich potato soup, and everything was helped down with cups of wine. Rice was seldom served, but instead we ate the babas-thick wheat pancakes with butter and ham shavings. Young trapas served at the table and before and after the meals grace was said by the oldest lama.

Afterwards I lay on rich rugs in my lama friend's cell, with butter lamps flickering before the golden Buddhas on an altar. Outside there was the hooting of owls and

The Yuenfoungsze (Shangri Moupo gompa) Lamasery playing
during lama dances.

screeching of wild animals, and now and then the sound of a bell from some distant shrine. Before dawn there was the noise of a drum, then the mysterious, hollow call of a conch shell. Then there was the dawn service with its murmur of recited sutras, punctuated by bells, conch-shell blasts and the wailing of trumpets. I got up at about six or seven and at nine there was breakfast of butter tea, sauerkraut, hard-boiled eggs and fried pork, accompanied by the inevitable babas. At about ten there was again a call to prayer and I went to the main hall. The lamas entered in a stately procession, each wearing a tall curving yellow hat with fringes. They seated themselves, cross-legged, on low benches and began to recite sutras spread on low tables in front of them, while the blare of trumpets, conch shells, bells and drums punctuated certain passages. Two trapas with long-spouted pots passed from lama to lama filling little white cups with wine. This was always done in rainy or wintry clays to protect them from chills and to keep up their strength during long services.

Behind the main hall and dining-room there lay a miniature city sprawling over the hillside. It consisted of one-storey houses with small gardens, all walled in. These were the residences of the high-ranking lamas. Each compound was occupied by one or two lamas and their attendants. Their old parents or male relatives could also stay with them; and a room could always be found for a guest for a few days.

I and my friend Changtehkuan, a Chinese from the Duchy of Bonzera, often stayed with a close relative of his mother's, who was a Tibetan. This venerable lama, who was in charge of the sacred music, was not really very old but he had a magnificent long beard, which is a rarity among the Tibetans, of which he was inordinately

222

proud. He shared his apartments with another lama and had his old father staying with him. His house had two wings; one was their living quarters and the other contained a shrine of his favourite deity. The old man loved flowers and in his jewel of a little garden he tended his pots of crooked plum- and cherry-trees: his miniature bamboo grove and his cluster of roses.

Rich merchants and officials from Likiang came to stay with their lama friends for a week or two. I always avoided them as their ideas of relaxation were diametrically opposed to mine, and they either smoked opium all day long or played mahjong. They could never understand my desire to climb the mountains or visit the tribal villages.

Quite high above the lamasery, on a precipitous spur of the mountain, there was a curious shrine, always padlocked and sealed. I climbed to it several times but saw nobody. At last a friend explained to me that this was a hermitage where some thirty-five young lamas had been shut up for meditation and study for a period of three years, three months, three weeks, three days, three hours and three minutes. Guided by a guru, usually an old, saintly and learned lama, these young men chose a sacred word or text to meditate upon. The favourite word, I was informed, was 'Aum', whose mystic meaning could seldom, if ever, be properly understood, but which contained power and enlightenment. Between meditations a regular course of Tantric theology was pursued. On the expiration of the seclusion each man became a lama in his own right and, if he chose, he could go to Lhasa to undergo further training and take examinations for higher initiations. I was told that two years more would be needed before the hermitage could be unsealed in a

223

brilliant ceremony and the young lamas released. In the meantime, they stayed there strictly incommunicado with food passed through a small window by an old caretaker.

I had almost forgotten about the young lamas when later, to my surprise, I was invited by my lama friends to go to the lamasery for the great day of the opening of the hermitage. The news spread quickly and the whole town talked of nothing but the forthcoming event.

I started with my friend Changtehkuan on the eve of the ceremony. The road to the lamasery was crowded with groups of people in their best dress: old gentlemen, in formal Chinese garb, proceeded on horseback, escorted by their sons or attendants: women, in black mitres and silk tunics, carried in their baskets the *houkous* and all sorts of dainties. *Pangchinmei*, also with baskets, walked in droves with the local beaux in the rear. The lawn in front of the lamasery was covered with picnicking families sitting on rugs. The over-flow of people was such that few expected to find shelter at night within the lamasery or in the lamas' apartments. We put up with our long-bearded lama, but his house too was crowded and we had to sleep three in one bed. All night long there was singing and dancing outside the lamasery. The invited dignitaries and merchants played mahjong or smoked opium in adjoining houses.

Next day, early in the morning, the service started in the main hall. All the grand lamas, attired in yellow silk jackets and new red tunics, were there chanting the *sutras*; but, advised by our lama friend to hurry, we started on our way to the hermitage. Had we tarried, we should not have reached it at all so great was the press of the milling multitude.

From the terrace of the hermitage the view was breath-taking in the early morning sunshine. Clouds of incense issued from the lamasery, and the sound of great trumpets, the throb of a huge drum, the wail of conch shells and the tinkling of bells reverberated in the narrow valley. At last the great procession to the hermitage started. Senior lamas walked first, gold chalices in their hands sparkling like flames, followed by richly attired dignitaries and a vast crowd. The scene was indescribable in its splendour and beauty, with bit Satseto sparkling in the background, deep blue sky and green pines and rhododendrons in bloom forming a vast stage setting for the glittering conclave. There was a short service before the sealed gate. Then the Grand Lama sprinkled it with holy water, dipping a bunch of the sacred *kusa* grass into the gold *kumba* (chalice). In the presence of the Pacification Commissioner and elders of the city, a gold key was inserted into the padlock, seals removed and the gate was flung open.

I thought the hermitage would be a mean, crowded place with a row of cells, like cages, along a narrow corridor, without light or air. It was nothing of the kind. Instead, I saw a vast oblong courtyard with age-old shady trees and masses of flowers. In the centre there was a tall and spacious prayer hall with a brightly polished floor. It was here that the lectures were delivered to the neophytes. All around the courtyard there were single-storey buildings divided into light and comfortable rooms. These were the students' private apartments. In front of each room, in the courtyard, there stood a small kiosk with a golden Buddha and dozens of brightly burning butter lamps. A stall in front of each kiosk was heaped with sweet meats and there was a row of small cups filled with wine. Each graduate stood by his kiosk welcoming friends and acquaintances with a bow. Expecting a group

YuenFoungsze Lamasery.

of ascetic and emaciated young men worn down by lack of food and the severity of their mystic exercises, I was confronted with bright-eyed, well-fed men in resplendent vestments who laughed and chatted and pressed us to eat and to drink, while themselves setting a good example.

Tables were produced in no time, and food, brought by the parents and relatives, was spread. The *houkous*, in the centre of each table, spewed smoke and flames like miniature volcanoes and a joyous feast was soon in progress. I was led to a terrace where several tables were prepared for the dignitaries, and was seated with the jovial Pacification Commissioner and the high lamas. The food was superb and the wine still better, and by the time we got up it was late afternoon.

The meadow in front of the lamasery was crowded with richly caparisoned mules and crowds of relatives in preparation for the triumphal send-off of the newly made lamas. Each young lama was affectionately assisted into the saddle and led off with infinite care by his admiring folk, some of whom cried unashamedly with joy and unutterable happiness. It was the culmination of a cherished ambition, and an unparalleled honour not only to the family concerned but to the whole district from which the young lama came. Not all the graduates came from the Likiang district. Some were from Tongwa and Hsiangchen, from Bongdzera and Lotien and other little-known regions. They were Tibetans and Nakhi and members of other tribes who had adopted Lamaism, and were now to be the torches of the light of truth, going to dispel the darkness of *avidya* (ignorance) in their barbaric lands and to be the shining, priceless jewel of faith.

Nature itself smiled on the men during this felicitous day. The air was warm and scented, the sky so cloudless and blue; the Snow Mountain waved a long white plume, as if in greeting, from the glittering crown of its summit. The city was *en fête* and there were delirious celebrations in many houses that evening before the departure of holy caravans on the morrow.

It will be several years before this glorious festival is repeated. It takes a long time to find and prepare a group of serious-minded and ardent neophytes willing to endure such a long seclusion for the sake of faith and spiritual glory. Perseverance in studies and intellectual honesty are required. The full implication of solitude, obedience to guru, renunciation of worldly desires and tastes is not easy to inculcate and still harder to practise. The wise High Lamas have to exercise an infinite care not to include in the group any undesirable person. Any debauchery, or the scandal of escaping inmates, would destroy for ever the high repute of this holy and famed hermitage. The comparative comfort of existence, similar to some Taoistic hermitages in China, presents greater temptations than the life in certain Tibetan and Christian retreats, where the emphasis is on the mortification of the flesh. The problem of man was understood better at this hermitage. Man is not only a spirit: he has his physical nature as well. It is not with the destruction of one aspect of his being by the other that he fulfils his existence. It is by a harmony of the two that he becomes perfect. Jesus, Gautama and Gandhi emphasized this balance between the two extremes and it was for this reason that they were able to render their great services to humanity. Mortification, carried to excess, is no good either to man himself or to humanity. The greater victories come to the man who does not concentrate on murdering his body but utilizes its strength and energy in developing his spiritual

Yuenfoungsze Lamasery (Shangri Moupo gompa). The venerable lama.

gifts. A withered tree bears no fruit.

The sacred peak of Shangri Moupo was not of significance to the Tibetans only. At its back, in front of an immense sheer white cliff called Loupaper, there was a huge stony platform on which the Nakhi Shamans, called dtombas, held a conclave once in ten years. This was preceded by much feasting and drinking in tents and then the dtombas arranged a series of shamanistic dances representing various felicity ceremonies such as the Longevity ceremony. They were attired in Chinese figured mandarin robes and wore five-petal diadems on their heads. The dance was a slow one, always turning on one leg and swaying; it was monotonous but strangely rhythmic and, to me, very hypnotic. In one hand they held a magic sword and in another a ndseler. A ndseler is a cymbal, made of an alloy of gold, silver and brass, to which, as a striker, a small brass weight is attached on a string. The sound of it is most beautiful and quite unlike anything produced by a triangle or a similar orchestral instrument of the West. There is little doubt that the dtomba practices were closely affiliated to those of the Mongolian Shamans. They had originated in the remote past long before the great religions made their appearance in the world. There is a close affinity between the Dtombas and Bonists, that is to say, the adherents of the 'Bon' or Black Church of Tibet. The Bon Church was the dominant cult of Tibet before the establishment of Buddhism. It is founded entirely on the practice of black magic and communication with evil spirits through necromancy and other morbid and macabre rites. The cups, made of human skulls, and flutes of human bone are used freely in certain religious services. There are a number of Bon lamaseries in Kham, where these practices take place, and it was occurrences such as these that helped to make Tibet known as a land of horrible occult rites and other unspeakable mysteries.

It cannot be said that the dtombas represented an established church like Lamaism. They worked independently, the art passing from father to son. They had a loose association, but it was by no means a recognized institution or club. They knew each other and, when occasion offered, they combined together for large ceremonies, and they were needed for the exorcising, during special ceremonies, of the demons of suicide and other calamities. As such occurrences were frequent, their trade was quite lucrative. They claimed control over spirits both bad and good, and as their performances always produced a trance or semi-trance they were a somewhat unbalanced people and were very heavy drinkers.

I believe that the Chinese Taoist cult of Changtienssu, established during the Han dynasty, borrowed many of its magic practices from the Bon lamas. It was this Taoist Church, the lowest of all, that encouraged the unwarranted and contemptuous opinion in the West about Taoism. Europe and America still have not realized that the true Taoist Church of China are the Lungmen Church with its sublime teaching of Lao Tzu, practised in all its purity, and the second church of Cheng-I Taoism which specializes in the knowledge of nature and man's relation with the world of spirits. Much of what is best in Chinese civilization and the character of the Chinese people is entirely due to the philosophy and teaching of these two churches.

The higher Taoism buttressed by the written teachings of Lao Tzu and Chuan Tzu, conceives the Universe as a product of Tao, which means the Universal Mind, independent of the being itself, of space and of time: in other words a conception of God. Lao Tzu advisedly did not use the word 'God' because the Chinese language does not possess such an all-embracing and all-inclusive term. Immediately the word 'God' is used in the Orient it conjures up in the human mind a vision of a glorious, effulgent Man sitting on a flaming throne somewhere in immeasurable space. The teachers of Christianity in the Orient have always been handicapped by this all— important definition, and the Bible, provided for the different churches and sects implanted by the missionaries in China, has never been given by its translators a unifying term for God.

Lao Tzu, in his teaching, does not specifically mention Earth or its affairs: he simply and unequivocally states that the Universe is the product of Tao (Great Mind) which, by the Power of its Will, brought forms out of the formless, differentiated them by the flow of numbers and series, and activated life by the eternal rhythm of Yang and Ying which made all things and events in space and time relative to each other.

Therefore, since both the visible and invisible worlds are the creation of one and the same Mind, their difference is only relative and it becomes understandable that an interplay, between them is possible and natural.

CHAPTER XI

POLTERGEISTS

$\mathcal{T}$HE Nakhi, like many other people still unaffected by the materialistic Western civilization, lived in close and intimate contact with the world of spirits. They believed that the immensity of space was inhabited by big and small deities, spirits of the dead and a host of nature's spirits both good and bad. The relationship between mankind and these many spirits was not considered hypothetical or conjectural but factual and authentic. Psychic phenomena neither surprised nor alarmed them unless they were of a disagreeable nature. Unlike the taboo imposed by religion in the West on communication with spirits, no such restrictions existed in Likiang and the communications themselves were looked upon as the normal and eminently practical means of solving certain intricate problems of life when other methods had failed. If there was an apparition, materialization or direct voice, people did not shrink from it but investigated the matter with sympathy and interest.

In a word, a visitor from the unseen was treated as a person, with proper courtesy.

It was firmly believed that the dead survived. They did not live somewhere in the blue sky beyond the clouds but existed somewhere near, just on the other side of the veil. The veil could be lifted or, at least, a hole could be made in it for a short talk with the dear departed. It was not considered necessary or desirable to bother them too much for two reasons. One was that they had already accustomed themselves to their new existence and that it was a bad thing to remind them too much of earthly affairs and thereby induce them to become earthbound. The second reason was that if it should ever be demonstrated that the life beyond is as happy and felicitous as it is pictured in Nakhi scriptures, there would be the temptation to end it all and to migrate to a happier plane of existence in a hurry. As it was, the suicides in Likiang were too frequent and easy, and such revelations might cause a stampede, bringing the whole Nakhi race to a premature end.

The dead, therefore, could only be approached in time of a severe crisis in the family when, for example, someone was dangerously ill, with all hope in drugs abandoned. Then a professional medium, called *sanyi*, was summoned and his visit was always arranged in the dead of night, when the neighbours were asleep. He chanted the incantations from the scriptures, accompanying himself on a small drum. He danced a little. Then he fell into a trance. There was no direct voice. The man gasped out what he saw. It might, for instance, be a tall old man in a purple jacket, slightly lame, leaning on a black stick. 'Oh, that is Grandfather!' cried the family, prostrating themselves. Then the sickness of the patient was described. 'The old man is smiling,' reported the *sanyi*. 'He says the boy will recover in seven days if he takes this medicine.' There followed a slow dictation of what to take and when to take it. The family prostrated themselves again as the old man was reported to be going away. On the other hand, the old man might have said that the case was hopeless and that the boy would be with him in three days.

People always said that such prescriptions or prophecies were infallible: either the patient recovered with the aid of the prescribed medicine or he was dead on the day and hour announced by his departed ancestor. Moreover, murderers could be brought to justice through interviews with their dead victims and certain family affairs cleared up. Conversations with the dead in dreams were a frequent occurrence in Likiang and were given much credence.

As I have already explained, the *dtombas* controlled a vast realm of malignant and destructive demons, who plagued mankind with their malicious interference. They ensconced themselves in the households, where disharmony occurred, and ragged telepathically at the disordered thoughts of the miserable or the depressed, inciting in them the ideas of revenge, murder or suicide. These demons are pictured in the Nakhi sacred manuscripts as being with a human head, of a repulsive appearance, and a snake body. The *dtombas* claim that these snake-like creatures can be seen by men subjectively under the effect of prolonged drink or in insanity. This is rather in accord with the Western conception of the visions during *delirium tremens*. The whole idea of the *dtomba* ceremonial dances is to induce these malignant creatures, once they had invaded the house, to come out, so to speak, into the open. Then they are ceremoniously feasted, exorcised and conjured never to return.

The deities are in a class by themselves and cannot be coerced or commanded. To these belong the powerful Nagaraja clans. The Nagarajas are the heroic spirits of great Nagas or serpents, and it is clear that they can be identified with the biblical seraphim who were the angels with snake bodies. Like the seraphim, all Nagarajas possess beautiful human faces and can manifest themselves in an entire human form. Many women fall in love with these handsome denizens of the spirit world and bear, as a result of the union, specially gifted and good-looking children. The Nagarajas are propitiated with milk and dainties at special ceremonies. They are always treated with particular courtesies. The Nagaraja cult is not confined to Likiang but is very popular in Burma and Siam. Nagas were worshipped in ancient Angkor Thom also and the Naga motif is still predominant in temple decorations in Indo-China and Siam. In China the cult survives as the worship and reverence of the Dragon — the clawed Naga — which rules oceans, rivers and mountains. One of the objects of Fengshui in China is to determine the sites of houses and tombs so as to conform to the Dragon's disposition and will.

It is believed that the Nagarajas sometimes live on the material plane incarnated, of course, in a snake form. One of them lived close to my Iron Mining Co-operative, and near the village which was on a hill covered with sparse woods. The deity stayed in a small cave and milk and eggs were placed at a respectful distance from the opening. Not satisfied by these willing sacrifices, the Naga emerged from time to time to swallow a chicken or young pig, thus becoming rather an expensive visitor. I was fortunate to catch a glimpse of it one evening. It was a huge king cobra, old and venerable, and its upraised head, I had time to notice, had a comb like a cock's. We quickly moved away as king cobras can run with the speed of a galloping horse, and if bitten we would have died within half an hour.

In addition to the spirits of the dead, malevolent demons and Nagarajas, Likiang was a veritable playground for *siao-shentze*, which in the West are usually termed poltergeists. I liked the Chinese version, which means 'little spirits' or, by extension, 'little gods'. It is now freely recognized in the West by those interested in psychical research that such psychic phenomena are almost commonplace among people who believe in them. It seems that these unseen intelligences prefer to manifest themselves in a congenial atmosphere created by the impressionable acceptance of simple people who live in close communion with nature. In Europe and America, even in China, these poltergeistic manifestations are considered as an inexplicable nuisance. Many people believe, of course, that they are devil's tricks to subvert the faithful, and when these unusual performances start, many shrink in pious horror and rush to have them exorcised.

The Nakhi people, whilst not welcoming such manifestations of the unseen forces, were nevertheless very level-headed and practical when they occurred. They believed implicitly that the phenomena were originated and directed by intelligent spirit-beings— not the spirits of the ancestors but creatures of an order either below or above the human level. The accepted opinion was that the displacement of objects, rapping and other phenomena were not purposeless acts to frighten or annoy the occupants of a house, but were designed by the intelligences to attract attention as, evidently they had no other means of making themselves known. The purpose of this interference in the human sphere was, clearly, to communicate something to the family, or, perhaps, issue a warning about some impending misfortune which might be forestalled. Thus, instead of cursing or insulting the unseen intruders or shrinking from them, people addressed them courteously and tried to find out, by a timely seance, what the matter was.

The most celebrated case of persistent poltergeistic phenomena in Likiang, was the Lai family's old house in one of the principal streets near Madame Lee's wine-shop. The family was considered to be the richest in town, but it was agreed that their vast fortune seemed to have originated soon after the phenomena had started. It was a curious case and it is related by Fitzgerald in his book *The Tower of Five Glories*. I went to the house a few days after my arrival in Likiang and saw where the roof had been broken through in many places by the huge boulders which still lay on the floor as they had fallen. The walls were deeply scarred by the tongues of a flame which had appeared from nowhere. The place was utterly uninhabitable. A few years later it was pulled down.

This was the story, as related to me by friends. The Lais had been a moderately well-to-do family and they had only enough money to build that modest one-storey house. One evening, as Mr. Lai was lying on his couch smoking opium, he noticed a strange disappearance and reappearance of objects. Turning over on the bed to relight his pipe, he saw, to his intense surprise, that the little lamp was gone. Laying his pipe on the table, he got up to investigate. Turning round, he saw the lamp in its old place but this time the pipe was not there. Day after day these curious happenings increased. Friends came to watch in fascinated amazement as dishes were carried by invisible hands from one table to another; playing-cards scattered over the bed; bottles of wine and cups moved round and many other acts, some of them highly comical, were performed. There was no hint of anything unpleasant or destructive. Finally, Mr. Lai decided to arrange a seance at which it was discovered that there were two 'little spirits' in action and that both, so they said, were females. They declared that their purpose in molesting Mr. Lai and his family was to demand that Mr. Lai should rebuild the famous iron chain bridge over the Yangtze at Tzelichiang, some eighty *li* from Likiang on the busy Likiang—Yuenpei caravan route. This hanging bridge, about 150 feet long, had been built long ago by a pair of lovers, who had escaped from the fury of pursuing parents, and who, with great difficulty and only just in time, had crossed the raging river by boat to safety. In gratitude for their almost miraculous escape from two mortal dangers and in fulfillment of a vow they built the bridge. With the passage of time the eighteen chains, anchored to the huge boulders on each side of the gorge, where deep down the great river boiled, became loosened and worn out and liable to break at any time.

Mr. Lai, during the fateful seance, retorted that it was easier said than done to undertake such a work, and that he was not a rich man. Why did the spirit ladies not go to somebody else with such a request? They replied that they came to him because they knew him to be a man of drive and purpose; as for finance, they would see what could be done.

Ever since that day the Lai family began to prosper

exceedingly. In no time at all they became the richest merchants in Likiang. No one knows exactly how, but some people averred that the little spirits brought or materialized gold and silver ingots into Mr. Lai's room. Others thought it was opium, which was even better for trade than gold. A few conjectured that perhaps some vital trade secrets had been disclosed to the family by those omniscient spirits. One thing is certain – the spirits were always present in the house and continued to amuse the merchant and his friends with their clever and good-natured pranks. Then the day of reckoning arrived when the 'little sisters' declared that since Mr. Lai was now a very rich man, the time had come to begin work on the bridge. But as always happens, when a man is becoming rich, his appetite grows with eating. Mr. Lai dolefully protested that he was still a poor man and must accumulate more funds before he could undertake so expensive a job. 'Now or never!' cried the two infuriated spirits through the medium. In a flash, they changed from being charming angels into intractable, avenging demons. The pleasant and luxuriously furnished house was turned into an abode of desolation and fear. Tongues of flame licked the walls at unexpected places and times. Boulders crashed now and then in the very midst of the drawing-room. Pebbles were thrown into the food dishes and crockery was smashed. This continued for many weeks. Poor Mr. Lai did not know what to do. His name became associated with bad luck in town and people were afraid to pass his house at night. All sorts of conjurations and exorcisms were resorted to, but without avail.

Fitzgerald describes in his book how a Chinese colonel visited the house, armed with two pistols and surrounded by his soldiers. 'I am not afraid of you, you rogues!' the colonel shouted, brandishing his pistols and entering the drawing-room. Before he had finished his tirade, a round stone, as big as a fist, hit him on the head and he had to be rushed away for treatment. A missionary, whom I met afterwards, boldly entered the house carrying a cross and the Bible. 'Where Christ is,' he shouted, 'no evil spirits may abide' A huge boulder crashed right by his feet and he rushed out in a panic.

With a heavy heart, grieving over the ruination of his house and the heavy outlay of capital, Mr. Lai had the bridge reconstructed. But the destructive manifestations did not abate. Another protracted seance was arranged in the presence of a local Buddhist priest. The 'little spirits' declared that they were disgusted with Mr. Lai's avarice and wanted to continue punishing him. However, they yielded to the priest's entreaties and a compact was made by which Mr. Lai would build a small shrine by the bridge; there was to be an attendant priest, and a daily offering of rice, wheat, wine and other edibles to be made in perpetuity. Mr. Lai carried out the agreement to the letter and then, with a great ceremony, the 'little spirit ladies' were escorted to their new dwelling. The manifestations ceased and later on the old house was demolished and a new one built in its place.

I have never been seriously interested in communications with the dead: but poltergeists have always attracted me and I have devoted more than thirty years of my life to their observation and research whenever possible. I had long ago persuaded myself that these phenomena do occur and that poltergeists do really exist. In China, whilst staying for long periods at certain Taoistic monasteries, I had the opportunity of observing a number of interesting psychic phenomena but did not take part in them. I was particularly impressed by the long and difficult ceremony of exorcising an energumen at a Taoist monastery near Soochow. It was a most horrible proceeding.

My observations of the phenomena, in which the 'little spirits', or so-called poltergeists, participated, left me with a firm conviction that they had nothing to do with the spirits of the departed. They were not really human at all and even their intelligence did not conceal their lack of many characteristics we usually associate with men. For one thing, they did not possess love: they were joyous and they could be friendly, but that was about all. They could be easily pleased and just as easily displeased. In their nature, they were either malignant or benignant, and St. Paul's warning to 'try the spirits whether they be good or evil', before dealing with them, was very much to the point. I found out from practice that levity, frivolity, scepticism and conscious fraud during a seance attracted malignant spirits, but that a warm, friendly atmosphere generally led to contacts with benignant entities. A short prayer generally repelled bad influences. Laughter could interrupt a seance for good.

Armed with this knowledge, little as it was, I arrived in Likiang to find it a haven for anyone interested in psychical research. And the years spent in Likiang led me to experiences and experiments which showed that most of the poltergeists could be dealt with by carefully arranged contact through a seance with the spirit agencies involved; that seances could lead to poltergeistic phenomena without any reference to the spirits of the dead, and that the disturbances were not aimless and irrational but had a definite purpose in view. Indeed, if pohergeistic manifestations were aimless and senseless, then there would be more of them since they would require neither rhyme nor reason.

On the whole, the 'little spirits' do not seem interested in human affairs and they undertake their appearance only in special cases when certain specific interests of theirs seem to be involved. Ties of friendship and kindness seem to have an effect on them, and perhaps the concern of the two female spirits in the reconstruction of the bridge across the Yangtze was due to their past friendship with the adventurous lovers.

Another case concerned the hill which extended, at the back of our house, towards Double Stone Bridge. They repeatedly enjoined the people, through manifestations and seances, not to disfigure it by quarrying. But it was an easy and desirable place to obtain stone and the gangs of Minkia stone-cutters always tried to nibble at it. One gang started quarrying at the back of the hill. Within a week big boulders were thrown at them and a man's foot was crushed. Then they moved to a place near Double Stone Bridge on the road from my house to Madame Ho's wine-shop. They put up low shacks by the roadside and were cutting stone for a week or two without accidents. Then the warning came: pebbles were put in their wine-cups and stones thrown into their cooking pots. These Minkia were a cheerful, friendly lot, always singing and joking, and I used to stop to chat and drink with them when passing. I was delighted when they began telling me about the phenomena. One evening I was asked in, took the proffered bowl of wine and waited, sitting together with them around the fire. I watched my cup attentively and noted that nobody was very close to me. Bringing it to my lips I saw a round pebble in it. Then a hat from the man opposite was placed on my head. Within a few moments all the hats were exchanged by invisible hands, and other pebbles followed into our cups. But no one could spot the very act of the placing of the pebbles into cups or the changing of the hats. Then stones were gently thrown round our feet.

This continued for several days. Afterwards heavy boulders were thrown into the shacks, breaking the pots. At last a falling rock smashed somebody's foot. Next day the Minkia had a secret seance and were told to get out as fast as they could or grievous things would happen to them. So the quarry was abandoned and only a small cave under the over-hanging cliff showed where they had worked.

About a month or two afterwards I was passing the place in the evening. Some poor Tibetan pilgrims were preparing to pass the night in the cave. A woman and a child were sitting inside, the man was feeding a mule tied to a post by the cave. A sacred sheep munched grass by the roadside. Sheep are usually taken on a pilgrimage on which they carry a small load of provisions tied to a miniature saddle. They acquire merit from the long tramp to holy peaks and shrines and are never killed afterwards.

Early next morning I received the news of a terrible disaster and rushed to the cave. The whole hillside had crashed down on the family and the mule. Only the sheep continued to munch its grass unconcernedly by the roadside. Tons of rock and earth had buried them completely. People dug there for weeks without uncovering the bodies and, finally, the work was abandoned.

CHAPTER XII

SUICIDES AND DTOMBA CEREMONIES

*L*IKIANG could really hold the doubtful honour of being the world's suicide capital. There was not a family that did not number a suicide or two among its members. Suicide was looked upon as a convenient and desirable way of escape from a tangled love affair, a severe loss of 'face', a grievous quarrel, a mortal insult, an unhappy married life and from a host of other unfortunate situations. There was no opprobrium attached to it and the unhappy man or woman was not threatened with eternal burning in a fiery furnace. Not that there were no furnaces in the Nakhi hell, but they were reserved for offences of a more heinous character. Yet it was believed to be true that suicides were definitely outside the pale of the paradise where the ancestors of all the Nakhi dwelt in leisurely enjoyment of the luxurious plenty of white yaks and fleet horses, vast expanses of rich fields and flower-strewn meadows, palatial houses, and wine, women and song.

The men and women, who had died by their own hand or suddenly, without the benefit of the magic coin in the mouth which opened the gates of paradise, remained as earthbound spirits, flitting here and there in a rather pretty no man's land between the living and the dead. It was not a bad place and it closely resembled the material contours of the mother earth; there were hills and valleys, rivers and lakes and lush alpine meadows, overgrown with the gorgeous *yuwoo* flowers.[1] But existence in this pleasant place was rather aimless. They could eat the nectar of the *yuwoo* flowers and drink the dew, they could lounge on the clouds, talk to friends, if they had any, and indulge in shadowy love-making as much as they wanted. But sooner or later they got tired of it all and realized that they were neither fish nor fowl. They longed for their families but they could not reach them. It was impossible to return to earth, and the infrequent exchange of words with the near and dear through the *sanyi* medium were distressingly unsatisfying. Nor could they join the other departed members of their family as they did not know the way to the gates of paradise, which were guarded by malicious and unkind spirits. They were usually saved by their living relatives or parents who ordered the *dtombas* to perform a Harlallu ceremony which ultimately opened the gates of the ancestral paradise for them to enter.

Suicide was not committed haphazardly in an undignified or casual manner as in the West, where people throw themselves under a tram or train, jump from tall buildings or put their heads in gas ovens. The Nakhi, like other Orientals, considered the entry into the Beyond a serious and ceremonious affair. It was as unseemly to

---

[1] The word *yuwoo* literally means suicide; thus there was a special variety of flower called the Suicide Flower.

cross the Threshold in a hurry, dishevelled or in untidy dress, as to attend an audience at the king's palace in dirty rags with perhaps a pail and broom in hand.

The *yuwoo* was a ceremonial suicide and had definite rules for stepping out of the body in a decorous and dignified manner and in proper surroundings. If the suicide was to be committed at home, the drawing-room was the right place for it. If it could not be done at home, as in the case of runaway couples, a secluded and beautiful spot in an inaccessible part of the mountains was the prescribed rule. The intending suicide had to be properly attired as though invited to an official feast. If the human personality persisted in the Beyond in the likeness of its earthly form, no doubt the dress persisted too and it would have been folly to wear dirty or improper clothes, perhaps for eternity. Besides, sooner or later there might be a passage to the ancestral paradise, and what would an ancestor say to a descendant entering the celestial mansion in rags.

All the various ways of ending life had not been definitely prescribed but a reliable variety of sure and lethal methods was recommended for the purpose. The best and surest was the root of black aconite boiled in oil and it was reasonably swift. It did cause great suffering, but it had the advantage of paralysing the larynx instantly so that no cries or groans could betray the whereabouts of the expiring suicides to any search parties. It was much preferred also because it did not disfigure the body as would death from drowning, hanging or a fall from a cliff. But its real value lay in double suicides, when it guaranteed the death of both lovers absolutely. No mischance was possible. A simultaneous jump from a cliff, into a lake or a river, a stabbing or even a hanging always carried the possibility that one party to the pact might survive, and perhaps not unwillingly. But these methods were not altogether disdained, so that there was a sufficient variety to provide an endless topic of discussion and suggestions for morbid neighbours.

The suicide pacts between girls and boys accounted, in my opinion, for at least 80 per cent of the suicides in Likiang. Next on the list were the unhappily married women and the rest were due to miscellaneous causes. This unusual and alarming prevalence of suicide among the young people was due entirely to the marriage system of the Nakhi which had never fitted the passionate character of these free and independent people. In their fervour to implant Chinese civilization and culture among their people, the Nakhi rulers had introduced a strict and uncompromising Confucian marriage code, the provisions of which caused much untold misery and death in this otherwise happy valley. According to old Chinese custom, it is the parents who arrange marriages for their children without the slightest regard for their likes and dislikes. As a matter of fact, most of the engagements are concluded between the families when their children are still in their infancy or even whilst they are still in their mothers' wombs. It is considered highly improper and unnecessary that the prospective brides and grooms should meet each other before their marriage. It is only during the wedding ceremony that they see each other for the first time and nobody else is interested in whether they like each other or not after the wedding night. They have to stay together and there is nothing more to be said about it. No engagements, concluded by the parents, may be broken off in any circumstances.

With the Chinese, who have been trained for thousands

of years in obedience to parents and in filial piety, this system has worked fairly well. They are docile and friendly by nature, and to many real love came gradually after marriage. But with the Nakhi this system never worked. They had practised, ever since the beginning of their race, free love like their cousins the Tibetans and the Liukhi who still do. This tradition was part of their very blood and still expresses itself in their gaiety, their dances and the free mixing of sexes which even Chinese morality had been unable to suppress. As few secrets could be kept in such small communities as Likiang and its surrounding villages, boys and girls knew well in advance whom they were going to marry and when. Sometimes there was mutual liking between future partners and all was well. But in many cases feelings were not reciprocated or it was dislike that was mutual. From this sprang a continual re-grouping of the eternal triangles, and clandestine love was rather the rule in Likiang than the exception. Sometimes the unhappy lovers separated when the formal marriage took place, and sullenly paired with their unloved spouses, but more often than not, when love was too strong, they decided to end it all. This was especially the case when a baby was on the way, for a bastard was a disgrace of unparalleled proportions. The girl would be killed by her parents anyway, and the only escape was a suicide in which her lover was honour bound to join.

The idea of a suicide pact, it seems, had been established centuries ago by a Nakhi girl, named Kamegamiki, as the only way out of her entanglement with a handsome boy. She was to be married to a wealthy but plain man and could not bear the prospect. In accordance with the then prevailing etiquette, she did not broach tile subject of suicide to the young man by word of mouth direct but conveyed the meaning in verse through the music of the Jew's-harp which is a national musical instrument of the Nakhi and much used in love-making. Accompanying her whispered words with the harp she made a long and plaintive recital in which she used all her power and charm to persuade her lover of the hopelessness of their position, out of which the only escape was through death. He was not at all keen to follow her into the grave and raised many objections to her plan, expressing them in suitable verse, again with the help of the Jew's-harp. But she was a persistent and possessive woman and finally she drove him to distraction with her promptings.

At last the boy yielded and promised to commit suicide with her, but on the condition that she put up the necessary capital. He wanted to get a suit of fine clothes and other articles of a gentleman's attire, and a lot of good food and good wine. Perhaps, he thought, she would be unable to raise so much money; but, to his dismay, she produced the cash on the table without much difficulty as, evidently, she was a rich woman. He was trapped. They proceeded to a secluded spot in the mountains, spent an idyllic time until the provisions ran out and then, it is said, took the poison. This story and the verses are recorded in an ancient manuscript, called the Book of Kamegamiki. The top page is illuminated and shows the lady in a wine-red tunic and a petunia-blue skirt. Her great dark and lustrous eyes, even in the picture, seem to promise and beckon and their intensity still rivets the attention.

This story has inspired suicide ever since; it is recited by the *dtombas*, as a prelude, when performing the Harlallu ceremony, and the procedure of using the Jew's-harp in concluding the suicide pact has been strictly adhered to. As the boys did not have a penny of their own, the girls

were always called upon to finance the ceremony of
yawoo. They had to get new clothes, food and wine. Then,
hand in hand, they slipped away into the mountains,
where they ate and danced and made love to their hearts'
content until the end. But even in the face Of death, the
Likiang girls showed their superiority over the weak
male. Many boys did not want to die but were stampeded
into doing it by their strong-willed sweethearts. It was
related to me that once a girl drove her lover at the point
of a sword and, scaring away the people who wanted to
stop them, she forced the trembling lover to the brink of a
high cliff and calmly pushed him over. Titan, with perfect
Composure, she ran herself through with the sword.

Mass suicide pacts were not unusual and it was related
to me that once six couples were found hanging in the
forest on the Horse Saddle peak, next to the Shangri
Moupo. Once a pair of unhappy girls were found
standing, locked in an embrace, in a small lake below the
Snow Peak. They had tied their ankles together, weighed
them with a stone and jumped in. When a boy or a girl
was missing from home for more than two days, the
parents always suspected the awful truth. There was no
time lost in organizing a thorough search, and in a few
days the bodies of the unhappy lovers would be found
at some far-away spot. The parents wailed and beat their
breasts and began to make arrangements for the Harlallu
ceremony. Sometimes the trail was still hot when the
outraged parents started the chase. Judging from their
grief and lamentations, one would suppose that they
would have been overjoyed to catch their children before
the deed had been done. It was nothing of the sort. Were
the lovers to be caught alive, they would be reviled and
perhaps beaten to death by parents or neighbours from

the necessity of saving face. This face saving was the inflexible and immovable Moloch and had precedence over parental love. It demanded blood sacrifices, in one form or another, irrespective of all other considerations. The lovers knew this only too well and took great care not to be found alive. If a girl's sworn lover had died far away from Likiang, she was honour bound to follow him into the grave.

It is surprising that the Liukhi of Yungning, living practically next door to Likiang, never had suicidal tendencies. But they had kept to their custom of free love and married or lived with anybody they liked. There were no heartbreaks there that could not be repaired, and tile oblivion of death was not sought before its appointed time. Marriage amongst the Tibetans and Black Lolos was also on the basis of free choice and mutual love, and they had no such suicides. In Likiang the prevalence of free and easy suicides could also be traced to the *dtombas'* pernicious influence. The rich emoluments from the Harlaltu ceremonies kept the *dtombas* in clover and it was in their interest to encourage and maintain a high rate of suicides. Therefore, they kept up a subtle and cunning propaganda among these credulous people about the desirability of suicide as a logical solution of the grave problems of life. It was they who took pains to represent existence in the suicides no man's land as blissful, and they certainly succeeded in their salesmanship. Their teachings during the centuries had brought the whole tribe to such a fine point of equipoise between life and death that it became a matter of touch-and-go, and sometimes a petty quarrel or a flash of rage sent a person beyond the veil.

Such examples of thoughtless and cruel avarice were

not confined to the *dtombas* alone. I remember a detestable and blasphemous episode which occurred in Likiang during the war years. A small group of Gurkha soldiers and a few refugees from Burma had trekked into Likiang after a death march across those impossible gorges and ranges of the Salween and Mekong. Unfortunately some of them had dysentery and cholera. The Nakhi, never affected before by such epidemic diseases, succumbed in considerable numbers, and the Minkia carpenters had hardly time enough to produce the coffins. When their lucrative trade had slackened, with the abatement of the disease, they arranged sumptuous services at all Buddhistic temples of Likiang praying the Buddha and other deities to renew and keep up the mortality to the continued prosperity of their business. This reminded me strongly of a Tolstoy story in which a rich merchant, having garnered huge stocks of grain, was selling it at enormous profit during the famine. He vowed to God to build a new cathedral with big bells and all, if only God would keep up the famine in the land. That very night all his barns and store-houses were destroyed by fire.

The Harlallu ceremonies were a constant feature of life in Likiang. Strangers were not invited to witness them, but many friends made it a point to ask me as I was considered almost a member of their family. They always affected me deeply: perhaps it was the sense of the romantic in me that was thrilled by such a display of love unto death. I remember one particular case very well.

A girl in the village at the foot of the Saddle peak had a lover who was a soldier fighting with the army at Taierhchwang. One day his family received a telegram that he was killed in action. The girl cried bitterly when she heard the news from friends, but did not say anything.

Then one night she dressed herself in her best garments, made up her face, put on perfume, and in the morning the parents found her dead, hanging from a beam in the drawing-room. It was only in death that the lovers were forgiven by their sorrowing families and it was usual for the Harlallu ceremony to be a joint one. It was for such a ceremony that I was invited to the house of the dead soldier.

On arrival at the farm I found the courtyard swept clean and decorated with pine branches. The family, dressed in white sackcloth, was waiting about for the guests. Near the entrance there were erected two artificial trees, made up of a thin pole, bamboo stalks, leaves and branches of other trees. They looked rather like two Christmas-trees as they were gaily decorated with little flags and banners and charms. One tree was for the boy and the other for the girl. The boy's tree among other decorations displayed miniature articles of male attire — jackets and trousers, etc., cut out of coloured paper. There were also all the small articles that he had used and cherished, such as his favourite comb and his pipe, tobacco pouch, his mirror, razor and other little possessions. Her tree had her powder-box and lipstick, combs and pins, a simple vanity case, cheap ornaments and a perfume bottle, in addition to the paper models of feminine costume. It was touching and very pitiful.

In the centre of the courtyard there was a small mound of earth and sand, fenced in by wooden planks. A handful of multi-coloured triangular banners was stuck in the middle of the mound with the names and titles of the demons of suicide. Their likenesses, drawn by charcoal on a series of unpainted wooden tablets, were stuck in the sand around the banners. There were many of them—

horrible creatures with snake bodies and bestial human faces; some had their hair standing on end, others had little diadems and caps on their heads. Outside, by the hall door, there was a small, silk-draped altar on which the pictures of the deceased stood with offerings of fruits and sweets, and an incense burner. On the other side below there was a sort of curtained kiosk where the *dtombas* sat, intoning passages from the Book of Kamegamiki and other ancient manuscripts. A gong punctuated their reading. There were seven *dtombas* and they were dressed in mandarin coats of embroidered silk, with five-petal diadems on their heads; on their feet they wore the ancient-style Chinese boots with very thick soles. After their recital they moved into the courtyard and started a slow dance around the banners and the demons to the sound of a small drum and their sonorous *ndselers*. They lifted one leg high, turned slowly on the other and stepped ahead. Continually repeating these precise but monotonous movements, they chanted the incantations summoning the suicide demons to come and the dead couple to appear once more at their home. On and on it went, persistent, irresistible.

'Come! Come! Appear! Come!' they commanded in a metallic and hypnotic voice. There was a deathly hush among the family and the guests. Beads of perspiration appeared on the *dtombas*' faces and their eyes became inverted and glazed. They clearly moved in a semi-trance.

'Appear! Appear! Come! Come!' The words fell with each clang of *ndseler* and each beat of the drum. An hour passed and more. Still the rhythmic, intolerable command went on. Still the men stepped slowly and gyrated in unison. The tension mounted and was reaching a breaking point. Suddenly they stopped. There was a dead stillness and a gust of ice-cold wind filled the courtyard. Just for an instant, one brief moment, we all felt that the lovers had returned and stood there by their likenesses. I thought at first the impression was entirely mine: but, with a burst of weeping, the two families prostrated themselves as one man before the little altar. The guests looked startled. Nothing was seen and the impression was gone in a flash. But they had been there and everyone knew it.

The still weeping hosts now began to arrange the tables and a simple village funeral feast of the traditional eight dishes was served. A special table with similar dishes was put up for the demons and a row of dishes was placed on the altar for the departed. As the wine began to flow, the people regained their spirits and started talking and joking as if it was not a funeral at all. After the meal the *dtombas* killed two black chickens, putting the coins into their beaks as they expired. The chickens represented the deceased, and thus the gate to the paradise of their ancestors was opened and their connection with earth broken. Then there was another dance of the *dtombas*, armed this time with small, wooden swords. It was lively and resembled a spirited fencing as the demons, having been convened, fêted and propitiated, were now being driven out of the house to their nether regions and conjured never to afflict again the two households with their suicidal influence.

Sitting one morning at my desk about ten o'clock, I was called by the neighbours to come down quickly to a house near our village gate. There I found a young girl in a stupor. It appeared that early in the morning she had drunk four ounces of raw opium, dissolved in a bowl of vinegar, and in addition swallowed two or three gold rings. I gave her injections of caffeine and apomorphine, and did all within my power to make her vomit. But the enormous dose of the poison was already doing its work — she was breathing stertorously and her cheeks were purple. Her eyes were open but she was unconscious. I persisted in my efforts and by three o'clock in the afternoon she came round and was able to talk to her family for a while. She was extremely angry with me and knocked the medicine out of my hands. 'I want to die!' she cried. 'I must die! No one can stop me!' and she relapsed into unconsciousness again soon afterwards. I stayed with her till midnight, administering caffeine and other restoratives. Several times she responded again, only to cry out how much she wanted to die. Then she bade a very touching and affectionate farewell to her heart-broken parents and sisters and brothers. She seemed to be much better by midnight and I was persuaded to go home, but she sank rapidly afterwards and was dead at four.

It transpired that she had gone with other girls on a pilgrimage to the Fertility Temple on a peak near Likiang. There they met some boy friends and had a meal together which they themselves cooked. Upon her return to town an aunt of hers, a bad-tempered woman and a notorious gossip, scolded her. She called her an *apizdya* (slut) and many other names in which the Nakhi language is so rich. She also hinted that the girl had surely lost her honour and a baby would be on its way in due course. It was this undeserved reviling in front of all the neighbours which had unhinged this normally placid girl. She felt disgraced and the only way to prove her impotence, she decided, was by suicide. The bereaved and enraged family of the poor girl meted a typical Nakhi revenge on the wicked woman. They proceeded to her house and smashed everything to bits.

When someone is killed in a house or a woman dies there in childbirth, the place automatically becomes *chow* (unclean). The *dtombas* are then invited to perform the Chownaggv or Purification ceremony in which the demons of uncleanness and calamity are convened, feasted and driven out. It is a very expensive ceremony as a black ox, goat or sheep, with a black pig and a black chicken have to be killed. The ceremony takes place at night.

Hoshowen was a junior clerk at my office. He was a stocky and quiet young boy but sometimes rather truculent. When he was a child, his father had been ambushed by Tibetan robbers and cut up into small pieces. He lived with his widowed mother and an uncle on his father's side at a house about one li from our village on the road to Lashiba. My cook doted on him and adopted him legally as his son and heir. The boy became a victim of one of these foolish marriage arrangements which were common in Likiang, and had to marry the girl to whom he had been engaged immediately after his birth. At that time he was but a few months old while she was already fifteen or sixteen; so that at the time of their marriage, he was a boy of twenty-two and she was a ripe woman of thirty-eight and old enough to be his mother. She was, however, a good and hard-working woman and looked after him and her mother-in-law well enough. Unfortunately for her, both Hoshowen and her mother-in-law hated her. It appeared that the older woman had found consolation in her widowhood in the person of a man in the neighbourhood. The daughter-in-law was wise to this and despised her for it, and there were constant quarrels at that unhappy house which sometimes ended in fights between the two enraged women. Egged on by his mother, Hoshowen also began beating the poor woman. The climax came one day when the mother, in tears, told her son that she had been gravely insulted by her daughter-in-law that morning and nothing short of a good beating of the culprit could restore her face and honour. There must have been a terrible and degrading scene when the husband and his mother together pounced on the defenceless woman. They left her afterwards in the kitchen, bruised and whimpering, and retired to bed as it was already nightfall.

At midnight the poor woman, crushed by humiliation and despair, made a fire in the kitchen and burned her *pukai* (quilt) and trousseau. Then she dressed herself in her best garments as a married woman of good family, touched up her swollen face and lips, prepared a noose and then hanged herself in the drawing-room. No one heard any noise or knew anything until morning. They found her with her face purple and choking horribly. She was still alive but never regained consciousness and died soon afterwards. Then a still greater tragedy was revealed: she was gone about three or four months with child. The whole house became accursed and unclean. Lamas were hurriedly called and, after a short service, the coffin was escorted to a meadow outside the village. There it was placed on a pyre, and after another short service by the assembled lamas a torch was applied.[①]

The next act of the drama opened again at Hoshowen's house in the evening. The *dtombas* had been called, black

---

① The bodies of suicide, of women who died in childbirth and those who died a violent death, were alwayscremated by the Nakhi. This was a survival of their ancient custom. Burials were only introduced after the adoption of Chinese civilization.

animals prepared and tables and benches arranged for the usual funeral banquet. The lamas were sitting in the rooms on the first floor, intoning their litanies to the accompaniment of prayer-bells and small trumpets. Their butter lamps gleamed brightly. We went upstairs to watch their services. Everyone soon noticed that something was afoot in the adjoining rooms. There were loud raps, like pistol shots, coming from cupboards, wails and beams. Tables and benches crackled and moved very slightly over the floor. Everybody fled downstairs. I remained, fascinated as I always was by such phenomena.

The *dtombas* then started beating their drums, and as I did not want to miss the purification ceremony which was new to me, I went down to watch them. It was already ten o'clock and the moon was bright.

The stillness was uncanny as the dtombas started calling up the demons of uncleanness and calamity. Their likenesses had been stuck into a mound in the centre of the courtyard. They were dreadful, leering creatures, some headless, all with snake bodies — real devils this time. The black animals had been killed and there was blood spilled and smeared everywhere. The *dtombas* gyrated slowly to the measured clangs of ndselers. They were in a trance and there was something inhuman and mechanical in their mathematically precise movements. They looked like walking corpses with their pale faces and sightless eyes which had turned inwards. Their conjurations this time were different — they sounded insistent, potent, sinister. There was an atmosphere of unbearable expectancy and malignity. Almost palpably the forces of evil were filling the courtyard. People shivered and huddled closer to each other. It became cold and even the moon seemed to lose its brilliance.

The tables and benches, prepared for the feast, began to tremble and move. My neighbours watched them, frozen in silent horror. Suddenly Hoshowen's uncle was seized. He twisted and struggled on the ground, foaming at the mouth. People rushed to him, trying to hold him, but he shook them off like flies. His eyes were bulging out. A loud and strange voice came out of his convulsed throat. He turned to Hoshowen and his sister-in-law and shouted imprecations in that strange, unearthly voice. Again the people rushed at him trying to stop him and filling his mouth with leaves and anything within reach. Half choked, he subsided. The neighbours, with eyes of terror, fled and I was rushed home. Hoshowen fainted. We did not see the end of the Chownaggv ceremony. No one stayed for the funeral feast. Next day I was told that the uncle had been possessed by his brother, Hoshowen's father, who spoke in a direct voice, using his brother's larynx. He cursed his wife and his son for the poor woman's death. He said he would avenge her and that their punishment would come soon.

CHAPTER XIII

MARRIAGES

*M*ARRIAGES in Likiang, whether happy or unhappy, were always gay and colourful affairs. But however sumptuous they were in town, they could never be compared with even the poor weddings in villages. In the countryside there was more space and more leisure. Provisions, augmented by the gifts from neighbours and friends, were more plentiful, and therefore endless meals could be improvised without a thought of the heavy catering bills. The guests from distant hamlets could stay for days as, unlike in town, there was plenty of accommodation, if not at the bridegroom's house then at his neighbours'. In town a marriage was a minor and impersonal event, confined to a short stretch of the street, whilst in the village it was an affair of great importance, in which every family was intimately interested and concerned. It was anticipated with eagerness and the preparations were made months in advance. It was a great social event which renewed and strengthened the ties of affection with other villages and it provided an opportunity of seeing old friends, separated by long distances. I went dutifully to the weddings in town but must confess that my particular predilection was for country marriages. The further the village and the more primitive the people, the more pleasurable was my anticipation.

The marriage proceedings in town began a couple of weeks before the actual ceremony. Sitting at Madame Lee's bar I could always watch the little procession of the 'sending the wine ceremony'. The bride's family were officially given the date and hour of their daughter's marriage by the representatives of the groom's family. About ten matrons, splendidly attired in new black mitres, silk Lunics tied at the waist by sashes, and silk trousers tied up tightly at the ankles, and wearing embroidered slippers with upturned toes, proceeded in a military formation, four abreast through the street, looking neither to the right nor to the left. They were followed by about ten *pangchinmei*, similarly dressed but with their strange black Chinese caps with red buttons and their hair arranged in long queues. The leading lady carried a burnished brass pot of wine, decorated with pieces of red paper on which felicitous Chinese characters had been written. Another carried, on a copper tray, a pair of jade bangles. Others carried on their trays a comb, a bottle of perfume, a tooth-brush, a box of powder, and so on. Thus each matron and *pangchinmei* carried one or another article of toilette on a separate tray. They marched with great dignity and in silence through the streets, announcing to passers-by the approach of the happy day.

Before the marriage, the dowry was sent in procession to the bridegroom's house. It consisted of furniture, bedding and kitchen utensils of burnished copper and brass. The men carried the heavy pieces on bamboo poles and the women carried the rest in their baskets. There were wardrobes, tables and chairs, a pair of brass spittoons, a clock, two heavy quilts with embroidered silk covers, one representing a dragon for the bridegroom and the other with a phoenix for the bride. Then followed the utensils—copper buckets, basins, *houkous*, samovars, dippers, jugs and pans. The long procession was concluded with a series of heavy wooden chests with four legs, painted pale red; fastened by heavy, beautifully chased padlocks, they contained the couple's clothing for all occasions.

On the auspicious day the guests could be seen streaming towards the bridegroom's house. The men, old and young, dressed in their best, sauntered Singly or in small groups. But the women and girls always marched in military formations, platoon size, the matrons walking ahead and the *pangchinmei* bringing up the rear. Again each carried a copper tray with a gift prominently displayed in the centre, although it might be only a small red packet containing a couple of silver dollars.

On arrival at the house, each guest was courteously received by the bridegroom, dressed as a Chinese gentleman in dark Blue silk gown and black silk *makwa* (jacket), wearing a Chinese cap or European hat, with a huge red paper rose pinned to his breast. Immediately each guest proceeded inside to a table, usually in the corner, where he handed his present to a man who kept a special register of red paper. If it was cash, the amount and name of the donor was carefully recorded. If it was a measure of rice with four cones of brown sugar, which was the usual gift among the villagers, the rice was weighed and sugar appraised for its size, and again a record made with the name, sex and village of the donor. Afterwards the guest was handed a cup of tea by the bridegroom or his father and was free to mix and talk with other guests. The ladies usually joined the bridegroom's mother in an adjoining room. Then everyone waited for the arrival of the bride, who had to reach the bridegroom's house at the time determined by an astrologer. She must never be late, but as there were no reliable clocks either in town or in the country, she usually appeared much too early.

The bride arrived in a palanquin carried by two Minkia men. She was dressed always in a pink silk dress, old Chinese style, with a complicated headdress of false pearl beads, pompons, mythological birds and all. All this finery was usually rented, along with the palanquin, from one or other of the marriage and funeral shops in town. Arriving early she had to wait in her palanquin, sometimes for an hour or two, before the auspicious hour and minute came. Whilst waiting she had to simulate the utmost modesty and she usually buried her face in a red silk handkerchief. At last the time arrived and she was extracted by two bridesmaids and led to the gate. Firecrackers were let off. She jumped over the fire lit at the threshold to join the bridegroom. Rice was thrown over them and then, accompanied by a bevy of *pangchinmei*, she was rushed into the decorated bridal chamber where she remained during most of the feast that followed. There was seldom any special wedding ceremony. The very fact of her entering the bridegroom's house, for all the world to see, was a sufficient guarantee that she was the man's lawful wife.

Tables and benches by the dozen, mostly borrowed from neighbours, had already been laid out with the traditional marriage fare, with chopsticks and cups for wine. The guests needed no prompting and in a moment everybody was sitting and eating. Women sat with women and men with men. From time to time the bridegroom and bride came up to each table. An usher accompanied them with a tray with the cups of wine. They bowed to the guests, who rose and emptied the proffered cups, and with another bow they were off to the next table. By unwritten custom the guests did not tarry over their meal. As soon as they had finished their last dish of rice, they rose; the tables were hurriedly cleaned and rearranged, and another horde of visitors took their place. This eating in relay continued for hours. Neither did the guests, who had had their meal, tarry at the house. They promptly returned home. Such was the usual run of marriage festivities in the city.

One of the finest wedding parties in the countryside I ever attended was that of my good friend Wuhan. I had waited years for this happy event, and I was thrilled when one day his mother told me that, at last, she had paid the last installment on the purchase price of his wife and the couple could now be united in wedlock. I knew that this marriage party would be extremely joyous because of the unique feature of the forthcoming union. Wuhan already knew and loved his future wife and she loved him. As I have already explained, such a felicitous occurrence in the Nakhi marriage system was extremely rare. I knew also that Wuhan was a well-to-do and generous boy, beloved by his friends and relatives, and that he would see to it that his wedding would not be easily forgotten for the lavishness of his hospitality. Indeed his list of the invited was something to see. Even Madame Lee and her husband were included in the list, although there was doubt that this busy and important woman would be free to come. Every member of my household received the red invitation card, including the cook, and members of my office staff. There were long consultations about the amount of cash each was to send as a gift, what to wear and how to arrange the attendance at the feast without totally deserting the house.

The prospect of staying at Wuhan's village for two or three days and of meeting old friends and making new connections was very attractive. The villagers in that district had accepted me as one of their own and I knew I would be treated with easy familiarity and affection. I had warned Wuhan long ago that I wanted no special concessions or comforts and always wanted to be treated as one of his Nakhi friends. I told him that, like the others, I would bring my own bedding. He asked me to come early on the eve of the wedding day and sent a mule to fetch my baggage. As it was considered extremely elegant in Likiang for a bridegroom to be attired in Western garb for the wedding ceremony, I lent Wuhan one of my best suits, a shirt and a necktie. He was much taller than I was, but it did not make much difference in the village where the substance of the thing was of more importance than its fit.

Almost all the days in Likiang were glorious days. It was the land of the spring eternal, but the day I started on my walk to Wuhan's wedding seemed to be even more brilliant than usual. The beauty of this paradisical valley was never static or stale. It was renewed every day and something fresh and marvellous was added to it. The Snow Mountain was not a dead and stereotyped agglomeration of crags, ice and snow; it was a living goddess with her own way of life and moods. It never remained the same for more than a few minutes. It veiled and unveiled itself, trailed the bands of white vapour around its base or shot a white plume of snow into the azure sky. Its crown, in the form of a vast, opened fan, shot out the rays of gold and silver. The gurgling of rushing streams mingled with the song of larks and cries of herons. Flowers changed their colours and variety with each day and always the air was heavy with fragrance. Everything seemed to scintillate and sparkle in this wondrous valley; nature visibly breathed and moved and smiled. Every walk outside the town was an excitement and a revelation: there was intoxication in the warm breeze and a hint of dancing in the undulation of green mountains, the streams twisting and bouncing and birds and butterflies flitting in the air. The people too smiled, laughed and sang with the fullness of their joy and happiness in this secret paradise.

Wuhan's home had been transformed into a fairy palace. Gone were the stables and barns and the old courtyard. Instead there was a series of cool and elegant rooms decorated with carved screens and rich Tibetan rugs. The wide benches along the walls were also covered with rugs. A wide striped awning was spread over the courtyard and the floor was a soft carpet of fresh pine needles. All the ugly comers and crevices were smothered with pine branches and garlands of wild flowers. There were coloured paper streamers under the awning and a big fluttering ball of blown glass hung in the centre. A temporary kitchen was constructed in a shack outside the back wall and the women were already busy cooking for the morrow's celebrations.

The day before the wedding is spent by the bridegroom with his friends. This is his last opportunity to enjoy the freedom of a single man's life and to be alone with the companions of his carefree youth. Tomorrow he will be a married man, with new interests and responsibilities. He will see his schoolmates less frequently, unless he remains at school, and their relations will be more formal. We slept upstairs where the room had been cleared of its stores of grain and provisions.

In the morning the flood gates opened and the people streamed into the house. There were old gentlemen with long white beards, richly dressed women, women in their ordinary blue tunics, small boys and girls, *pangchinmei* and young men. Some came walking and some arrived on mules or horses. Gifts of money poured from men, but women's presents were, for most part, measures of rice or wheat, sugar cones, jars of white wine, eggs, fowl, joints of pork and cakes of yak butter.

The bride was brought by palanquin at about two o'clock in the afternoon. Firecrackers were let off, she duly jumped over the fire, rice was thrown and the feasting began at once. The first to sit down at the tables were the old gentlemen. By all the rules of etiquette I should have joined them, but I had told Wuhan before that I did not want to sit with them. Eating with them would have been an honour, but I knew from experience how ceremonious such gentlemen were. They talked little and in measured and calculated tones; there was much fuss about the procedure of eating and drinking — who should raise the cup first, how much to sip and what to eat first. All questions and answers had to be very formal and dignified. What I wanted were not the ceremonies or honour but the informality and hilarity of a congenial company. So I waited until the eiders had been fed and then took my seat with Wuhan's friends and relatives. We had a glorious time, eating, drinking and joking, and calling many times the groom and bride to drink ceremoniously with us. Wuhan's beaming mother glided between the tables and had a lovely smile and a kind word for every guest. Afterwards we sat in one of the rooms sipping tea. Unfortunately an uncle of Wuhan's on his mother's side came in. He was an old scamp and his nickname was Shebaba (Father of Obscenities). He was totally drunk and accosted all and sundry with comments of incredible indecency. There was an uproar among the old gentlemen and many women rushed, screaming and laughing, out of the house. Amidst shrieks and laughter, Wuhan and his cousin Wuyaoli set on the old man, trying to lead him away, until at last he collapsed in a corner and was carried out to sleep off his spirits in a hayloft.

The crowd became less dense when the neighbours returned to their homes for a rest. After sunset we had another meal. As darkness fell, the tables were all put together, forming two very long parallel tables with benches on each side and lit by pressure lanterns. After a long wait the old gentlemen returned and took their seats round one table and the women seated themselves at another. Wuhan sat at the head of the table, cups were filled with wine, the old gentlemen toasted him and ate the sweets and fruits. Soon they all rose to go. Then I and other friends were asked to sit at one of the tables. Small boys wriggled in beside us, while the other table was taken over by the *pangchinmei* and small girls. There was a unanimous cry that the bride should join her husband. After a pretended resistance, she appeared from her chamber and sat by Wuhan. Then a great inquisition started which I can only call a torture by spirits. Every friend challenged Wuhan to drink with him. Tiffs he could only avoid by a superior knowledge of the famous drinking games which came to the Nakhi from China. The loser had to empty his cup as a forfeit, but poor Wuhan was none too clever at them, and he had to empty many a cup, particularly as the small boys proved to be very adept challengers. Meanwhile, as was the custom, unbelievable indecencies were shouted at the newly weds which they had to bear in good burnout.

Soon the house began to empty. A great bonfire had been constructed outside in the meadow, and the girls, their cheeks aflame with wine, had already started dancing and soon the boys joined them. The dance was like a conga. The boy put his hands on the leading *pangchinmei's* shoulders, another girl put her hands on the boy's and so on until a long serpent of bodies slowly undulated round the fire to the tune of rhythmical singing. They walked slowly and made a side step at regular intervals. There were no musical instruments and the singing was improvised. A boy or girl would start some funny story and everybody had to continue in turn. It was interrupted from time to time by a refrain 'How pitiful that was!' because the narrative related imaginary dangers which continually beset the hero or heroine of the ballad. On and on they went, shuffling through the night without stopping, a dancer falling out from time to time for a short rest and drink of cold water without disrupting the dance. It became sheer hypnotism, this monotonous marching and the throbbing waves of sound. Beyond the pleasure they clearly derived from the dance, there was another, subtler meaning to it which showed the good manners and delicacy of the Nakhi. These dancers, about a hundred of them, came from distant villages. They knew very well that all available accommodation in the bridegroom's and neighbours' houses was overtaxed. They had nowhere to sleep, but to have made this obvious by loitering in

The author's frienf Wuhan with his first-born son, old mother and wife — all formally dressed.

the house, sitting on the benches round the tables or dozing off in corners would have deeply embarrassed the bridegroom's family; and in honour bound Wuhan would have had to try to find some place for them to sleep. The dance, tiring though it was, thus provided the fiction that they were not tired at all and preferred to spend the night on their feet. Indeed, the dance stopped only at dawn.

The privileged guests, myself included, were concentrated on the first floor and in a few rooms downstairs. We spread our *pukais* and rugs on the floor, undressed, and all slept together in closely packed rows. The Nakhi always slept naked, whether it was warm or not, but some of the boys stayed up all night playing mahjong or poker, and with the singing and laughter outside and the click of mahjong pieces there was not much opportunity for sleep.

A year or so after this happy wedding, when Wuhan already had a lusty little son in his arms, I had to go to my Copper Mining Co-operative on the Yangtze River, run by my friend Hoyei. I liked the visits there but I always dreaded the precipices that I had to pass on the way. The mine was ninety *li* (thirty miles) from Likiang and it was a long day's journey. As almost everywhere in Likiang district, the trail was one continuous panorama of mountain beauty and grandeur. After sixty *li* of comparatively level marching, we came to a point from which the great river became visible. There she flowed, like a liquid emerald, in the abyss that made my head reel. Like a green dragon she twisted, turned and foamed in gorges that staggered imagination. The trail dropped straight down, at least forty-five degrees, and down we went with our struggling horses. It was more a delayed fall than a regular descent. So steep was the path in some places that I had to break my descent by clinging to wayside trees. It was wonderful to see how our horses took it. Any moment I expected one of them to collapse with broken legs during the hours it took to negotiate this dangerous stretch. Then my real terrors began. A hanging bridge over a roaring stream a hundred feet below had to be crossed, after which the path ran along the wall of a sheer cliff with a fall of a thousand feet on the other side. Although I was led by Hoyei I suffered from nausea and my legs felt like jelly.

The village where the mine was located was perched on a small shelf over the roaring river; up to it narrow steps were cut in the rock, but there were no railings or protection at all from a bone-breaking fall. After lunch I was persuaded to visit a new copper mine they had opened somewhere along the river. They said the trip was quite safe and I agreed to go. The path led along a narrow shelf two thousand feet above the river. Cajoled and supported by Hoyei and his friends I somehow walked a mile or so. At one spot the rock shelf had collapsed and the path crossed the gap on the trunks of the trees driven into the face of the cliff. I could see through the crevices the river foaming far beneath my very feet. Then the path abruptly ended on a tiny platform jutting over the river. I became so giddy that I should have fallen off over the precipice had not my friends seized me in time. I collapsed, unable to go forward or backward, and I still do not remember clearly how I was dragged, or carried, back to the village.

The inhabitants of the village were the mountain Nakhi — simple and hospitable folk mostly clad in skin garments. They were quite poor as there was little good

The Yangtze River at the Copper Mining Co-operative.

soil around. Only down below, where the hissing river made a turn, was there a narrow lunette of green fields and groves of *mitou* – Likiang oranges—hanging like yellow lanterns on tall, dark trees. This type of orange, or perhaps it was tangerine, was an outstanding fruit of Likiang. It was very large, like a medium-size grape-fruit, with a puffy, pimply, and easily detachable skin. It was very juicy and had a very pleasant taste, quite unlike any other orange or tangerine.

Many people came to see me at the Copper Mining Co-operative and, quite unexpectedly, I was handed an invitation to a wedding feast the same evening. I was very glad to accept as I was assured that many strange tribes would attend. The Nakhi customs here were rather different from Likiang and, I thought, it would be interesting to see them.

The bridegroom's house was somewhere by the river and it was quite dark when, *mingtzes* in hand, we descended to the river through the hedges of giant *Euphorbias candelabra*. There was another terror in store for me. For at least a thousand yards we had to jump from boulder to boulder, over the dark waters rushing and swirling between. I was quite exhausted when we reached the scene of festivity. The house was on a ledge, just above the river, and the bonfires, lighted on the bank, were reflected in the racing waters. There were crowds of men and women inside and outside as we arrived. The youths, in blue turbans and clad in skin jackets and pants, played on flutes and *houloussehs*—a kind of bagless bagpipe made of bamboo stems with gourds for resonance.

I was heartily welcomed by the family, but this time I had to sit down to the feast together with the old men.

Fortunately it was a short meal. Afterwards Hoyei came up to me with the bridegroom.

'There are important guests here tonight,' Hoyei said, 'and we want you to meet them.' I followed them into an upper room. A very dignified lady in a blue skirt and crimson jacket sat at the table with her husband, an oldish man with a long moustache. She must be a Noble Lolo, I thought.

'Please meet the baroness and her husband,' Hoyei was saying. She rose, smiled and pointed to a place next to her.

'We are from the Black Lissu,' she said, 'and this is my husband.' I bowed.

'We live at the castle on top of that mountain across Yibi (the Yangtze),' she said, pointing. 'Lately we have had much trouble. Those dogs, the wild Lolos, have attacked us and burned three of my people's houses. Luckily we beat them off. I wanted to bring my sons and daughters here today but they cannot be spared. They are up at the castle defending it; she continued in a conversational tone. I sat down. She offered me a bowl of white wine and indicated the dishes of food of which I pretended to eat a little. She was very good-looking for her age which must have been forty-eight or flay. She wore a high silver collar with a clasp and long silver earrings terminating with hollow silver bubbles in the shape of eggs. Her husband's face was quite flushed from drinking and he looked very sleepy. Glancing round the room, I noticed several rifles stacked in the corner.

'These are our arms,' the baroness said. 'We must always have them handy.' Of course she was right. Only then I realized that the village we were in was just opposite the infamous Siaoliangshan where the outlaw

Lolos roamed, plundering and burning: but the Black Lissu were their brothers in spirit and quite a match for them. I wondered how it happened that the bridegroom's family were such good friends with this noble family: arms and opium running, I conjectured, as it was scarcely possible to raise such a question. The Black Lissu wanted arms just as badly as the Black Lolos, and they had the opium which the Chinese wanted. Fair exchange is no robbery, and it was on that principle, I was sure, that the intimate friendship with this dangerous couple was based.

The courtyard, which was very small, was just below the room.

'Let us go and watch the dancing,' said the baroness. I followed her. The snake-like file of youths and women was already undulating around the fire. There was no singing here but dance music provided by a dozen or so of the mountain boys playing on flutes and *houloussehs*. The music was soft and lilting and in no way different, in its rhythm, from a foxtrot.

'Let us dance!' decreed the baroness.

'I can follow the music, but I am not sure about the steps,' I protested.

'Never mind. I will show you,' she said, joining the dancers. I followed her with my hands on her shoulders.

'Ouch, you stepped on my toe!' she cried when I made a wrong step; and I apologized.

'Disgraceful,' she murmured. 'Look at that woman fondling that boy. She could be his grandmother,' she added, indicating with her head an elderly woman who was practically hanging on the neck of a handsome mountain boy dressed in skins. The people at this village were certainly uninhibited. Romance was rampant; and girls were dancing as if in a trance, clasping their boy friends around the waist and looking at them with melting eyes as if they were little gods. There was a blast of flutes, pipes and *houloussehs* and the boys rushed into the middle of the courtyard playing their instruments and executing a sort of Cossack dance, throwing their sandalled feet in the air. Then there was another dance which was exactly like the Big Apple, and like little furies the girls jumped on to the boys and were whirled by them until exhausted. It was already very late and everybody was getting drunk. I bowed to the baroness, who pressed me to visit them across the river where they were returning on the following day.

In the morning we went to see them off. Three rafts waited for them. Each raft consisted of twenty or thirty inflated pig-skins, held together by a flimsy bamboo frame. The rafts had been brought as far up the river as was possible. The baroness and her husband lay down on one raft and their suite occupied the others. The naked men, swimming in the water and holding the raft with one hand, helped to direct its course. The current was terrific, and the rafts twisted and bobbed up and down but soon they touched the other bank at the intended spot. Horses and retainers awaited the party there and they started crawling up the barren side of the mountain towards the forest and their castle.

Such were the marriages in Likiang and round about. For a girl who did not love her husband it was the end of her golden days when, as a *pangchinmei*, she roamed freely with her friends, boys and girls, dancing and romancing. In Likiang no one really objected to romances between a Nakhi girl and boy, but the people were roused if the romance was with a stranger. The motto was 'The Nakhi girls for the Nakhi boys and nobody else', and everyone was free within the framework of the tribe. A Minkia or

Chinese who tried to flirt with a Nakhi girl went in danger of his life, and as a matter of fact many were killed by the jealous Nakhi men. I remember a young Chinese, a refugee from the Japanese, who came to Likiang on business. Attracted by the apparent ease with which *pangchinmei* mixed with men, he started to court a pretty Nakhi girl. Soon afterwards, in broad daylight, he was ambushed by three Nakhi who concealed their faces with handkerchiefs. They shot him in the cheek and said, 'This is the first warning. Next time it will be in the heart.' The man left Likiang in a hurry.

When a girl becomes a matron, at once her long queue is cut off and she must always wear the black mitre of the married woman. She must sleep at a side room on the ground floor and is not permitted to run around with her former friends. The husband sleeps, almost as a rule, in the drawing-room. During the day his bed, adorned with rugs, serves as a day couch. Quite unlike China and other countries, there are no double beds and husband and wife are not supposed to sleep together throughout the night: if a neighbour found out that they did, they would be disgraced in the village. Even the *pukais* (quilts) are always made of single size and never double. This restriction does not apply to friends. Male friends, visiting overnight, always sleep together with the host, two or three in the same bed, and if their number is large, they are distributed in twos and threes in other available beds. Women do the same with their visiting girl friends. They all sleep totally naked and the room is heated to an appalling degree by blazing braziers. It is a lucky and much-valued guest who, as a special honour, is asked to share a bed with the grandfather of the house.

CHAPTER XIV

SOME LIKIANG FESTIVALS

ON the thirteenth day of the third moon, that is to say at about the end of March or beginning of April, there was a very lively and hilarious festival specially for women who were barren or had a desire to produce more children. It seemed to me that the men of Likiang were more than sympathetic to this worthy aim and showed a much greater interest in these festivities than did the women. The high point of the festival was a whole day pilgrimage to the peak, called Ghughlangyu, some six miles east of the city, where there was a small temple, worship at which, it was alleged, produced the desired results. It was best to reach the peak just before sunrise to enjoy the sight of the first rays of the sun striking the peak and Mount Satseto's glorious crown of ice.

On the eve of the festival all women and *pangchinmei* were very busy cooking, baking and burnishing their houkous and samovars. Men were excited, brushing their mules and horses and trimming their saddles, and large supplies of wine were collected. The pilgrimage began shortly after two o'clock in the morning. My friends always called to pick me up, armed with torchlights and *mingtzes*, as the moon, at this phase, was visible only till four o'clock. Once outside the town, the spectacle was unbelievable in its grandeur and beauty. Endless strings of flickering lights moved across the plain, converging at the foot of the dark and silent peak. Like a fiery dragon, composed of a myriad of little flames, they climbed and twisted along the face of the mountain. Lights were reflected in streams and canals, and merged with the reflection of the still bright moon. Each woman carried a blazing *houkou*, sparks and flames issuing from the chimney. It looked as if hundreds of small locomotives were running through the fields. By the time we reached the foot of the mountain there were hundreds of people there, talking and laughing. Tents were being erected on the meadows and in the woods, rugs spread and the *houkous* hissed, emitting a delicious smell of food, while a great procession climbed upwards with *mingtzes* and torches to light the path.

The climb was steep and we were quite exhausted by the time we reached the top. It was icy cold at this high altitude; there was hoar frost on the grass and shrubs and the water in the pools was frozen solid. The east glowed orange and gold and the Snow Mountain sparkled in the rays of the sun which we could not yet see. At last the rays struck us and rocks started to crack with a musical sound. We entered the small temple which was choked with people. The women prostrated themselves before the goddess Niangniang, the giver of children, and hastily put the bunches of incense and candles before the image. A small priapic god, golden and naked, was touched and kissed by the pious women who so ardently desired children. There he stood in front of the goddess, like a little boy ready to urinate, passing this little god, the girls giggled and blushed, averting their faces. Their turn had not yet arrived for such ceremonies.

It was not possible to remain long on the small platform of the peak owing to pressing crowds of new arrivals: so we started descending slowly. As we turned a corner there was a burst of music and singing from an ascending procession of Minkia women and maidens. The girls wore gaily embroidered jackets without sleeves: bright silk kerchiefs were tied around their heads, on which they wore sparkling diadems of semi-precious stones. The men with them played on flutes and cymbals and they all sang '*Nanmu Amitabha*' as they were slowly climbing upwards, holding candles and incense sticks in one hand.

Below it was like a scene from a great Oriental ballet. Beautifully dressed men and women sat on sparkling rugs around the shining *houkous*. There were tents of many colours, with richly caparisoned mules tied to trees. Groups of girls and boys promenaded in the woods gathering flowers. Many Minkia boys had red sashes across their shoulders and promenaded like peacocks whilst girls giggled and winked at them. A red sash across a young Minkia's shoulder at a festival proclaims the fact that he is still single and ready to be courted by a desirable girl. The handsome ones were soon surrounded by admiring girls who fluttered and buzzed like bees around a flower. One of them was at last captured by a pretty and determined girl, who led him away from the envious glances of her friends. From now on the lucky fellow had to pay attention to her only and a proper engagement ceremony might follow later.

The Fertility Festival continued till noon and then the tired and happy people filed slowly Back to the town or villages.

It was not far from this Ghughlangyu peak that Madame Lee had her tomb. All her family on her husband's side was buried there. She and her husband, already in the fullness of their years, expected serenely and in confidence to join the dear departed in the not too distant future. All the tombs had been recently rebuilt and renovated, and the time approached for a yearly sacrifice to the dead. As we were now old friends, I was invited to share in this joyous ceremony.

The tombs, some fifteen of them, were situated on a meadow in the foothills. It was a peaceful and beautiful spot. There were tall, shady trees and flowering shrubs. A brook gurgled in the ravine below, and the view down on to Likiang and the plain was magnificent. Each tomb was faced with stone and the front was decorated with a niche containing the names of the husband and wife, their ages and the dates of their death. A separate plot was earmarked for the future grave of Madame Lee and her husband. I had come in advance with Mr. Lee, and had enjoyed a walk in the hills. Later Madame Lee appeared with other women and her grand-children. They brought *houkous* as well as provisions, and when the food was cooked, it was arranged in bowls on a large tray with cups of wine. The old couple placed it on a ledge before the niche of Mr. Lee's parents and incense sticks were lighted. Then the couple prostrated themselves before the tomb several times, inviting the departed to partake of the proffered food and wine. The procedure was repeated before each tomb and by the other members of the family in their turn,

Mme. lee's husband and grandson in front of an aneestral tomb.

so that the ceremony took a long time. Finally the food was spread on the ground, and we all gathered round to enjoy what became quite a gay picnic.

There was nothing lugubrious about the proceedings and there was no sorrow or sadness. It was a joyous and serene reunion with the departed who, it was firmly believed, were present in the spirit. Had they appeared at this moment there would have been no consternation and no terror. They were expected and welcomed, whether they were invisible or visible, at this joint feast at which both worlds participated. Both were joined by love and affection and all knew that they would be reunited when earthly nature had taken its course.

After the meal the old couple went again, with their family, to prostrate themselves before the graves, expressing thanks to the ancestors for their attendance at the feast. They returned well satisfied and happy. They had had a full and rich life and they contemplated with pride their last home where they would sleep for ever amidst the beauty of the mountains and forests, perhaps listening to the eternal rustle of the pines and singing of the birds.

July, which was the critical month before the rainy season, had several festivals. With the rice already planted, the people did not have much to do and the evenings were devoted by the younger set to dancing and to flying the *kounmingtengs* — the lighted balloons. During the clay one could see the young men and *pangchinmei* pasting together the oiled sheets of rough paper to form the structure of a balloon. These balloons were then dried in the sun and were ready for use in the evening. Crowds gathered to watch. A bunch of burning *mingtzes* was tied underneath; the balloon swelled and quickly rose into the air to the shouts of excited spectators. The higher it rose the more good luck it promised to its owner. Some went up very high indeed and floated in the sky like red stars for several minutes. At the end they burst into flames and fell, sometimes causing fires by setting light to straw in unwatched farmhouses. Sometimes there were as many as twenty of these balloons floating through the dark sky. Balloon flying lasted for about a couple of weeks and it was great fun.

Then there was the Buddhistic festival of All Souls' Day, when, as in Japan, tiny boats were constructed of paper, small candles were lit in them and they were floated down the swift Likiang River.

But the greatest festival in July was the *Houpaochi* or Jumping through the Fire. Every household constructed a pyramid, two or three feet high, of wood splinters, *mingtzes* and incense sticks all tied together and gaily adorned with flowers. These bundles were placed upright in the middle of the street before each house. The day passed in feasting and drinking; at night a light was applied to each bundle and, as they began to blaze, the young people jumped over them. It was considered to be lucky and I did it myself without any serious ill effects.

This festival was not confined to Likiang valley but was observed as far down as Tali. Its origin was very old. People said it had started with the establishment of the great and powerful Nanchiao Kingdom some time during the Tang dynasty. At that time the whole region between Tali, capital of the kingdom, and Likiang was a series of small Minkia kingdoms. The King of Nanchiao wanted to extend his realm and personal dominion and, being cruel and cunning, hit on a very effective scheme. One day he invited all his brother kings for a conference and a great feast. One of those invited was the King of Erhyuen, a small principality some ninety li north of Tali.

The Queen of Erhyuen was as sensible as she was beautiful and she did all she could to dissuade her husband from attending the feast, as she felt sure that a sinister motive was hidden behind this unusual invitation. However, the king said that he was in honour bound to go. So certain was the beautiful queen that something evil was bound to happen, that she insisted on putting iron bracelets engraved with the king's name on her husband's wrists and ankles.

The King of Nanchiao had a special pavilion constructed and lavishly decorated for the feast. It was said that the woodwork of the pavilion had been fashioned out of particularly inflammable woods. When the visiting kings had been wined under the table by the hospitable King of Nanchiao, the doors were bolted and torches applied to the pavilion. Everybody inside was burnt to cinders and no one could identify the remains of any king except those of the King of Erhyuen. The queen was easily able to identify the bones of her beloved husband by the iron bracelets; so that he was the only king to receive a proper burial. The young queen was inconsolable and shut herself in her palace, but the ruthless King of Nanchiao heard of her great beauty and sent ambassadors to ask for her hand. The more she refused the more insistent did he become. At last she knew that she could not avoid this political marriage, and not wishing to be dragged to the king's court by force, she notified the king that she would be ready for the marriage as soon as she had burned her husband's royal robes, which was her last duty to him, as was the custom of almost all the monarchs in the Orient. Then she had a great pyre prepared on a hill near the city and the robes were spread over it. The torches were applied and, when the fire was at its highest, dressed in all her most beautiful robes of state, the queen jumped into the flames. The heroism and virtue of this beautiful and beloved queen have never been forgotten and the festival was established in her memory even in states which had no direct concern in the tragedy.

CHAPTER XV

MUSIC, ART AND LEISURE AMONG
THE NAKHI

*T*HE New Year celebrations provided the old gentlemen of Likiang with an opportunity to stage several concerts of sacred music in which they were adept. Madame Lee's husband was also a musician in his own right and heartily participated in these highbrow functions. The concerts were a unique institution and were so inspiring and interesting that I never failed to attend them. It was wonderful and extraordinary to hear the music which was played during the heydey of the glorious Han and Tang dynasties, and probably during the time of Confucious himself. This musical tradition was one of the most cherished among the Nakhi and was zealously transmitted from father to son. A well-to-do Nakhi in the city could only be accepted as a real gentleman if he knew this ancient music or was a fully fledged Chinese scholar. When I discovered this noble academic preoccupation of the Nakhi men, I felt a new respect for them. I forgave the Nakhi women for over-indulgence to their menfolk.

They gave them leisure, and at least a part of it did not go to waste. Spoilt they were, these Nakhi men, and many smoked opium to excess, but passing years mellowed them and turned their hearts to the attainment of culture and of the understanding of beautiful things. They had time for thinking and meditation. They had time to observe and drink deeply of the beauty of their marvellous valley and this did not fail to uplift and inspire them. Without being Taoists, they absorbed much of the wisdom of Tao, not through learning perhaps, but intuitively. Their happiness was great and they did their best to express it in the elegant and classical manner of their ancestors who had drunk deeply of Confucian idealism. The old Sage had always taught that music was the greatest attainment of a civilized man: and to music they turned to express the exquisite joy of living and to enhance the serenity of their old age.

A great blow was struck to Chinese civilization with the loss of Confucius's own Book of Music. It was probably destroyed, along with other classics, during the great burning of books undertaken by Chin Shi Hwangti, builder of the Great Wall of China. Yet it is impossible to believe that the tradition of that great music did not survive in some remote places.

The Nakhi were extremely fortunate in having had a long contact with a remarkable man and himself a musician, the great General Chukoliang of the Three Kingdoms period (c. A.D. 221-65). That was shortly after the disintegration of the Han dynasty. That cultured general spent years in and around what is now Likiang and even left, as a memorial, several huge stone drums at Laba (Shihku) only eighty li from Likiang on the Yangtze River. He spared no effort or money to implant

Chinese culture among the tribes, of whom he evidently preferred the bright Nakhi. Tradition says he himself taught them sacred music as he believed firmly in its civilizing influence. He left them a legacy of the musical instruments of that period and the sacred scores, and his able students and their descendants reverently preserved them in all their purity for succeeding generations.

There is nothing improbable in this. Chukoliang was a historical figure and his campaigns in ancient Yunnan are recorded history. That he was a man of outstanding cuhural attainments is also an undisputed fact. If Likiang has remained so little known and isolated, even to the Chinese, up to this day, we can only imagine how perfect the isolation was in those days. There had been invasions and military campaigns in Yunnan, but they affected the inner life of the Nakhi very little. Likiang was not a very great prize of war, being so small, remote and difficult of access. No Chinese general or his soldiers ever wanted to stay an extra day at so barbarous a place, with the bright lights of the capital and untold refinements of the Chinese life tempting them back.

So long as the Nakhi kings accepted the nominal suzerainty of the Chinese Emperor and sent some measure of tribute, they were left alone. Even the great conqueror Kublai Khan, who invaded Yunnan in the thirteenth century, advancing through the Kingdom of Muli with 1,200 chariots, barely glanced at the valley whose Nakhi king had offered his submission in advance. He was much more interested in investing Tall, whose proud Nanchiao king defied him, sitting in his impregnable Tower of Five Glories which accommodated a garrison of 50,000 men.

Thus Likiang has ever remained peaceful and isolated, and could devote itself to the perpetuation of cherished ancient arts. Indeed, it was China that had to sacrifice the purity of her music and drama to the whims of vulgar Mongol and Manchu conquerors. She had even to sacrifice her style of coiffure and dress, such as the long queue for men and the sheath-like dress of women. The conquests did harm to Chinese civilization and culture, and music perhaps suffered most at the hands of the invaders. The present-clay Chinese falsetto singing and the discordant and shallow music of Chinese theatres are no more representative of the ancient classical music of China than modern jazz is representative of classical Greek music. Some esoteric Taoist monasteries have preserved fragments of the classical music and they perform it in their ceremonies and dances, but the instruments and the score they use are far less genuine than those preserved by the Nakhi.

When I was in Likiang sacred concerts were usually held at some rich man's house. At intervals food and drinks were served both to the participants and the guests. The musical sessions were long and arduous but everybody was happy and attentive. The instruments were carefully arranged in a long room, sometimes in the enclosed veranda, and the atmosphere was reverent and definitely religious, with the scent of incense burning in great brass burners. There were the old carved frames on which multi-toned bronze bells were hanging in rows. Another frame had rows of chromatic jade pieces in the form of lunettes. A great and sonorous gong was suspended from a tall stand. There was a long *chin* or the proto-type of the modern piano lying on a long gable. Only very few people knew how to play it. And there were huge standing guitars, smaller *pipas* and several kinds of long and short flutes and pipes.

The old musicians, all formally dressed in long gowns

and *makwas*, took their seats unhurriedly, caressing their long white beards. One man acted as conductor. They peered at the score: a flute wailed and one by one other instruments joined in. Although I love music, I am not, alas, a musician and cannot describe the music that followed in technical terms. It was majestic and inspiring and proceeded in rising and falling cadences. Then, as a climax, the great gong was struck. I have never heard in China such a deep and sonorous gong: the whole house seemed to vibrate with its velvety waves. Then, rising from their chairs, the elders sang a sacred ode in a natural voice and with great reverence and feeling. Then the symphony continued, with notes of unimagined sweetness, falling like a cascade from the jade lunettes, and giving way to a golden shower of sounds from the chromatic bells. The chords from the great *chin* were like diamonds dropped into the golden melody, reinforced by a stopped diapason. Never was there any dissonance or retreat from harmony.

To a Western ear it might have appeared somewhat monotonous, but actually there was no repetition. It was only that the theme was unfolding in rhythmic waves of sound into which new motives were constantly introduced. It was a recital of the cosmic life as it was unfolding in its grandeur, unmarred by the discordant wails and crashes of petty human existence. It was classical, and timeless. It was the music of the gods and of a place where there is serenity, eternal peace and harmony. If it appeared monotonous to the uncomprehending people, it was because their hearts did not reach the right equilibrium and stability. They only understood the music which suited their own condition of struggle and conflict. They wanted to hear the shouts of their ephemeral victories and crashes of their defeats, the wails of their death throes and discordant screeches of their insane carnivals. The majestic rhythm of a universe left them cold. Chaos was nearer their nature and they wanted to hear the sound of explosions even in music. The ancient sages were the true children of nature and immeasurably closer to the Divine. They understood better the nature of melodies and harmonies and to them music was one of the surest means of communion with Heaven and subjugation of the animal in man. Let us hope that this treasure of music in Likiang may be secure from the ravages of the modern age.

It was not in music alone that the men of Likiang were proficient, and some of them devoted their life to painting. Flowers and birds were their favourite subjects and they decorated many ceilings and panels in the elegant homes of the wealthy. They did not paint for money or fame but simply to satisfy their craving for the expression of beauty in pictorial form.

Quite a few Nakhi became Chinese scholars and wrote elegant poetry and essays which were not disdained even in sophisticated China: and even the humble Hoyei of my Copper Mining Co-operative was a painter of talent and a poet. I still treasure a small scroll he painted and inscribed for me.

The concept of Time in Likiang was totally different from that in the West. In Europe, and especially in America, the greater part of Time is devoted to making money, not so much to sustain life in decent conditions as to accumulate more and more comforts and luxuries. The rest of Time, which remains unoccupied, is 'killed' in a manner which has now become routine and rigid. Because of the preoccupation with work and the ritual killing of

Time, there has grown up a comparatively new concept of the man who is so busy that he has no time at all. This idea of tile man who is so busy that he has not a minute to spare has been enthroned as the standard by which all humanity is judged. The normal man is now he who repeats that he is extremely busy and has no time and he is treated with great respect. Men whose time is totally or partially unoccupied are considered abnormal and inefficient and efforts are directed to make them normal, either by making them work or at least by training them to kill whatever Time is free.

This strange attitude to Time in the West is not due to an antagonism to Time itself but to the unreality of the modern world which man has created for himself. With his misdirected energy and his lack of understanding he has made his world so complex and so filled with the trivia of existence that he has lost himself in it, like a Minotaurian labyrinth, and for him it has become the only reality. True reality is thought of as a philosophical abstraction fit only for a few thinkers and not for busy men. As the true reality is the only one that gives man a full satisfaction in Time, the unreal world of activity and pointless rush can only give an illusion of life. Whenever the rush stops, Time proclaims the void, and it is to escape the void that the time must be killed. It is done by highly and systematically organized sport, radio, movies, tourism, clubs and parties — by anything that can conceal the frightening face of Time. The more the reality of life is avoided the more necessary it is to kill Time. But without reality whatever man perceives is nothing but illusion and vexation of spirit.

In the beautiful valley of Likiang, then still untouched by the complexities and hurry of modern life, Time had a different value. It was a gentle friend and a trusted teacher, possessing, there, a magical property which not only I but others had noticed. Instead of being too long it was too short; the days passed like hours and the weeks like days; a year was like a month, and my ten years spent there went by like one.

It was not true that we were so busy that we had no time to perceive all the beauty and goodness that was in that blessed valley. There was time for both. The people in the street interrupted their bargaining to admire a clump of roses or peer for a minute into the clear depths of a stream. Farmers paused in their fields to gaze at the ever-changing face of the Snow Mountain. A flight of cranes was breathlessly watched by the market crowds and the song of birds was commented upon at length by busy Minkia carpenters who leaned back from their saws and axes. The groups of apple-cheeked old men, with flowing beards, laughed and joked like children as they descended the hill, with rods in hand, for a fishing trip. A factory closed for a day or two as the workers suddenly wanted to have a picnic by a lake or on the Snow Mountain. And yet their work was done and done well.

No Nakhi ever wanted to leave the valley if he could help it. Even those who had seen the neon-lit glories of Shanghai, Hongkong and Calcutta always wanted to return to Likiang to live. The same was true of the Tibetans, Lolos and even Minkia. Those who had travelled described vividly their revulsion and horror of the great cities they visited, with their hot, treeless streets, box-like buildings, sordid and foetid slums, and soulless, rapacious people who milled through the streets in vast, drab, grey crowds. In Likiang, where every man and woman was an individual and a person, the very idea of the shuffling, anonymous multitudes of China and India made these independent people shudder. The idea of free people being shut up to work in airless rooms for hours was abhorrent to the Nakhi. Neither for love nor money, they declared, would they ever work in such factories as they had seen in Kunming and Shanghai.

CHAPTER XVI

PROGRESS

*T*HERE were forty-five industrial co-operatives by the summer of 1949. They included wool-spinning, weaving and knitting societies, brassware and copperware societies, a Minkia furniture-making society, a dry-noodle society, a plough-share-casting society, Tibetan leather and boot-making societies, and others. Two spinning and weaving co-operatives were run entirely by women and they were among the best. The chairman of one of them was an elderly woman of gigantic stature. She was illiterate but she watched all financial transactions with an eagle's eye. She bought all the wool herself and the yarn was disposed of under her strict control and supervision. She ruled the members — twelve women and three men — with an iron hand and sometimes beat the men into insensibility for any delinquencies or excessive opium-smoking. But she was just and honest and the members adored her for her ability; moreover, they were making pots of money.

It was easy enough to supervise the co-operatives which were in town, but some were far away in villages or mountains, like the Copper-mining Society by the Yangtze, where I met the Black Lissu baroness, and to these I had to make long expeditions from time to time.

The Ngatze Iron-mining Co-operative was both a curiosity and an experiment. It was the largest and had forty-three members. There were Nakhi, Tibetans, Boa, Miao and Chungchia among the members, and one Chinese. That it survived for a number of years with such a membership was something of a miracle and it was an unusual experiment in multi-racial co-operation. Strangely enough, its members worked in considerable harmony and were consistently friendly towards each other and to me. It was presided over by a very energetic but roguish man named Taichizu — a Nakhi from Wobo, a few steps below Madame Lee's wine-shop in Main Street. He needed careful watching, but I was never able to prove that he was a crook and the members seemed to be content with his management. Perhaps he did a little opium traffic on the side with the Lolos, as Siaoliangshan was not far off, but after all, this was not such a serious crime in these parts. His co-operative was forty miles from Likiang and was not far from my Upper Ngatze Paper-making Society. However, the difference in location of these neighbouring co-operatives was tremendous. Tai's mine was in a trench-like gorge perhaps only 4,000 feet above sea-level, and the Paper Co-operative was floating above it at 14,000 feet. I always combined my visit to the iron mine with one to the paper factory which by direct route was forty-eight miles from Likiang.

The trip to the Iron-mining Co-operative required some preparation. First of all, Tai and all the members there were very poor, and sometimes I thought they did not have a dollar between them. They had no bedding to spare, so I always took my own. Secondly, there was very little to eat there so that pork, vegetables and wine had to be brought from Likiang. It was really a two-day caravan journey, but as there was not a village or a hut between Likiang and Ngatze it had to be covered in one day. This made it a very strenuous trip. I always insisted on our departure from Likiang before dawn, never later than four o'clock, which permitted us, with a stop for lunch, to arrive at the iron mine about five o'clock in [he afternoon. After five it became dark in the valleys and gorges and I was afraid of losing my footing on the path which weaved along a series of precipices.

Sometimes I rode on horseback, but more often I preferred to walk the whole way. Our little caravan consisted of three or four horses, carrying supplies and bedding, and two or three tribesmen from the co-operative, usually Tibetans or Miao who had come to town the previous day with their horses bringing pig-iron. It was a long and tedious walk towards the Snow Mountain, in front of which there was a long and smooth alpine meadow which nature provided as the airport for Likiang and where only the row of white stones to indicate the runway was made by man. Still higher, there was another long plain to cross. It was dotted with low shrubs, and basalt rocks as sharp as razors protruded through the grass and cut the animals' hooves and men's sandals unmercifully. At last the low ridges ahead closed into a spring in a hollow and the traditional resting place for the people and caravans going to and from Likiang. We built a small fire, warmed our *babas* and pre-cooked food, boiled tea and had a pleasant, long rest, taking time over our meal. Then the road passed through a pine forest carpeted with flowers. On one side there was Sepilome — the Cassia gorge — filled with trees which later rose to meet our road. It was mysterious and beautiful beyond words. Here it was called Mbergkvho or the Buffalo Horn defile, and on its left side was a vast cave in which, legend says, lived a *letthisippu* — a ghoul who appeared as a beautiful woman to guileless men, enticing and then devouring them. It was in this gorge that my office boy Hoshowen's father had been chopped to pieces by robbers.

As the road climbed higher and higher the flowers increased in variety and beauty — lilies and dark blue tree asters, clark peonies, irises and ground orchids. At last we emerged on a vast plateau at Ngaba. Before us on the left was the whole Likiang Snow Range, its snow and ice-clad peaks glittering like a string of diamonds. Of these peaks the Gyinanvlv was the loveliest, with her glacier flowing down like a blue veil. Pines studded the great undulating plain, and peeping between them were the incomparable *incarvilias* with their blooms like crimson gloxinias. At 11,000 feet it was quite cold, and in winter Ngaba is covered with snow and the wind is so strong and icy that many poor people have died on the way. The road forked left to Taku, a pretty village on the Yangtze, and then right, where we soon entered a great forest. We began to descend, the forest becoming more and more beautiful. Moss hung like strands of hair from age-old trees; there were bright green clumps of bamboo and all kinds of creepers. It was cool and moist in the green darkness and alive with the sounds of animals; cascades splashed on the road and a distant roar of waterfalls shook the air which was heavy with the fragrance of giant rhododendrons in bloom and the scent of pines and spruces. Through the trees we could see for miles and miles below the torrents tumbling into green valleys and dark gorges, the vast expanse of forests and the emerald meadows on which here and there were the black dots of Lolo dwellings: and above all this floated the purple and white sci tillating snow peaks, remote and inaccessible.

For many hours we crept clown through this enchanted forest and came at last to the village of Ngatze, which was all an earthly paradise should be. It was particularly wonderful in winter months, when after the snow and icy winds of Ngaba — winter at its cruellest — you arrived here in a few hours to find roses smothering the houses, bees buzzing among the flowers and vivid butterflies fluttering everywhere. What a delight it was to pick from the vine or to eat a blood-red tomato, ripened in the warm sun, whilst right in front of you, through a gap in the green mountains, you could see a snowstorm raging between snow peaks. The village was in a green bowl, like a gem encased in a frame of forested mountains.

The road dipped down sharply once we left Ngatze. The deep thunder of a savage torrent somewhere in the deep trench into which we were almost literally falling came nearer, and zigzagging with infinite care we at last reached the mighty stream. Shaking the earth, it rushed, boiled and raged among the great rocks that hindered its path. This was the famous Gyipergyina — the Black and White Water, or Heipaishui in Chinese. Of all the mountain streams in Likiang it was the most powerful and the noisiest. We could see high up its parents — the White Water on the left and the Black Water on the right — combining their fury to give birth to this terrible child. It was still Swollen by melted snows and rains and the roar was so deafening we could not talk to each other. Soon we reached the iron mine and were at home.

In spite of its ferocity I loved the Heipaishui and always looked forward to staying for a few days at the Iron-mining Co-operative. To me this powerful torrent was a living being and I spent hours listening to its thunderous conversation and contemplating its enormous energy and vitality. At night, when all other noises subsided, its thunder seemed to change. No longer continuous and muffled, its separate notes became distinct and I could hear the varied voices, the whispers and hisses, the groans, and even the gaiety all of which it was compounded. I used to watch the Heipaishui playing with the pebbles and stones, hurling them at the rocks; or undermining and shifting by degrees with almost human precision huge boulders the size of small houses, which, with all resistance spent, toppled and crashed screechingly on to the rocks below.

The work at the Mining Co-operative started early in the morning. Some men dug the haematite out of the pits on the hillside, where the ore was very rich and contained, I was told, about 80 per cent of pure iron. Entire hillsides consisted of haematite, but extraction by hand was so primitive that they worked only the richest veins. The ore was brought by baskets to an opening near the stream and there the men, sitting on the ground, broke the stones into small fragments ready for smelting. A great furnace, constructed of stones, bricks and clay, bound with wooden poles on the outside, stood near by. The fragmented ore was dumped into the open top of the furnace, followed by a layer of charcoal, then another layer of ore, and so on until the furnace was full. Finally the top was sealed and the furnace fired. A water-wheel slowly worked giant bellows made out of a huge tree-trunk. After a whole day's burning a small window was opened at the base of the furnace and the blazing stream of molten iron slowly poured out on the ground, solidifying into a thin sheet of primary iron. This was broken into large slabs and dragged aside for weighing, breaking and then loading into another smaller furnace near by, which was worked on the same principle. Soon a small door was opened in the furnace and a man extracted with long iron tongs a blazing lump of iron and deftly put it on the anvil. Immediately a group of assistants joined him, and with heavy hammers they pounded the lump, in a minute or two, into an oblong pig which was thrown aside on the ground to cool. This operation was a monopoly of the Miao and Chungchia, who were considered great specialists at it. These pigs were then weighed and stored for disposal.

Such was the uncomplicated working of this co-operative. Once a week a small caravan of horses took the pig-iron to Likiang, where it was sold to my Ploughshare-casting Co-operative and a few other smithies, the rest going to Hoking, Chienchwang and Hsiakwan, where they cast good kitchen boilers, and made such things as horseshoes and nails, knives and scythes.

The Tibetan and Nakhi members dug the ore and fragmented it. The Boa looked after the making of the charcoal. The Miao and Chungchia beat the iron, and a lone Chinese, named Ahting, was a sort of an errand boy, bringing caravans to Likiang, buying provisions and doing all sorts of odd jobs. He was rather a scamp, and a portion of his income came from a widow at Ngatze village with whom he was living. The Tibetans were from Chungdien, on the other side of the Yangtze, and they were very simple folk, friendly and cheerful. The Boa and Nakhi were from the mountains around and were very primitive, rather suspicious and really wild and willful. But the most primitive and difficult to manage were the

Miao and Chungchia members who lived close by in the valley downstream.

The Miao and Chungchia were very closely related, and there was only a minor difference in their dress or their writing, and therefore I shall refer to them collectively as the Miao. In my opinion, they represented the most perfect example of an outgoing, dying race. Like the division of the Lolos and the Lissu into Black and White, the Miao were divided into the Flowery, Black and White Miao. The Flowery Miao live on the borders of the Yunnan and Kweichow provinces and they get their name from the picturesque and colourful costumes they wear. It may be said that they are more approachable and less introvert than all other Miao. The other Miao are styled White and Black merely because of the colour of their clothes and are certainly the most primitive of all the Miao. The ones near the co-operative were the White Miao, with whom the retreat from the world and other people became almost fetishism at times reaching absurdity. It was not only the presence of a stranger, a foreigner or Chinese in their midst which frightened them, but even the mere news that someone was coming to their village sent them all scampering for cover in the surrounding forests.

When at first I went with Tai to visit their villages close by, there was nobody left in the houses but pigs and dogs. This ridiculous situation only changed much later when I became friendly with the Miao members of the co-operative. They were so shy at first that they scattered whenever I arrived. Then, reassured by Tai and other members, they began at least to remain in their place when I came up to watch them beat the iron. Then I melted the ice by inviting them for a drink after their day's work. This they could not resist, and after a few such occasions we became, at last, quite good friends.

Then we decided one day to go to their villages and they guaranteed that their people would not run away. They went with me holding my hands, like children led by a nanny. I was told by Tai, and then noticed it myself, that if I smiled, everything was all right, but as soon as my face became serious, they were frightened and tended to run away. And so, when dealing with them, I always tried to wear a grin on my face.

We climbed over the cliff on to a broad shelf where their fields lay. There was a curious rock lying in a depression on which a small pagoda, constructed of straw and bark, was standing. It was a Miao shrine. The path dipped into a little valley where the Heipaishui spread, no longer a roaring torrent but a broad and shallow river with every stone and pebble visible in its clear waters. The Miao huts were very low and dark, and their women, in white petticoats, sat inside weaving hempen cloth on primitive looms. In some of the low trees near tile huts, I noticed huge nests, and was wondering what kind of birds built them when suddenly I saw children's heads popping out of them. 'These are our children,' my Miao friends told me; 'they always sleep there at night. We are very poor and have no bedding. At night it is very cold so the children sleep there together for warmth.' Indeed there they were — huddled in the dried leaves with only a rag between them to cover themselves.

The poverty of the Miao was unimaginable. There was nothing in the huts resembling furniture or utensils. There were some vessels made of bark, bamboo or wood but no beds and no bedding. The men themselves were in rags, seminaked, with no protection either for modesty or from cold. Even the older children had no clothing at all; though the girls had a kind of a small triangle to act as a fig-leaf. Most of them had big bellies from eating bulky and indigestible food, and their skin, unlike the glossy and firm skin of the Nakhi and Tibetans, was a pasty grey and felt like an old, crumpled newspaper. But how could one help them? They rejected almost everything which could assist them to improve their lot. I offered them the seeds of various vegetables and corn. No, they said, they would not plant them; they did not eat such things; they did not know how to look after them and they would not grow there anyway. They were not prepared even to give them a trial. They accepted simple medicines gratefully—eye lotion, quinine, sulphur ointment—but even these they used lackadaisically and laid them aside in some dusty corner when improvements did not come at once. They needed money but had almost nothing to sell, except perhaps a chicken or two or the eternal pig. The work at the co-operative helped, but it was not enough. The money was needed not so much to buy food, of which they had just enough, poor though it was, but to buy a wife and arrange a wedding feast. That must be done. The wedding feast was the only time when all these villagers had plenty to eat and plenty to drink. These were the rare and important events when they could glimpse a ray of joy and happiness and forget for a day the unutterable misery of their existence.

Sometimes I brought them gifts. At first I made the mistake of giving them such things as soap or electric torches as I ordinarily gave to the Nakhi and other tribes; these the Miao put in a place of honour and never used them, as if I had given them an ormolu clock or a Sevres statuette. Then I took to bringing them old clothes, a pound or two of salt, cheap cloth, or cones of brown sugar and jars of wine, and for these they were pathetically grateful.

There was nothing the Miao could do. Centuries ago, pressed by the expanding population of China, they had retreated from Kweichow to these wild and empty valleys and gorges where they could hide themselves from their aggressive neighbours. But now they found themselves pressed again: and this was the last frontier. There were no more empty spaces, no further retreat, nowhere to hide.

Even going to Likiang they avoided the people on the road. Huddled in small groups they gazed fearfully at any approaching group of strangers or a caravan and made a long detour to escape meeting them face to face. A harsh look or a loud word sent them scampering in unreasoning panic. Sometimes they called at my house but never stayed long. The way my cook looked at them, and the people coming and going through my office, terrified them.

After two or three days' stay at the Iron-mining Co-operative, I used to ascend to my Paper-making Co-operative at Upper Ngatze. Its manager, my good friend Aiya Aiya, usually came down the night before to fetch me. He was an extremely nice, capable young Nakhi and a very hard worker. To avoid the day's heat, which was unbearable in the fold of these tremendous mountains, we started early in the morning. The Heipaishui was crossed by a stone bridge a little way upstream from the Iron-mining Co-operative. Then the path started climbing sharply along a low ridge running by another stream which was a tributary of the Heipaishui. This country was rather dangerous as it was a sort of no man's land, covered with great forests, and peopled by many comparative newcomers such as the Szechuanese squatters, Tibetans from Chungdien, Miao, White Lolos and displaced Nakhi and Boa.

There were two tea-shops on the way and we rested there. On one occasion Aiya Aiya looked rather anxiously at another table where some tribesmen were sitting. I noticed that he was trying to isolate me from them. I asked him what was the matter. He said that many of the local tribesmen, including the Miao, were adepts in casting evil spells. It was accomplished not by occult methods but by throwing a microscopic pellet of poison called *ndouk*, by a flick of the finger, into the person's cup of tea or wine. Without anything being apparently wrong with him, the man's health steadily declined and he died in a couple of months. I pointed out to Aiya Aiya that I was not a likely subject for such poisoning as I had not clone anything wrong to these people, but he was not persuaded. He said they had a different mentality from ours and often followed strange, irrational fancies, doing many abominable things just for the fun of it.

Further up the mountain we passed a village called Sadowa, populated by Szechuanese squatters who were peaceful farmers by day and, it was alleged, ruthless robbers by night. The climb from this village became more arduous and we entered a vast forest, which enclosed a little village in a hollow, surrounded by a thick fence made of tree branches. It was a leper enclave in which several families of the Szechuanese Chinese and others, afflicted with the dreadful disease, were living. Then, past midday, we made one last effort and climbed, at an incredible angle, through a thick wood, to the small platform on which the Paper-making Co-operative was situated. It was a long, rather low building begrimed with the smoke of wood fires which were burning in it day and night owing to the cold. In front there were three large and deep square stone tubs. Further down there were two huge vats with furnaces underneath and a shallow, stone-lined oblong pool. A small, surprisingly powerful and noisy, ice-cold stream rushed from the top of the mountain, past the building, revolving a wooden wheel connected to a crusher. In a tiny fenced field a few cabbages and turnips grew; a few big pigs and some chickens roamed at large and there were two fierce Tibetan mastiffs chained to the log fence.

The co-operative had eight members. Aiya Aiya was the manager and he was assisted by his old father who never left the place. The rest were mountain Nakhi and Szechuanese, one of whom was the technician. The material for the paper was a kind of mountain bamboo called *arundinaria*. It was slender, of purple colour, and grew in dense patches at an altitude of not less than 15,000 feet. Several members had gone early on the morning of our arrival to cut it and would be returning with large bunches of it slung over their shaggy horses. After lying on the ground for some time open to the elements, it was put through the water-power crusher and dumped into the oblong pool; lime was heaped on it and there it stayed until properly processed. When soft, it was loaded into the vats and boiled with chemicals. The resulting pulp was transferred to the stone tubs, where a juice from the roots of a species of dwarf pine was added; it was then ready for making into paper. A frame of horsehair was dipped carefully into the tub and lifted with a thin layer of the pulp which was deftly deposited on a clean wooden board. This congealed almost at once. Then another layer was added on to this initial sheet and so on until a stack was formed which was taken away and a new one started. All the time more pulp solution, water and root chemicals were added into the tub. The stacked paper was separated and the sheets hung on long poles in the building to dry with the help of braziers. When the sheets were dry they were stacked again in reams and were ready for sale. The paper was yellowish in colour, thick and too rough for writing on. It was used for wrapping and other household purposes; but its main use was in childbirth, fulfilling the function of sanitary napkins and towels. It was very cheap and the margin of profit on its production was extremely meagre.

I nicknamed the Paper-making Society the 'Co-operative above the Clouds.' The view from the place was breathtaking. It was like looking from an aeroplane. Its height was 14,000 feet and one could see for miles around: as far as the dark trench, where the Iron-mining Co-operative was, and to a series of mountain ranges which, like colossal waves, ebbed away and melted into the blue haze of distant horizons. Sometimes clouds came, but they did not reach us. They floated below like a limitless silvery sea out of which the peaks protruded like purple islands.

The furthest co-operative society I had was at Erhyuen, about eighty miles south of Likiang. It was in real Minkia country. Erhyuen was the capital of that small kingdom whose beautiful queen committed the ceremonial suicide by immolating herself on a pyre after her husband had been murdered by the Nanchiao king.

The road to Erhyuen branched off the main caravan trail from Likiang to Hsiakwan at Niukai, where there were so many hot springs. Erhyuen was a small town but very picturesque as it lay in a perfect amphitheatre of green, forested mountains behind a large lake which completely isolated it from the plain except for a narrow causeway, spanned at intervals by high camel-back bridges. Heavily loaded boats passed underneath the bridges along the channels cut through the vast growths of rushes and lotus plants.

The countryside around Erhyuen was green and full of lush pastures, and here I had formed a Butter-making Co-operative. It was under the patronage of a very influential and powerful local family, named Ma, which was very progressive, patriotic and was determined to improve, through the introduction of new industries, the lot of the local Minkia, with all of whom they were more or less related. It was war-time then and Kunming, with its swollen foreign population, hungered for good butter, which it was very difficult to procure from abroad. Some butter was of course already being made at Erhyuen, but it was made in the wrong way, was dirty and went rancid almost at once.

About twenty young Minkia men, all from good farming families, who had cows of their own, joined together. I wrote to friends in America and they promptly donated a good-sized cream separator, which was flown out to Kunming and which I brought, with great trouble, to Erhyuen. A very creditable churn was made by our Minkia Carpenter Co-operative and the cans and other containers were made by the Copperware Co-operative out of solid copper duly lined with tin. The Ma family provided a clean building for the purpose. The downstair rooms were devoted to butter-making and upstairs we lived together. It was impossible for the members to start the process of butter-making by themselves, for they had some very funny ideas about hygiene and machinery; so I had to spend more than a month at Erhyuen, working like a slave, and teaching them the art of making butter in European style.

Every morning I got up at six and after breakfast we received the milk from neighbouring farms. It came in hermetically closed cans and was duly weighed and tested with a lactometer. If too cold, it was slightly warmed. Then it was poured into the separator. I shall never forget that separator. Day after day I had to turn it for hours on end, for it was almost impossible to teach the boys to do it properly by not accelerating too fast and then maintaining strictly the same rate of revolutions. It was a month before they could grasp this essential fact and even then I was never quite sure of them.

I had great respect for cream separators, especially big ones; I have always thought them to be dangerous if not treated properly, and with all my efforts I tried to inculcate this respect into the co-operative members. The boys always agreed, but I could see from their faces that they still regarded this machine as a sort of a new and amusing foreign toy. However, the machine itself decided to co-operate with me in teaching them a lesson. One day I went out of the milk room for a minute, leaving the handle to be turned by one of the boys. I do not know what he did but he probably over-accelerated, and there was a terrific explosion. I rushed back to find a shambles. The milk bowl and plates were scattered all over the room in pools of milk, crockery was broken and the heavy centrifuge lay in a corner on the floor beside a screaming boy. It appeared that, as the boy had increased the speed erratically, there had been a big electric spark and the heavy, madly spinning centrifuge had jumped right up at the ceiling. It scraped the boy's leg and burned a wide patch of skin almost to the flesh because of the high velocity of its revolutions.

After this accident they acquired respect for modern methods and things went much more smoothly; and soon we were making up to fifty pounds of butter every day. It was sent, in little barrels, by truck to Kunming, was cut there into 1-lb., $\frac{1}{2}$-lb., and $\frac{1}{4}$-lb. blocks, wrapped and sotd at a store. The business was good and had every promise of growing.

The list of my most interesting co-operatives would not be complete without mentioning the big Leather and Shoe-making Co-operative which became the pride of Likiang. It was composed of twenty-three young Nakhi men, between eighteen and twenty-five years of age, with the exception of the manager who was thirty-eight. It was affectionately called by the Likiang people the Wa Wa Co-operative, that is to say, Children's Co-operative. All the boys had worked as apprentices to some local shoe-makers and I used to know many of them long before the society's formation. Influenced by my talks on co-operation and its advantages, they had decided to emancipate themselves and start a business of their own on the co-operative basis.

At first the society was rather helpless because they knew only how to tan one or two kinds of very crude leather and the shoes they made looked as shapeless as potatoes. So I sent one of them, duly selected by themselves, to Chungking to be trained at a really good Shanghai leather-tanning factory. He spent two years there and learned shoe-making as well. At last the poor man, disfigured by smallpox which he had picked up at the war capital, returned to Likiang with a load of chemicals and instruments which he had bought out of the proceeds of a loan I arranged for the society. Then things began moving and in no time at all the co-operative turned out rolls of beautiful leather of several qualities. The shoes were now strong and elegant, and yet the price was extremely low.

They were clever and willing, these boys. They had natural good taste and they turned to good account the copies of Montgomery Ward's catalogue that I provided. They constructed perfect copies of what was worn at that time on Bond Street or Fifth Avenue and probably at one-twentieth of the price. They made excellent top-boots too and, in addition, footballs, revolver holsters, military belts and a host of other leather articles. They captured, almost in the twinkle of an eye, the patronage of the local beaux and military officers. The orders poured in. In a few months Likiang had under-gone a considerable sartorial change. The men in town and in the villages simply had to have the elegant shining black and brown shoes of the latest style, and to go with them they also ordered equally elegant trousers of European style.

Some of the boys lived at the co-operative, others at home. They had no salary but only an allowance sufficient for the immediate needs of themselves and their families. At the end of the year, when the profits were divided, they all got a bonus in accordance with the work they had performed. A sum was set aside as a reserve fund and a percentage was carried to the 'common-good fund'. This fund was used primarily for funerals and weddings, and it was settled that each member was entitled to one wedding paid for out of the common-good fund, and each year a limited number of weddings were financed in this way by drawing lots. The profits were good and soon the society opened its own store in Main Street. Large consignments of shoes, top-boots and footballs went to Kunming, Paoshan, Hsiakwan and even to Tibet.

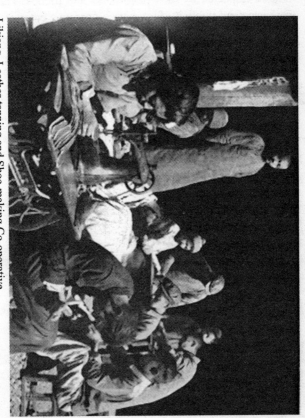

Likiang. Leather-tanning and Shoe-making Co-operative.

The loans contracted by the society from banks were repaid. The ragged apprentice members now emerged as prosperous and substantial citizens — well dressed, well fed and respected by their neighbours and friends. They were excellent publicity for what co-operative enterprise, properly established and conducted, could do for the craftsmen.

CHAPTER XVII

HOKING BRIGAND

*T*HE year 1949 opened inauspiciously. The dark clouds of civil strife, upheavals and hatred hovered on the horizon. The Nationalist regime was fighting a rearguard action and its control was shrinking rapidly. Yunnan itself was in the balance. Its powerful and ruthless, though just and popular, governor had been replaced by a general, who had been born outside south-west China and knew nothing of its problems. He did nothing for this remote province except plunder the ex-governor's fortune of gold and silver and put his nominees in the Provincial Government. At one time the province came near to open revolt and the Central Government appointed as governor the nephew of the former strong man. But it was too late-the damage had been done-and the uncle, smarting from humiliation and the loss of his vast fortune, threw in his lot openly with the Red regime already entrenched in Peking. Bands of Communist guerrillas roamed through the province, seizing a small town here and a village there. Although Likiang was still peaceful there was restiveness in the air as caravans brought more and more news of troubles elsewhere.

I believe it was in March that the jolly, roly-poly Pacification Commissioner went to Yungpei, a prosperous town across the Yangtze River, some three or four days east by caravan. There was some dispute there and, as it was a territory under his jurisdiction, the commissioner thought that his presence and mediation would help to settle it. In a fortnight or so Likiang was stunned by the news that there was an uprising at Yungpei, engineered by an army officer named Lokyun. This Lokyun, it was rumoured, had interned the Pacification Commissioner and disarmed his bodyguards. There was little reliable news, but in a week or so the caravan traffic to Yungpei ceased as the caravan men reported that their cargoes were being plundered there. The iron-chain bridge over the Yangtze River was closed to commercial traffic and a heavy guard posted at the Likiang end of it.

Lokyun himself was evidently a crafty fellow. He did not admit that anything was out of order at Yungpei. Telegrams, signed by the commissioner, sending orders to the Likiang authorities continued to arrive regularly as the telegraph line remained undamaged, but the Likiang magistrate and elder's felt sure that these messages had been sent by the commissioner under duress.

Having evidently consolidated his hold on Yungpei, Lokyun made the next tactical move. A long message was sent to the Likiang Government ostensibly from the Pacification Commissioner, bearing as it did his seal. It informed the government that Lokyun, burning with fierce patriotism and righteousness, had taken over the government and affairs at Yungpei and had decided to 'liberate' at least north-western Yunnan from corrupt officials, both Central and Provincial, to introduce just and incorruptible local self-administration (under his authority, naturally) and to lay down a new deal for the poor and under-privileged. He (the commissioner) himself was persuaded of the integrity and high motives of Lokyun, he heartily endorsed this idealistic movement, and would assist it with all the power at his command. Furthermore, the message continued, the armed forces and people of Yungpei were filled with brotherly love and sympathy towards the brave and noble people of the sister city of Likiang, and were determined to help them to overthrow the present corrupt and ineffective administration and the dominance of powerful and rapacious landlords and merchants.

The rambling document concluded with the assurance that Lokyun's liberation movement had nothing to do either with the Communists or Nationalists, but was a spontaneous growth generated by the discontent and misery of the oppressed people of Yunnan. The government and people of Likiang were respectfully requested to welcome the liberation force which would be dispatched in the near future and treat its members as their nearest and dearest brothers.

There was some confusion among the authorities and people of Likiang upon receipt of this lengthy message. Some people thought that the Pacification Commissioner was still in authority; perhaps it was a genuine document really sent by him of his own free will; after all, he was not a fool and, if he said the man was honourable and idealistic, it might indeed be so. Perhaps it was an emergence of another strong man on the provincial stage. Such phenomena in Chinese national and provincial histories were by no means rare. If Lokyun was indeed such a man, perhaps it might be better to join up with him at the outset and thus be in a favourable position when his rule over the province had been firmly established. Others, more sceptical, advised caution and a wait-and-see policy. After all, they argued, Lokyun was not a Nakhi and his army was composed of outside Chinese. Why should the Nakhi submit precipitately to a stranger's yoke? Besides, Likiang was the biggest and richest city in the region and quite a prize if Lokyun's forces, probably little disciplined, should decide to help themselves. Likiang had already experienced in its long history such 'friendly' invasions.

Cautious counsels prevailed and it was decided to find out more about the merits of the new movement. A telegram was dispatched to the Pacification Commissioner asking him to come to Likiang alone and tell the city more about the advantages and benefits of the movement and the virtues of its comparatively unknown leader. There was no reply for several days. In the meantime, the cunning Nakhi sent spies to Yungpei, who returned in a few days in great alarm. Yungpei had been thoroughly looted, they reported, all leading citizens were under detention and the commissioner was kept by Lokyun in isolation. Gloom descended on Likiang, and the people in the shops and streets talked of nothing but Lokyun. Soon a new message was flashed from Yungpei. The Pacification Commissioner wired that, in response to the Likiang Government's request, he was coming to Likiang with Lokyun as his most valued guest. As a mark of respect for so famous and honoured a city as Likiang, an escort of honour of some 10,000 picked troops would accompany them.

Great was the consternation in town. Many shop-owners disappeared from behind their counters, for being practical women they began collecting into the back room all their most valuable goods, and we could see that our neighbours were starting to pack. Small caravans of horses and women with heavy bundles streamed furtively out of town towards the Snow Mountain, lamaseries or Lapo where, they thought, their valuables would be safer in the hands of relatives and friends if the worst came to the worst. Then a big gathering of the people was summoned by the magistrate and other high officials. There was a long and heated discussion about Lokyun's imminent arrival with so strong an army. At last a unanimous decision was taken. Likiang should not surrender; Likiang must fight; all Nakhi would fight— both men and women. A message to this effect was wired to the Pacification Commissioner, aimed, of course, at Lokyun, and messages also sent to the sister cities of Hoking, Chienchwang and Tail Hoking, in particular, was asked to join in the resistance.

A mobilization order was issued asking every able-bodied Nakhi to come to Likiang from his village, bringing whatever arms he could find, his bedding and a small store of necessary provisions. Another message was sent by runner to Chungdien, asking the Tibetans to help. This last step was taken only after much deliberation, for the Tibetans were always a dangerous ally. Were the city defeated and captured by Lokyun's men, Tibetans would help them to plunder it. If Lokyun was defeated, they might decide to remain in Likiang just the same and help themselves to whatever they liked. But they were fierce and fearless fighters and as loyal to the Nakhi cause as the Nakhi themselves. The very mention that the Tibetans were on the march seldom failed to put the fear of God in the hearts of an enemy. It was largely for this psychological reason that the decision to invite the Tibetans was made.

News and rumours of the invasion started to pour in daily, then hourly. At first it was reported that Lokyun was coming with 10,000 troops; next day it was 20,000; then it was 40,000, until a grandiose total of 100,000 was freely discussed in the streets. It was impressive to watch the inborn courage, bravery and magnificent warrior spirit of the Nakhi which now displayed itself. There was no longer panic or confusion; only confidence, discipline, order and affectionate solidarity. They treated each other as a brother or a sister, who had gathered together to protect the beloved family.

The first step was to remove the flooring and then to dismantle the chains of the great suspension bridge over the Yangtze. They were detached from the boulders, to which they had been anchored on the other side of the river and they clanged heavily as they dropped into the turbulent stream. A series of patrols were posted on the bank to prevent a crossing by the ferries which were removed to the near side of the river. The villagers began pouring in from plains and mountains. Some carried heavy antique muskets reminiscent of the Three Musketeers' days; others had flint-lock guns; many carried bows and arrows, spears and swords, halberds and lances and other arms of bygone ages. Comparatively few had up-to-date rifles and revolvers. There were some firearms at the *yamen* and these were quickly distributed. Most of the *pangchinmei* came forward and joined their brothers and sweet-hearts. In addition to the baskets, in which they carried their men's provisions and blankets, these girls also brought their own weapons such as rifles, spears, swords or just long, sharp knives. All the newcomers were hospitably quartered by the citizens and my house too became like a barracks. Of course, we all had to feed them, but it was not too onerous, and they were polite, friendly and uncomplaining.

Soon it was reported that the invasion units had been sighted on the other side of the river. Bamed and disconcerted by the Nakhi's war-like measures and their hostile attitude, the invaders moved hesitantly down the river towards Hoking. Ultimatum after ultimatum poured into Likiang demanding unconditional surrender. The reply from the Nakhi always was, 'Come and take us if you can.' Only Hoking sent a cowardly message of welcome and submission, promising Lokyun open gates and hospitality. The stalemate continued for three days.

In the meantime the Chungdien Tibetans arrived. They were hefty and hearty fellows, ferocious-looking and very picturesque. A cavalry unit, armed with rifles, spears and swords, they swaggered through the town on their shaggy ponies. They invaded my house, under the pretext of needing treatment for most varied ailments, and consumed many a large jar of *ara* (white wine) which I had the foresight to prepare. My cook was in a panic and rushed to me almost hourly, urging me to send my things away to a friend of his in a village for safe keeping, or at least to let him bury my silver dollars in a pot under the privy. I told him not to make a fool of himself. He was flee, I added, to do anything he wanted with his own fortune. But I was not particularly happy about the situation, though I had a good deal of confidence in the Nakhi and Tibetans and their magnificent determination to resist at all costs. If Likiang was to be lost, I wanted to share their humiliation and misfortune as I had shared, during so many years, their life and their happiness.

At last the critical moment arrived. Under cover of darkness, Lokyun's forces crossed the river in specially constructed ferries opposite Hoking. From that point it was only a short march to that town across a mountain range. Both the Nakhi and Tibetans moved down the valley to Chiho, some forty *li* away, where the border between the ancient Kingdom of Mu and the former Minkia states (now Hoking district) lay. Likiang looked forlorn and abandoned. The shops were shuttered and few people appeared in the street. Every member of my 'Children's Co-operative' went to the front, arming themselves, like the men from our village, with the steel axes which I had previously received from Kunming and with other tools and machinery sent as part of the American assistance programme to our Co-operative Movement. I sat alone in our abandoned office. All the clerks, Hozuchi and the old couple's son went away to fight. Only my cook and myself were left.

Under the weight of an intolerable tension and anxiety I went to Madame Lee's shop. It was shuttered, but the old lady was there. She was calm, though her face looked worried. She said the people were now waiting to hear how Hoking was treated by the 'great liberator' Lokyun. We did not have to wait long. As I came to her place next day and sat sipping wine, the runners from the south came into the city. Very soon the truth was known and the people gathered in small groups excitedly discussing the news. As many in Likiang had suspected, Lokyun was no liberator and no revolutionary. He was a brigand, a robber of utmost rapacity the like of whom had not been seen in Yunnan for many decades. On entering Hoking, he extorted enormous sums of money from the merchants and wealthy landlords. His men looted and plundered to their hearts' content. The shuttered shops were smashed with axes and silks and satins were scattered knee-deep in the streets. In the streets the women had their gold earrings torn off their ears, the men had their rings snatched from their fingers and their jackets and trousers pulled off. Mirrors, clock, clothing, utensils and other articles were carried off in heaps and sometimes scattered by the road-side and in ditches. The whole to arm was left as a shell of its former self. So Likiang now knew what to expect. Even old Madame Lee was infused with a warrior spirit and picked up her big chopper threateningly when somebody talked of Lokyun.

Flushed with their 'bloodless and easy' victory over chicken-hearted Hoking, the robbers now advanced on Likiang, with most insolent threats. They abandoned all pretence and openly declared what they would do to Likiang when they had taken the city. They appealed to the cupidity of the poorer Nakhi, asking them to join up with them and afterwards share the loot.

When they reached the Nakhi defence lines a great battle ensued. It was not true that the brigands numbered 100,000 or even 10,000. Perhaps the regular band was in the neighbourhood of 5,000 Yungpei men. The rest were their camp-followers—relatives and friends, mostly women, boys and the like who picked up the loot, as it came, and assisted to transport it to the other side of the river whence it was forwarded home. They were like the ravens and ghouls which wait for the end of the battle to snatch what is left. The Nakhi men fought bravely and well, and the girls by their sides distinguished themselves by their ferocity and fearlessness. It was reported that one *pangchinmei* killed five robbers with her own hands. The charge by the Tibetan cavalry rounded off the Nakhi attack. The brigands were utterly defeated and driven back to the gates of Hoking. Lokyun escaped, but the fat Pacification Commissioner was captured and brought back to Likiang. The wounded returned to the city and I spent all my time dressing their injuries, and for a couple of clays my house looked like a hospital.

The inglorious Hoking now requested the Nakhi to pursue the robbers across the river and to recapture their loot. However, it was decided not to take any action as Hoking had previously refused to support Likiang in united action.

When the Nakhi and Tibetans made sure that the robbers had gone they returned to Likiang and were welcomed with open arms. There was a series of feasts for the victors and they received all kinds of gifts. The Tibetans lingered for a fortnight, still not being sure of the situation. If they had something else on their mind, they did not show it. Anyway, they were pacified and made happy with feasts and wine and gifts of cloth and provisions. Finally they received a sizable present of hard cash which, to them, was a satisfactory recompense for their sacrifices. Well satisfied, they returned to their native Chungdien.

The defeated brigands and their leader Lokyun, in their frenzy, rushed across the mountains from Hoking and looted Chienchwang. Still not satisfied, they went further to Erhyuen, where they took the little town by surprise. Eye-witnesses told me afterwards how the bandits took every room in Mr. Ma's new mansion apart, looking for gold and jewellery. What they could not take away, they destroyed, and large bevelled mirrors were smashed just for the fun of it. They did not even leave our Butter-making Co-operative alone. They smashed everything to bits in the milk room. I really do not know what possessed them to take away the cream separator which was so useless to them and which had given me so much work; but they carried the heavy machine for almost five miles and then dumped it into a ditch by the lake. Mr. Ma told me afterwards that he was sure they thought it to be a new kind of machine-gun.

The unfortunate Pacification Commissioner was, of course, very ashamed of the role he had been forced to play in this unfortunate affair. It was a very severe loss of face as far as Likiang was concerned, but it was not irreparable, for after all the town of Likiang had not been harmed. No doubt he was taunted and reproached by the magistrate and Likiang elders, but from all accounts their attitude was surprisingly lenient. The situation at Hoking was different. Hoking had been invaded, looted and devastated, and the people there laid all the blame on the commissioner. They now claimed that they had opened the gates of the city to Lokyun only on the strength of the written assurances signed by the commissioner himself; otherwise, like Likiang, they would have resisted. Besides, the commissioner was a Holding resident himself and thus one of its trusted elders. Actually he was from a district near Tali lake but had bought a mansion and had long established himself at Hoking. Thus the Hoking people claimed that he had betrayed them doubly, both in his official capacity and as an elder and guardian of Hoking. They demanded from the Likiang authorities his extradition to Hoking for whatever punishment they decided. In the meantime they held his family there as hostages. This was vastly more serious than his position in Likiang. With the people of Hoking he had lost face utterly and irretrievably; nor could he offer any explanation to the Governor in Kunming. He had to go down to Hoking, and he went. His house was about ten *li* before reaching Hoking. He said he was tired by long travel and wanted to rest before entering the city. He retired to his study. An hour later a shot was heard. When they opened the door they found him dead, sitting before his desk with a bullet in his head.

I was very sorry to hear of the old commissioner's passing. He was a kindly old man and he was very good to me and my co-operatives. Whenever there was any trouble or unpleasantness he always tried to smooth matters over for me and he was very helpful with documents and passes whenever I had to travel to Kunming. The destruction of my Butter-making Co-operative at Erhyuen and the devastation wrought on that pretty little place made me very sad, and it seemed like a personal loss. It seemed part of me — a real product of my own enterprise and sweat, and a really new industry in that part of the country.

Somehow things had changed and Likiang was not quite the same after this harrowing experience. The old sense of security and certainty had gone, and the people had lost some of their zest for work and even for play. Lokyun was gone but the damage he had done fingered. Hoking market was dead and so was Chienchwang's and Erhyuen's. People had lost money and goods, and somehow they seemed to have lost heart too. No one cared to buy or sell. There was unrest everywhere, petty robberies and a flood of rumours. The caravan roads, never too safe before, further deteriorated with the appearance of small groups of bandits — well armed and seemingly unafraid of anything. Some said they were the remnants of the Lokyun band; others thought they were something else. The telephone line to Hoking had been repaired, but the telegraph line to Kunming was still blocked by the retreating brigands. The arms issued by government to the villagers had not Been returned. People said they expected more trouble. Why? Where? When? No one knew and yet there was tension and suspense. Something was expected, something new — something fearful perhaps.

Soon there were rumours in the street that Chienchwang had 'turned over'. What it exactly meant people themselves did not quite know. They said that Paoshan on the Burma Road had 'turned over' quite a long time ago, perhaps a month or two. Now a group of men from that place had reached Erhyuen, 'turned it over' and were at present in Chienchwang. Who were these men? Nobody was certain. Were they the Communists? No, they themselves said they were not. Yet they wore a sort of uniform, a very simple one of indigo blue colour, and had a peculiar cap on their heads. They proclaimed the end of the landlords, the supremacy of the poor people and the abolition of luxurious living. As a first step, it was reported, they requisitioned some of the best houses and imposed a strict curfew on the town. No one was permitted to leave without permission, and usually such a permit was withheld from the landlords. Passing caravans were searched by them and certain goods and arms were taken. They prohibited the use of sedan chairs to all men under sixty and some travellers from Likiang to Hsiakwan were brusquely pulled out of their chairs, made to pay off the bearers at the full rate to Hsiakwan and were told to continue their journey on foot. A committee of the poorest people had been elected and was ruling the place in close collaboration with this mysterious group of men.

Piecing these rumours and reports together I could not help feeling that I knew who the mysterious reformers were. The pattern of their work and actions was only too familiar. A dread foreboding filled my heart.

CHAPTER XVIII

THE LAST OF LIKIANG

$\mathcal{B}$ESET by anxiety and uncertainty, with an undercurrent of fear, I sat at my desk. There was no desire or energy to work and indeed there was no work to do. No one in town or in the villages seemed to be interested in anything, much less in co-operatives. People whispered and talked in small groups and then went about their business listlessly. Suddenly, in my perplexity, I decided to go and find out from my trusted and intimate friend Wuhan what was really happening. He was well connected both in town and in the villages and surely he could enlighten and advise me. At that moment there was a sound of steps on my staircase and Wuhan himself entered. It was an almost unbelievable coincidence, a real case of telepathy. He said he had come to invite me to his village on the morrow as he was performing the *Muan* Peu ceremony. He had no time now to talk, he added, as he had to buy incense and other things for the ceremony and to hurry back home to make the necessary preparations.

I left the house very early next morning and was at Wuhan's farm before ten o'clock. As was the custom, he spent the night fasting with some friends and *dtombas* at the holy place and was now fully dressed for the ritual. We proceeded to the holy place, which every Nakhi village has for the purpose of these sacrifices. It was a small clearing, and was enclosed by a grove of age-old trees surrounded by a broad wall of boulders and stones, at one end of which stood a long altar also made of rough stones. There on the altar, between two candlesticks, was a triangular ploughshare and offerings of grain. Special incense sticks of gigantic size stood on both sides of the altar. Wuhan prostrated himself several times before the altar, holding incense sticks in his clasped hands. Such was the simple ceremony, but it was one of great importance and solemnity among the Nakhi. Only the elder male in the family was entitled to perform it—the father or, if he were dead, the son. Different clans of the Nakhi performed this ceremony at different times. Wuhan belonged to the famous Gvghugh clan, whilst some of the villagers were of the Gvdza clan.

In this sacred ceremony the head of the family made a sacrifice to Heaven, symbolized by the mystic Mount Somero, the Centre of the Universe, where God and His lieutenants, the lesser deities, dwell. The triangular ploughshare represented Mount Somero in a visible form. The bountiful Heaven was humbly thanked for the plentiful harvest of grain and other foodstuffs, the continued prosperity and the health of the family and the domestic harmony it had vouchsafed during the past year, and was implored not to withhold its favours to the family during the current year.

The same kind of ceremony was practised by the Black

Lolos and other members of the Nakhi race, collectively known as the Chiang. The origin of the ceremony is as old as mankind itself and antedates all known religions. It was the same type of sacrifice with the same purpose as that related in the Bible when, at the dawn of the human race, Cain and Abel sacrificed the fruits of their labour, and when Noah, after the landing of his ark, thanked God in a similar manner. It was the harvest festival practised by all races at all times of their history. It was practised by the Emperor of China, who sacrificed in great humility at the resplendent Temple of Heaven in Peking, and it is practised now, although in a slightly different form but with the same intent, by the Eastern Orthodox Church during the evening service when the priest, blessing the bread, oil and wine, thanks God for His abundance, love and great mercies and invokes His blessings for the future. It was made a focal point in the beautiful liturgy of St. John Chrysostom, 'Thine from Thine to Thee from All and for All.'

A feast, at which the sacrificial food was utilized, always followed the *Muan Peu* ceremony, but only close relatives and members of the clan were invited. When the guests had gone and we remained alone I broached the subject of my worries to Wuhan.

'Wuhan,' I said, 'we have been good and intimate friends for a very long time and I want you to tell me absolutely frankly what is happening in Likiang, what do you think will happen and what can I do? I feel worried and unhappy.'

He stared at the ceiling for a long time. Then he leaned towards me and began to talk in a lowered voice, although there was nobody around except his old mother and wife, neither of whom knew English or Chinese. He explained to me that the mysterious reformers at Chienchwang, Erhyuen and Paoshan were the Communist advance guards who came to infiltrate among the population and pave the way for the 'liberation' of that part of Yunnan ahead of the arrival of the regular Red armies which were moving from Szechuan and Kweichow. At the moment Likiang was already infiltrated and everything was ready for the coup; they were waiting only for the arrival of certain important leaders, who were coming in secret from Kunming. He said it would be a matter of a week or two, or perhaps even a few days, before the city officially 'turned over'. He himself did not know much about communism or communistic principles and tactics. However, he thought, there might be trouble all around. In his opinion the best course for me would be to go to Kunming and stay there for a while to see what happened. We parted in sadness — a premonition, perhaps, that it was my last visit to this peaceful and happy farmstead.

I returned home in a very gloomy mood. Likiang was changing day by day; it was filled with an atmosphere unclean, murky and pregnant, and I was afraid lest it gave birth to a phantasmagoria of the things one desired least but was unable to avoid.

I stayed at home most of the time. Somehow I now had little desire to go out in the streets. The wine-shops of Madame Lee, Madame Yang and Madame Ho were no longer the open gates through which I had entered the life of Likiang, the nursery of friendships. No longer were they, for me, centres of interest and knowledge, even though through their windows new kinds of strangers were to be seen passing in the streets. They passed with grave and cold faces. There was a suggestion of ruthlessness and arrogance as they peremptorily parted the crowds to make their way. I wanted to do something and could not. I lost my appetite and could not sleep well. Thoughts whirled in my brain day and night. Was this a new crisis in my own life also? Did I have to go on the road again? Where to, how and when? The idea of leaving Likiang, perhaps for ever, appeared intolerable. Nowhere in my turbulent life had I tasted such peace and such happiness as in Likiang. To me it was paradise. I thought I had worked hard to win it, and yet it seemed to be slipping away. I knew it was a paradise to me only and I never tried to convert those outside to my private belief or induce them to visit me. In spite of my long residence here and in China, I was still Western enough to realize that the idea of 'earthly paradise' was not the same in the West. In Likiang there were no hotels, no cinemas, few bodily comforts, no funicular to the top of Mount Satseto and no natives to 'perform' for a tourist's fee; in contrast there was the ever-present danger of disease to constitutions weakened by too much hygiene.

My happiness in Likiang did not spring only from an idle enjoyment of the flowers and their scent, of the brilliance of ever-changing snow peaks and of a succession of feasts. Neither was it in the absorption in my work with co-operatives or in service to the sick and poor. It was in an even balancing of these two aspects of life, but to become perfect it needed the belief in the love and goodness of God and the friendship and trust of the simple and honest people among whom I lived. When these things had been granted me, I felt at last at peace with the world and, what is more important, with myself. I believe that this sort of happiness is perhaps a foreshadowing of the true paradise, unlike what is pictured by the theologians of many religions. Who would want a paradise resembling a *cafe de luxe* where the departed can enjoy food and drinks free of charge throughout eternity whilst contemplating the splendours of heavenly scenery? And it is no substitute for paradise to be eternally preoccupied with sickness, misery, filth and rags. Paradise is perhaps the transformation of both through wisdom and love and the knowledge that the work has been well done.

At last the dreaded day arrived. It was announced that Likiang had been 'liberated'. A Communist Executive Committee was promptly established and took over. The magistrate was arrested along with a number of town elders. The head of the local militia, Captain Yang, fled and they arrested his third wife. All the scamps and the village bullies, who had not done a stroke of honest work in their life, suddenly blossomed forth as the accredited members of the Communist Party, and swaggered with special red armbands and badges and the peculiar caps with duckbill visors which seemed to be the hallmark of a Chinese Red.

I was introduced to the Executive Committee. It consisted of a number of newly arrived members of the Paoshan Liberation group. They were some of the dreaded Makung (Malayan Communists), Chinese of a peculiarly uncouth and brutal-looking type, reminding me of certain gangsters who were employed as truck drivers on the Burma Road. They had trekked into Paoshan direct from Malaya, passing through Chiengmai in Siam, which was the favourite route between Yunnan and Malaya for the Communist agents. Some of these to whom I spoke had a pretty good knowledge of Russian and evidently had had their training in the U.S.S.R. A few other members were, surprisingly, Nakhi whom I had not known before, and who had recently arrived from Peking where they had probably been trusted officials of the Red Government. They were quite civil and looked much more intelligent and cultured than the Malayans, and seemed to have more authority.

The debut of the new government was the shooting of Dr. Lee's brother, that wretch who had nearly poisoned me with chloroform at a party. Everybody had to go to witness this execution. I did not go as I am not a lover of morbid sights, and was later fined two dollars for non-attendance. Afterwards I had to pay many fines for this sort of offence. Next day there was a procession of the elders and others accused of opium-smoking and other crimes against the people. The wife of Captain Yang was among them. With bound hands they shuffled along, carrying on their backs huge placards announcing the nature of their crimes. It was a sorry and pitiful sight.

To celebrate the 'liberation' a mammoth meeting was arranged on the racecourse which everybody had to attend. After the meeting, carrying hundreds of banners and placards with the images of Stalin and Mao Tse Tung, the crowd passed through Main Street. Just at that very moment there occurred a terrific thunderstorm and they marched, drenched to the bone, while the hastily painted Mao Tse Tung and Stalin dissolved on their banners under the deluge.

To protect the revolution, the militia had been disarmed first and then reorganized into a new unit, a real little army, to which all the young men now belonged. Not to be outdone, and in the spirit of the new equality of sexes, many girls dressed in the soldiers' Blue uniforms, cut off their hair and became soldiers too, staying at the same barracks and eating together with the men. Yet there was no suggestion of immorality because love was prohibited along with wine and fine food. These recruits were given very little to eat and what there was was very poor. However, to forestall grumbling, the officers ate together with the men, and these tactics went well with the village bumpkins, but others were not deceived. The officers were members of the Executive Committee which held its sessions always in the dead of night; and these sessions were not held on empty stomachs, for sumptuous dinners, wine and even opium preceded the business.

Many of my village friends were among the recruits and they always found time to sneak into my house through the back door which was quite close to the barracks on the hill. They were as hungry as dogs and we always kept something for them to eat such as a rich soup or fat pork with rice. They had not a cent between them and I used to make them small loans, enough at least for cigarettes.

Three days after the liberation parade, Dr. Rock arrived by chartered plane on one of his periodical visits. I had had no means of advising him beforehand of the political changes and he nearly collapsed as I greeted him with the words, 'Welcome to the Red Paradise!' He was treated civilly, although they searched his baggage, and the funds he brought with him were not confiscated. We spent the night at a village near the airport and went to town next morning. We felt isolated amidst this new set-up and saw each other almost every day to exchange the latest news.

Life in Likiang had changed almost beyond recognition. There were daily parades of boys and girls everywhere with the eternal singing of the tune of 'John Brown's Body' and hymns of praise for Mao Tse Tung. Old Nakhi dances were prohibited and replaced by the new Communist dances which were neither attractive nor becoming.

Many people donned the Blue uniforms. Hired labour was abolished and all the village people had to work collectively. After their work, though tired and sleepy, they had to listen to interminable indoctrination talks at daily meetings and afterwards to dance the compulsory Communist dances. It was prohibited to eat chicken and pork and drink wine, except very occasionally. Poor villagers no longer found buyers in town for their eggs, poultry and pork, and even the firewood was not much in demand. They had to return to their villages without the money they hoped to obtain from the sale of their products for other pressing needs.

There was at the time in Likiang a group of very poor Lotien boys who usually came for seasonal farm work. Under the new regulations they could not be engaged as they were hired labour. They were desperate and starving, without money or food and clothed only in a few rags. I could not stand the sight of their suffering and despair and invited all of them to my house to stay for a few days. I fed them, supplied them with such clothing as I could find and gave them enough money to enable them to return to Lotien.

There were continual arrests, usually in the dead of night, decreed by the dread Executive Committee, and secret executions. It was reported that an old man at Boashi village was shot by a squad commanded by his own son.

The local merchants had been 'fined' and had to pay out thousands of dollars to the Executive Committee. These 'fines' or 'contributions were not fixed and further levies were hinted at. The failure to pay up was a signal for the arrest of the victim and probable liquidation at a future date. Not a few merchants had already been arrested and their execution was pending; and the magistrate was also on the list. The inveterate opium smokers and eiders were either locked up in jail or permitted to buy their freedom by further stupendous 'fines'. The local *jeunesse doree* were also recruited into the militia and had to exercise and march on almost empty stomachs. All of them had been opium smokers and I can well imagine their sufferings.

The *dtombas* were proscribed and many of them lived in fear of their lives, expecting to be arrested any moment and executed. The lamaseries were desecrated, images and priceless tankas burned or smashed, sutras destroyed and lamas either arrested or scattered. The lamasery halls were declared to be the future seats of popular schools, as if there were not enough buildings elsewhere for this purpose. The temple of the god Saddok was likewise desecrated and everything inside it smashed. Lenin's dictum, 'Religion is the opium of masses', was probably more zealously enforced in Likiang than it had been in Russia.

One day a group of the new officials appeared at my gate and, without much ceremony, confiscated all the machinery and tools donated by America for the benefit of our co-operatives. They also took all my accounts and receipts for the loans we had made to them. Afterwards they proceeded to the co-operative societies themselves and confiscated their knitting and sewing machines which I had previously sold them officially on behalf of our office. I tried to find out the reason for such drastic and precipitate action. 'All this belongs to the people now,' the officials said. 'We are going to create our own people's co-operatives on a grand scale. Where a co-operative society of yours had thirty members, ours will have 3,000 members.' What could I say in the face of such economic absurdity? But I pointed out that, as it was, the present co-operatives were for the people and of the people and the machinery and tools were imported for them. That meant nothing. A couple of men, their eyes aflame with greed, attempted to search my private rooms and carry away my stock of medicines. Others, perhaps still retaining a spark of decency, dissuaded them. I told them they were at liberty to take anything they coveted, even my personal belongings.

After these incidents and several remarks, overheard from the Malayan members of the Executive Committee, that I was an agent of 'Western Imperialism', I at last decided that I must leave Likiang, and quickly, before the Russian advisers and the regular OGPU from Peking came. I talked it over with Dr. Rock, who wanted to leave anyway for reasons of his health whilst the going was still good. We went to see the Executive Committee, and if there was any opposition to our departure from the Malayan members, it was quickly quashed by the Nakhi members who were clearly their superiors. Dr. Rock and myself still had the affection and respect of the Likiang people and our prestige was high. The committee authorized our departure by chartered plane, but on the condition that it should bring from Kunming several thousand silver dollars which the government there owed to Likiang teachers. But communications with Kunming had been severed, so Dr. Rock had to send a runner to Tali to send the telegram. We waited anxiously. A reply finally came that the plane would pick us up on the 24th or 25th of July.

I never mentioned to anybody that I was going away for good. I only said that I was going to Kunming to fetch the new consignment of medicine which had arrived there for us from the International Red Cross in Chungking. Even when packing I took with me only my typewriter and a suitcase with my clothing and a few books. I had to abandon my library, victrola, medicines and many other belongings. Dr. Rock likewise left many treasures behind.

For two days I went round the town talking to friends and acquaintances, saying good-bye to them. Even to my closest friends I did not say that I was not returning, but they were not stupid and I knew they sensed it. I sat for a little while with old Madame Lee. She said her shop was as dead as a doornail and she did not know what to do now. Wine was prohibited and she did not dare to make new stocks or sell old ones. Cordially she wished me good luck and blessings in her own way. Madame Yang was upset and tearful; the committee was after a nephew of hers suspected of being pro-Kuomintang. She was genuinely sorry to see me go. The 'merry girls' appeared funny in their male military uniform; the soldiers' caps gave them, however, a coquettish look. They were rather insolent and full of their own importance, but even they became sorry when I told them I was going away, and all said they hoped that I would return from Kunming soon. Madame Ho looked gloomy and worried. She had had to pay a heavy contribution to the committee, and they were likely to come for more any day.

Wuhan came in the evening. He was terribly worried. The village scoundrels, now in the flush of their power, were after him and his little fortune. His brother-in-law, gentle and inoffensive Wuhsiha, was strung from a tree on the accusation of his wife, who disliked him because of his inborn sexual weakness. It was shocking news. I bade him go back and not bother about seeing me off. We had a very touching farewell. Howenhua, a friend of mine, came trembling and reported that his old father, a landlord at Chiho, was shot by the village committee. Although Likiang still maintained its outward appearances, there was a naked reign of terror in the villages, especially at Boashi, which I had to pass the next day.

In the morning it was raining heavily. My cook was very ill. Hozuchi picked up my meagre baggage, put it on his basket and we started for the airfield forty-five *li* away. Only Wuhsien dared to accompany us; he was a devoted friend. But the downpour was too heavy, the roads flooded and I persuaded him to return. Hozuchi and I plodded on and on and reached the village by the airfield late in the afternoon. Dr. Rock was already there. We tried our best to dry our drenched clothing by the fire. Outside the house was guarded by village militia as if we were criminals.

Next day we went to the field early. It was a bright, sunny day, and we thought the plane must surely come. The day dragged on until, about sunset, we returned to the village, deeply disappointed. Just as we were on the point of unpacking our bedding, there was a roar and the plane landed. We rushed back to the field. Some newcomers were disembarking and there were many heavy chests on board with the silver brought for the schools. There was no time to be lost. The chests were dragged off the runway. We piled our baggage in and I said good-bye to the tearful Hozuchi, pressing some money into his hand. The field was ringed by the village militia and by the curious. I looked at the Snow Peak, perhaps, I thought, for the last time. Had I but known the future at that moment! For in December of 1952 this great mountain convulsed and split. Tremendous shocks rocked Likiang and the towns and villages as far as Holding and Erhyuen and even more remote districts. For a whole week the earth heaved and trembled. The terrified people rushed to the fields and forests for safety and lived there in whatever clothing they had been wearing, at the mercy of the elements. Returning to the city they found havoc, and the houses which had not been levelled were plundered by robbers. Boashi and Lashiba, the two villages which saw so many bloody excesses by the Reds, were totally destroyed. Chienchwang had not a house standing; even its city walls collapsed. Hoking was also totally destroyed. No wonder the superstitious people thought it was a retribution for the destruction of the temple of Saddok, titular deity of the Snow Mountain and of Likiang.

The sun had already dipped behind the towering peak of Mount Satseto, but its parting rays still painted in Orange and gold the eternal ice and snows of its fan-shaped crown. Glaciers became dark blue in gathering shadows. The silver Dakota, resting on the flower-strewn alpine meadow, looked portentous and mysterious, a messenger of the gods sent from outer space. Like the fabulous Garuda, it had come to snatch us up, to take us into the unknown, and to plunge us into a new way of living So this was the end of the dream that had come true, to the happiness that passed all understanding.

The shadows were thickening. It was becoming cold. The terrific blasts of wind, which usually come after sunset, were already roaring down the great mountain. No time must be lost lest disaster should overcome the courageous man-made Bird which dared to approach the Throne of the Gods. There was a last wave of the hand to friends, and local Nakhi peasants and lamas who were there to see us off. The propellers began to revolve. With misty eyes we fastened our belts. The plane taxied to the

far end of the alpine meadow and then started with a roar.
A crowd of Nakhi and Tibetans waved to us as we ran
clown the valley and rose into the air. Slowly we passed
our beloved Likiang, with its tiled roofs and running
streams, and started climbing to cross the Nanshan Range.
The last glimpse was of the great River of the Golden
Sand winding through its deep gorge amid the sea of
mountains. Then it became dark.

Thus, due to political upheavals, ended my stay, of almost
nine years, in the little-known and all but forgotten
ancient Nakhi Kingdom of south-west China. Even
during my youth spent in Moscow and Paris I had been
unaccountably attracted to Asia, her vast, little-explored
mountains and her strange peoples and, especially, to
mysterious Tibet. The Fates, stern to me in many other
ways, have been kind in vouchsafing me long travels
in Asia which even now, I have a feeling, are not at
an end. I had always dreamed of finding, and living in
that beautiful place, shut off from the world by its great
mountains, which years later James Hilton conceived in
his novel *Lost Horizon*. His hero found his 'Shangri-La' by
accident. I found mine, by design and perseverance, in
Likiang.

Singapore, Summer 1955

图书在版编目（CIP）数据

被遗忘的王国=Forgotten Kingdom: 英文 / (俄罗斯)
顾彼得著.—昆明：云南人民出版社，2007.8
ISBN 978-7-222-05101-0

Ⅰ. 被… Ⅱ. 顾… Ⅲ. 散文－作品集－俄罗斯－现代－英文 Ⅳ. I512.65

中国版本图书馆CIP数据核字（2007）第115671号

责任编辑：段兴民 董继梅
封面设计：陶汝昌
责任印制：洪中丽

书　　名	被遗忘的王国
编　　著	【俄】顾彼得 著
出　　版	云南出版集团公司 云南人民出版社
发　　行	云南人民出版社
地　　址	昆明市环城西路609号
网　　址	www.ynpph.com.cn
E－mail	rmszbs@public.km.yn.cn
邮　　编	650034
开　　本	787×1092　1/32
印　　张	11
字　　数	95千
版　　次	2007年8月第1版第1次印刷
印　　数	1-5000册
印　　刷	云南朗明印务有限公司
书　　号	ISBN 978-7-222-05101-0
定　　价	25.00元

尊敬的读者：若您购买的我社图书存在印装质量问题，
　　　　　　请与我社发行部联系调换。
发行部电话：(0871)4194864　4191604　4107628(邮购)